Lecture Notes in Business Information Processing

581

Series Editors

Wil van der Aalst, *RWTH Aachen University, Aachen, Germany*
Sudha Ram, *University of Arizona, Tucson, USA*
Michael Rosemann, *Queensland University of Technology, Brisbane, Australia*
Clemens Szyperski, *Microsoft Research, Redmond, USA*
Giancarlo Guizzardi, *University of Twente, Enschede, The Netherlands*

LNBIP reports state-of-the-art results in areas related to business information systems and industrial application software development – timely, at a high level, and in both printed and electronic form.

The type of material published includes

- Proceedings (published in time for the respective event)
- Postproceedings (consisting of thoroughly revised and/or extended final papers)
- Other edited monographs (such as, for example, project reports or invited volumes)
- Tutorials (coherently integrated collections of lectures given at advanced courses, seminars, schools, etc.)
- Award-winning or exceptional theses

LNBIP is abstracted/indexed in DBLP, EI and Scopus. LNBIP volumes are also submitted for the inclusion in ISI Proceedings.

Michael Dorner · Rudolf Ramler ·
Dietmar Winkler · Johannes Bergsmann
Editors

Software Architecture as the Backbone of Software Quality

18th International Conference on Software Quality, SWQD 2026
Vienna, Austria, May 19–21, 2026
Proceedings

Editors
Michael Dorner
Technische Hochschule Nürnberg Georg
Simon Ohm
Nuremberg, Germany

Dietmar Winkler
Center for Digital Production (CDP)
GmbH & TU Wien
Vienna, Austria

Rudolf Ramler
Software Competence Center Hagenberg
GmbH
Hagenberg, Austria

Johannes Bergsmann
Software Quality Lab GmbH
Linz, Austria

ISSN 1865-1348   ISSN 1865-1356 (electronic)
Lecture Notes in Business Information Processing
ISBN 978-3-032-24215-0   ISBN 978-3-032-24216-7 (eBook)
https://doi.org/10.1007/978-3-032-24216-7

© The Editor(s) (if applicable) and The Author(s), under exclusive license
to Springer Nature Switzerland AG 2026

This work is subject to copyright. All rights are solely and exclusively licensed by the Publisher, whether the whole or part of the material is concerned, specifically the rights of translation, reprinting, reuse of illustrations, recitation, broadcasting, reproduction on microfilms or in any other physical way, and transmission or information storage and retrieval, electronic adaptation, computer software, or by similar or dissimilar methodology now known or hereafter developed.
The use of general descriptive names, registered names, trademarks, service marks, etc. in this publication does not imply, even in the absence of a specific statement, that such names are exempt from the relevant protective laws and regulations and therefore free for general use.
The publisher, the authors and the editors are safe to assume that the advice and information in this book are believed to be true and accurate at the date of publication. Neither the publisher nor the authors or the editors give a warranty, expressed or implied, with respect to the material contained herein or for any errors or omissions that may have been made. The publisher remains neutral with regard to jurisdictional claims in published maps and institutional affiliations.

This Springer imprint is published by the registered company Springer Nature Switzerland AG
The registered company address is: Gewerbestrasse 11, 6330 Cham, Switzerland

If disposing of this product, please recycle the paper.

Message from the General Chair

The *Software Quality Days* (SWQD) conference and tools fair was first organized in 2009 and has since grown to become Europe's largest annual industry-oriented conference on software quality, supported by a strong and vibrant community. The SWQD conference program is designed to provide a stimulating mix of practice-oriented presentations, scientific contributions presenting new research topics, tutorials, and an exhibition area where tool vendors present solutions for the software quality domain.

This professional symposium offers valuable opportunities for professional development, the exchange of ideas, and networking. Participants benefit from keynote speeches, technical presentations, exhibitions, and tutorials delivered by experts from both academia and industry.

The SWQD conference welcomes professionals and researchers interested in the wide range of topics related to software quality, including software process and quality managers, software testers and test managers, product managers, agile coaches, project managers, software architects and designers, requirements engineers, user interface designers, software developers, IT managers, release managers, development managers, application engineers, DevOps specialists, and many others.

The guiding theme of SWQD 2026 was *"Software Architecture as the Backbone of Software Quality"*. Evolving product, process, and service requirements—such as distributed engineering projects, mobile applications, the involvement of heterogeneous disciplines and stakeholders, extended application domains, and the emergence of new technologies—introduce new challenges. Addressing these challenges may require adapted methods and tools to meet the continuously increasing demands for quality and security in modern software systems and applications.

May 2026   Johannes Bergsmann

Preface

The 18th *Software Quality Days* (SWQD) international conference and tools fair brought together researchers and practitioners from business, industry, and academia working in the areas of quality assurance and quality management for artificial intelligence, software and information technology. Over the years, SWQD has established itself as one of the largest conferences in Europe dedicated to software quality. SWQD 2026 was organized by fortiss GmbH (Munich, Germany), Software Competence Center Hagenberg GmbH (Hagenberg, Austria), Center for Digital Production GmbH (Vienna, Austria), TU Wien, Institute of Information Systems Engineering (Vienna, Austria), and Software Quality Lab GmbH (Linz),.

In recent years, the SWQD symposium has received a steadily growing number of scientific contributions. Since 2012, the conference has included a dedicated scientific program with peer-reviewed papers published in scientific proceedings. For this edition, we received 16 submissions from researchers worldwide. Each submission was reviewed by at least three members of the program committee.

Based on the single-blind review process, six papers were accepted as full research papers, resulting in an acceptance rate of 37%. In addition, two short papers presenting promising research directions and work in progress were accepted to stimulate discussion and exchange between researchers and practitioners. Furthermore, the proceedings include an invited keynote paper by Henry Muccini, providing a critical discussion of the strategic role of software architecture design, from traditional monolithic systems to emerging agentic software systems.

The accepted contributions from academia and industry cover a wide range of topics, including software testing, static quality assurance, software design, process quality, documentation, and software architecture in the context of artificial intelligence. The papers in this volume are organized according to thematic areas aligned with the guiding conference theme, *"Software Architecture as the Backbone of Software Quality."*

- Process Quality and Quality Assurance
- Software Architecture and Design
- Software Development and Documentation
- Software Testing and AI

May 2026

Michael Dorner
Rudolf Ramler
Dietmar Winkler

Organization

General Chair

Johannes Bergsmann — Software Quality Lab GmbH, Austria

Program Committee Chairs

Michael Dorner	Technische Hochschule Nürnberg Georg Simon Ohm, Germany
Rudolf Ramler	Software Competence Center Hagenberg GmbH, Austria
Dietmar Winkler	Austrian Center for Digital Production GmbH and TU Wien, Austria

Proceedings Chair

Dietmar Winkler — Austrian Center for Digital Production GmbH and TU Wien, Austria

Organizing and Publicity Chair

Petra Bergsmann — Software Quality Lab GmbH, Austria

Program Committee

Silvia Bonfanti	University of Bergamo, Italy
Maximilian Capraro	DATEV, Germany
Michael Felderer	German Aerospace Center (DLR), Germany
Henning Femmer	South Westphalia University of Applied Sciences, Germany
Stefan Fischer	Software Competence Center Hagenberg GmbH, Austria
Gordon Fraser	University of Passau, Germany

Julian Frattini	Chalmers University of Technology and University of Gothenburg, Sweden
Roman Haas	CQSE GmbH, Germany
Jens Heidrich	Fraunhofer IESE, Germany
Eckehard Hermann	University of Applied Sciences Upper Austria, Campus Hagenberg, Austria
Helena Holmström Olsson	University of Malmö, Sweden
Frank Houdek	Mercedes-Benz AG, Germany
Marco Kuhrmann	Reutlingen University, Germany
Harald Lampesberger	University of Applied Sciences Upper Austria, Campus Hagenberg, Austria
Christian Macho	University of Klagenfurt, Austria
Eda Marchetti	ISTI-CNR, Italian National Research Council, Italy
Paula Monteiro	University of Minho, Portugal
Jürgen Münch	Reutlingen University, Germany
Dietmar Pfahl	University of Tartu, Estonia
Josef Pichler	University of Applied Sciences Upper Austria, Campus Hagenberg, Austria
Rick Rabiser	Johannes Kepler University Linz, Austria
Miroslaw Staron	University of Gothenburg, Sweden
Andrea Stocco	Technische Universität München, Germany
Rini van Solingen	Delft University of Technology, Netherlands
Hugo Villamizar	fortiss GmbH, Germany
Ehsan Zabardast	Blekinge Institute of Technology, Sweden

Additional Reviewer

Ivan Esau	South Westphalia University of Applied Sciences, Germany

Contents

Keynote

Architecting for Quality: The Strategic Role of Architecture Design
from Monoliths to Agentic Software Systems 3
Henry Muccini

Process Quality and Quality Assurance

On Effort Awareness for Just-In-Time Defect Prediction 25
Peter Bludau and Alexander Pretschner

Business Intelligence Architecture for Process Quality Monitoring
with BDD 42
Stefan Biffl, Matteo Martinelli, Hossein Rahmani, and Marco Picone

Software Architecture and Design

Using LLMs to Evaluate Architecture Documents – Results from a Digital
Marketplace Environment 65
Frank Elberzhager, Matthias Gerbershagen, and Joshua Ginkel

AI-Assisted REST API Design with Large Language Models 82
*Jorge Martinez-Gil, Christoph Daxerer, Mario Winterer,
Cornelia Neumüller, and Matthias Krump*

Software Development and Documentation

Generative AI for Software Development: Study on Current Utilization
in Upper Austria 101
Simon Mairinger and Thomas Ziebermayr

Automating Documentation of Complex Data Processing Flows
with Large Language Models 113
*Parisa Mahya, Jorge Martinez-Gil, Mario Winterer,
Cornelia Neumüller, and Matthias Krump*

Software Testing and AI

Improving the Quality of GitHub Copilot Generated Unit Tests 127
  Max Schallermayer and Markus Schnappinger

LLM Agents for Autonomous System Testing: A Semi-structured
Literature Review 147
  Stefan Fischer and Werner Kloihofer

Author Index 169

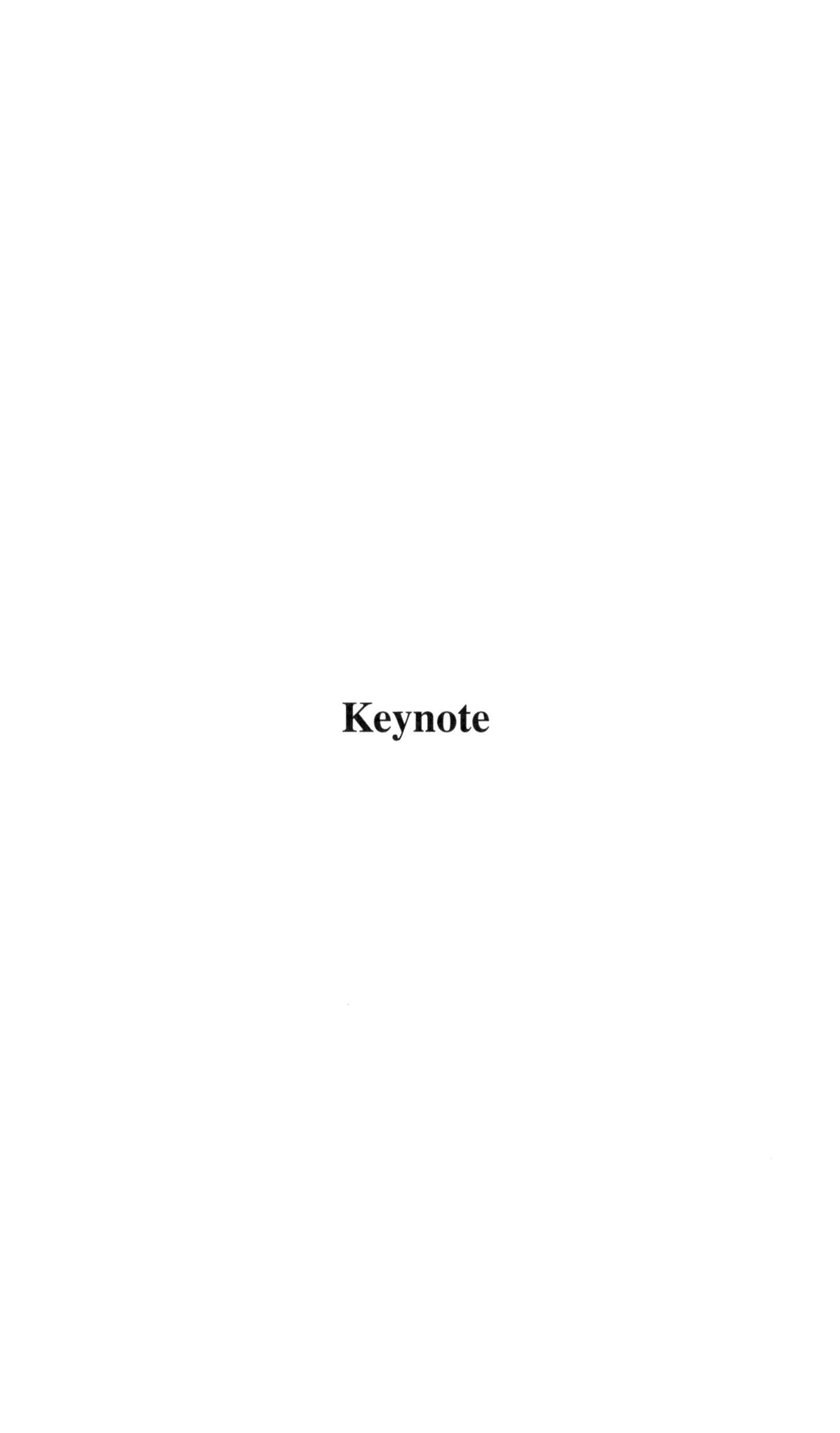

Keynote

Architecting for Quality: The Strategic Role of Architecture Design from Monoliths to Agentic Software Systems

Henry Muccini[(✉)][iD]

FrAmeLab @Software Engineering Research Group,
University of L'Aquila, Via Vetoio, 67100 L'Aquila, Italy
`henry.muccini@univaq.it`

Abstract. *If a building collapses, we do not blame the inspectors who checked the windows; we blame the foundation. Why, in software, do we still expect testing to save a failing architecture?*

Software quality must be viewed as an emergent property of architectural decisions rather than a post-development discovery. It is not achieved through testing alone; it is secured through intentional design. This paper, based on the keynote for Software Quality Days 2026, explores the foundational and evolving role of software architecture design as the primary driver of quality assurance. By adopting a "shift-left" imperative, we move from a reactive "detect and fix" mentality to a proactive "prevent and design" philosophy.

We first examine the role of architectures for quality engineering. Then, we discuss the techniques architectural design supports to achieve quality. The paper ends with an overview of the strategic role of architectural design for quality assurance from monolithic applications to agentic systems.

Keywords: Software Quality · Software Architecture · Agentic AI

1 Introduction

In the contemporary landscape of software engineering, software quality is frequently relegated to a post-hoc verification activity, characterized by reactive discovery during testing phases. However, as system complexity scales, this paradigm proves insufficient. Scientific rigor demands that quality be treated as a structural property that must be initiated *a priori* through intentional design. This proactive engineering of quality attributes is the primary domain of software Architecture.

Software architecture constitutes the synthesis of significant design decisions that form the system's backbone. It defines the structural constraints and the non-functional boundaries within which the implementation resides. By *"shifting*

© The Author(s), under exclusive license to Springer Nature Switzerland AG 2026
M. Dorner et al. (Eds.): SWQD 2026, LNBIP 581, pp. 3–22, 2026.
https://doi.org/10.1007/978-3-032-24216-7_1

left" on quality assurance, we allow for the formal analysis of trade-offs—such as the tension between performance and security—long before development begins. This architectural backbone has undergone a profound evolution, adapting to the shifting requirements of system topology and computational paradigms.

During the era of *monolithic* and *multi-tier client–server* enterprise systems, architecture quality was already a multi-dimensional concern. Architects addressed not only internal modularity and cohesion, but also performance, availability, security, scalability, and operability—typically within a single deployable unit or a small number of tightly managed tiers. In these systems, many quality attributes could often be engineered through centralized control points (e.g., a single database, shared transaction manager, centralized authentication, and controlled deployment topology). While emergent behavior can certainly arise even in monoliths—through concurrency, shared state, configuration, or complex dependencies—it was usually confined within clearer runtime and operational boundaries, and mitigated using established architectural styles, patterns, and tactics (e.g., layering, caching, pooling, replication, and access-control mechanisms).

The transition to *microservices* did not introduce architecture quality concerns from scratch; rather, it redistributed and amplified them. Decomposition into independently deployable services increases autonomy and evolvability, but moves key quality responsibilities into inter-service communication, data ownership, and runtime coordination. As a consequence, system-level qualities such as reliability, performance, and security become more dependent on orchestration effects, network behavior, and partial failures, making emergent behavior more frequent and harder to diagnose. This shift elevates the role of patterns and tactics for distributed systems (e.g., circuit breakers, bulkheads, sagas, idempotency, backpressure), along with observability and continuous verification, to manage the new failure modes and preserve architectural intent under constant change.

The integration of *machine learning* (ML) components into traditional deterministic systems necessitates taking into account the stochastic nature of models and the volatility of data. Currently, we face the *Agentic AI* frontier, where LLM-based agents introduce autonomous reasoning into the system. In this probabilistic era, the architectural backbone must act as a set of sophisticated guardrails to ensure the desired qualities.

This paper explores the trajectory of this evolution, arguing that architecture remains the singular constant in the quest for software excellence. It is structured in such a way that Sect. 2 introduces the significance of software architecture as the primary software quality artifact; Sect. 3 explains how architecture design and analysis support the achievement of software quality goals. Section 4 discusses the strategic, and evolving, role of architecture design from monolithic applications to nowadays' AI-enabled and agentic software systems. Section 6 concludes this work.

2   Architecture as the Primary Quality Artifact

A rigorous scientific definition of software architecture exceeds the visual abstraction of components and connectors. It is more accurately described as the collection of significant architecture design decisions made by different stakeholders to address competing concerns [1,2]. User stories, constraints, business goal and contextual information are passed to architects whose decisions shape the overall skeleton of the system. Once implemented, architecture decisions are characterized by a high cost of change [3,4], in contrast to source code that remains relatively easy to modify. Using the civil engineering metaphor, if code represents the interior design of a building, architecture represents its backbone: a late correction of a deficiency in the foundation (the architecture) is orders of magnitude more costly than refactoring the interior finishes (the code). Consequently, *quality must be engineered into the structural design a priori.*

Architecture is the primary artifact where non-functional requirements — mostly being referred to as Quality Attributes (QAs)—are addressed. While functional requirements dictate what a system does, the architecture determines *how well* it performs those functions under various constraints. However, the efficacy of an architectural design is measured by its ability to support not simply specific QAs, but rather to handle the inherent tension between orthogonal competing "ilities". Architecture is fundamentally a discipline *of trade-offs*, since optimization in one dimension often necessitates degradation in another.

For instance, the architectural decision to prioritize near-real-time responsiveness through aggressive data polling and high-frequency synchronization may achieve superior performance metrics and user experience. However, such a design necessarily increases the duty cycle of hardware components, thereby elevating the system's power requirements and overall carbon footprint. Conversely, optimizing for sustainability by implementing "lazy" evaluation or batch-processing patterns reduces energy consumption but introduces latent delays that may compromise strict performance service level agreements. Consequently, a rigorous architectural methodology does not treat design as the quest for an absolute or perfect state. Instead, it is defined as the systematic negotiation of trade-offs, where design decisions are validated based on their ability to achieve a sufficient and balanced reconciliation of competing constraints within a multi-dimensional design space.

3   Software Quality Through Architecture Improvement Techniques

Architecture quality is not ensured by a single artifact or review, but rather by a set of complementary techniques that (i) make quality concerns explicit, (ii) evaluate architectural decisions early, and (iii) continuously preserve architectural intent as the system evolves. In the following, without any claim to offer a complete overview of the state of the art, we summarize major techniques that have been widely adopted in both research and practice to achieve and sustain architecture quality systematically.

This section analyzes how to design for quality (Sect. 3.1), how to evaluate an architecture for trade-offs (Sect. 3.2), how to document architectural artifacts and decisions (Sect. 3.3). Then, the focus moves to best practices for reusable architectures (Sect. 3.4), followed by early validation through model-driven engineering (Sect. 3.5), to conclude with continuous verification of evolving architectures (Sect. 3.6).

3.1 Quality-Attribute–Driven Design

A foundational mechanism for achieving architecture quality is to treat quality attributes—such as performance, availability, security, sustainability, trustworthiness—as first-class drivers of design rather than as secondary constraints. Bass et al. [4] emphasize the use of explicit quality-attribute reasoning and tactics in architecture practice. In this approach, architects formulate quality-attribute scenarios (*stimulus and its source, response and its measure, environment, and artifact*) and select architectural tactics and structural strategies that are known to influence the targeted qualities [4]. Importantly, this makes trade-offs explicit—for example, recognizing that higher availability via redundancy may increase operational complexity and cost—thereby constraining the architectural search space and clarifying decision priorities.

Purpose: Synthesize/design an architecture to meet prioritized quality goals.

3.2 Scenario-Based Architecture Evaluation and Trade-Off Analysis

Among the most established classic approaches for quality assurance at the architectural level are scenario-based evaluation methods, which assess an architectural candidate against stakeholder-relevant quality concerns before significant implementation effort is invested. These methods are particularly valuable because they make quality risks explicit, structure stakeholder discussion, and expose design trade-offs early, when changes are less costly [5–7].

SAAM (Software Architecture Analysis Method) is an early systematic method based on scenarios, with a strong focus on modifiability and change impact analysis [6]. By evaluating how an architecture accommodates representative change scenarios, SAAM helps identify tightly coupled components and structurally fragile areas. ATAM (Architecture Tradeoff Analysis Method) extends this scenario-based reasoning to multiple quality attributes (e.g., performance, availability, security, modifiability) and explicitly supports trade-off analysis [5]. Through structured stakeholder elicitation and architectural examination, ATAM identifies risks, sensitivity points, and trade-off points that influence the achievement of quality goals.

CBAM (Cost Benefit Analysis Method) complements ATAM by adding economic reasoning to architectural evaluation [7]. It supports the comparison of alternative architectural strategies in terms of expected benefit, implementation, and operational cost, and overall value under budget and schedule constraints.

Overall: Taken together, SAAM, ATAM, and CBAM provide a rigorous basis for architecture-level quality assurance by producing an explicit, scenario-grounded view of risks, trade-offs, and value before deep implementation begins. At the same time, the effectiveness of these methods depends on the quality of stakeholder input and the evaluators' experience, which can introduce an element of subjectivity.

Purpose: Evaluate/analyze architecture options to meet the quality goals.

3.3 Documentation for Architecture Quality: Multi-view Specification, Decision Capture, and Traceability

Architecture quality is difficult to sustain if architectural intent, key decisions, and their rationale are not explicitly documented and maintained over time. In practice, quality degradation often emerges not only from poor initial design choices, but also from the progressive loss of architectural knowledge during system evolution. For this reason, documentation for architecture quality should combine three complementary mechanisms: (i) *multi-view specification* of the architecture, (ii) *decision capture* through Architecture Decision Records (ADRs), and (iii) *traceability* links across quality drivers, decisions, architectural elements, and downstream artifacts.

A first pillar is *multi-view architectural specification.* ISO/IEC/IEEE 42010 defines architecture descriptions in terms of stakeholders, concerns, viewpoints, and views, emphasizing that no single representation is sufficient to address all relevant concerns [8,9]. This is particularly important for quality assurance, since qualities such as performance, security, deployment, and operability require different viewpoints and review lenses. Multi-view descriptions therefore improve communication and reviewability while reducing the risk of architectural erosion [4,8,9].

A second pillar is *decision capture.* ADRs provide a lightweight mechanism to document architecturally significant decisions, alternatives, rationale, and consequences [10]. Empirical and reflective studies show that ADRs support knowledge sharing and continuity in practice, while also reinforcing design awareness and architectural reasoning within teams [11–13]. Their contribution to architecture quality is therefore both technical (preserving rationale) and socio-technical (supporting consistent decision-making).

A third pillar is *architectural traceability.* Traceability links quality drivers, architectural decisions, and the structures that realize them, enabling impact analysis, conformance reasoning, and maintenance [14,15]. In particular, traceability helps preserve alignment between architectural intent and evolving implementation artifacts, which is essential when systems change rapidly.

Overall: multi-view specification, ADR-based decision capture, and traceability are distinct but mutually reinforcing techniques: views improve concern coverage and communication, ADRs preserve rationale, and traceability maintains the chain from concerns to decisions to realization. Together, they provide a compact but effective foundation for sustaining architecture quality over time.

Purpose: Document architecture solutions and design decisions.

3.4 Leveraging Reference Architectures, Styles, Patterns, and Tactics

A recurring strategy for achieving architecture quality is to reuse and adapt architectural knowledge at different levels of abstraction. In particular, *reference architectures, architectural styles/patterns*, and *architectural tactics* play distinct but complementary roles: reference architectures provide domain- or organization-level guidance, styles and patterns structure the solution space at system level, and tactics operationalize quality-attribute improvements through targeted design decisions.

Reference architectures support quality assurance by capturing reusable architectural knowledge, constraints, and recommended structures for a family of systems. They help reduce unnecessary variability, promote consistency across teams, and provide curated defaults that can improve interoperability, maintainability, and governance. Prior work has shown that the effectiveness of reference architectures depends on the congruence among their goals, context, and design, and that different reference architecture types are appropriate for different adoption settings [16, 17]. More recent mapping evidence further confirms the growing use of reference architectures across domains, while also highlighting differences in maturity, stakeholder involvement, and industrial uptake that affect their practical impact on quality [18]. Thus, reference architectures are most useful when treated not as rigid templates, but as structured quality-oriented guidance that can be tailored and justified in context.

At the system-design level, *architectural styles* and *patterns* provide reusable solutions to recurring structural problems and encode known trade-offs among quality attributes. Pattern-oriented architecture literature emphasizes that patterns are not isolated prescriptions, but part of a broader design vocabulary (and often a pattern language) that supports coherent reasoning across design decisions [19, 20]. In practice, selecting a style (e.g., layered, event-driven, microservices, modular monolith) strongly shapes modifiability, deployment complexity, performance behavior, and operational coupling; finer-grained patterns (e.g., circuit breakers, sagas, anti-corruption layers) then address recurring concerns within that chosen structural context. Contemporary architecture guidance also reinforces this distinction between high-level structural choices and lower-level design mechanisms, framing styles/patterns as reusable means to realize architectural characteristics under explicit trade-offs [21].

Architectural tactics operate at a more fine-grained level than styles and patterns: they are design decisions aimed at improving a specific quality attribute response (e.g., introducing redundancy for availability, caching for performance, or encapsulation boundaries for modifiability). Tactics are particularly important because they bridge quality scenarios and concrete design moves, enabling more methodical architectural design [22]. They also interact with patterns and styles rather than replacing them; in practice, patterns often realize bundles of tactics, and tactic choices can constrain or refine pattern selection [23]. Finally, recent work on detecting and tracing tactics in code highlights an important quality-assurance implication: tactics must remain visible and monitorable during implementation and evolution, otherwise the original quality intent can be lost even when the high-level architecture appears unchanged [24].

Overall: these mechanisms address quality at complementary levels. Reference architectures provide reusable architectural guidance across systems, styles and patterns structure the solution within a system, and tactics target specific quality responses within that structure.

Purpose: Best practices for designing quality architectures.

3.5 Early Validation Through Modeling and Model-Driven Simulation

Early validation of architectural decisions can be achieved through *model-based analysis*, i.e., by using architectural models as analyzable artifacts before substantial implementation effort is invested. Compared to purely qualitative reviews, modeling enables architects to obtain executable or formal evidence about behavioral and quality-related properties while design alternatives are still inexpensive to change. In this sense, architectural modeling complements scenario-based evaluation methods by providing stronger analytical support for validating assumptions and comparing candidate solutions.

A broad body of work shows that software architecture models can be exploited through model checking, simulation, and model-based testing. Model-checking approaches support early reasoning about correctness and behavioral properties at the architectural level, with different trade-offs in terms of expressiveness, scalability, and automation [25]. In parallel, model-driven architecture-based testing and architecture-driven testing approaches use design and architectural models to derive or guide test artifacts, thus improving test planning and helping preserve alignment between architectural intent and implementation-level verification [26,27]. More generally, methodological overviews on software architecture validation highlight model-based techniques as a key means to assess architectural adequacy early and systematically [28].

Within this space, *model-driven simulation based on architectural models* is particularly relevant for quality evaluation under dynamic conditions (e.g., varying workloads, deployment choices, and interaction patterns). Prior work has shown how architectural descriptions (including UML-based models) can be transformed into simulation models to assess quality behavior before implementation [29], and how DEVS-based approaches support architectural simulation for joint functional and quality evaluation [30]. Simulation has also been used in layered modeling-and-simulation architectures for agent-based systems [31] and in architecture-centric frameworks for situational-aware cyber-physical systems, including CAPS/CAPSim, to analyze system behavior and support code generation from architectural models [32–34].

A major application area is *performance validation at the architecture level*. Early software performance engineering work established the importance of evaluating performance at the architectural stage, where decisions about concurrency, communication, deployment, and allocation have the highest leverage and are hardest to fix later [35,36]. Model-driven approaches further advanced this perspective by enabling transformations from design/architecture models to analyzable performance models [37]. The Palladio ecosystem operationalizes this idea through the Palladio Component Model, supporting architecture-level modeling and simulation for prediction of quality-of-service properties and comparison of alternatives [38–40]. Recent work extends this line to continuous performance engineering in microservice-based systems by linking architectural models with runtime data [41].

Overall: modeling and model-driven simulation provide a rigorous foundation for early architectural validation: they allow architects to analyze behavioral and quality properties, compare alternatives quantitatively, and strengthen confidence in architectural decisions before deep implementation commitment.

Purpose: early validation.

3.6 Continuous Architectural Verification Through Automated Checks

Modern software evolution can rapidly undermine architecture quality unless conformance is verified continuously. This need is consistent with the *continuous architecture* perspective, which emphasizes that architecture and implementation co-evolve in Agile/DevOps contexts and therefore require recurrent validation rather than one-off assessments [42–44].

A key technique is to express architectural constraints as executable checks in the delivery pipeline. This includes automated conformance rules (e.g., forbidden dependencies, layering constraints, coupling thresholds), API and schema compatibility tests, and contract testing between components or services. More generally, *architecture fitness functions* operationalize architectural characteristics as measurable, repeatable tests: rather than assuming that architecture "stays good," teams continuously evaluate whether key properties (e.g., latency SLOs, resilience expectations, dependency rules, security baselines) are preserved across releases [45].

The importance of continuous verification is further reinforced by research on architecture evaluation under uncertainty and continuous development. Systematic evidence shows that many evaluation approaches still struggle to connect design-time and run-time concerns, especially in dynamic environments [46]. In response, recent work on architecture evaluation in continuous development argues for adapted evaluation practices and dedicated feedback loops that provide useful architectural feedback during ongoing development, rather than only at major milestones [47]. Similarly, continuous software architecture analysis highlights the need to align architecture analysis activities with incremental and iterative development rhythms [44].

Overall: continuous architectural verification reframes architecture quality as a property that must be *continuously enforced and re-assessed* through automation and feedback. This reduces architectural drift, makes violations visible early, and better matches the realities of continuously evolving systems in Agile/DevOps settings [42,43,47].

Purpose: continuous verification.

4   The Strategic Role of Architecture Design for Quality Assurance: from Monolithic Applications to Agentic Systems

As software engineering progressed from early monolithic systems to today's AI-enabled and agentic applications, software architecture remained a primary vehicle for engineering and sustaining system quality. Importantly, this evolution was not a direct leap from monoliths to microservices. Enterprise systems adopted *componentized* and *tiered* architectures well before microservices—including client–server and N-tier (e.g., 3-tier) structures, component-based software engineering (CBSE), and later service-oriented architecture (SOA). Each step redistributed quality responsibilities across architectural boundaries and increased the need for explicit design rationale and architecture-aware analysis.

Accordingly, this section examines how architectural design and analysis for quality assurance evolved across four stages: monolithic applications (Sect. 4.1), componentized enterprise systems (Sect. 4.2), microservice-based systems (Sect. 4.3), and AI-enabled and agentic applications (Sect. 4.4).

4.1   Architecture Design and Analysis for Quality in Monolithic Applications

In monolithic applications, architectural quality is pursued within a single deployable unit (and often within a small number of tightly managed tiers), but it has long been a multi-dimensional concern. Besides enforcing *internal modularity*—through stable module boundaries, dependency directions, and responsibility allocation—architects also design for performance, availability, security, scalability, and operability, frequently leveraging centralized control points such as shared databases, transaction managers, and authentication mechanisms [48,49]. In this setting, architecture design and analysis focus on preserving cohesion and controlling coupling across layers and subsystems, while using established styles, patterns, and tactics (e.g., layering, caching, pooling, replication) to meet quality goals under relatively well-defined deployment and operational boundaries.

Classic software architecture analysis methods (e.g., scenario-based and trade-off-oriented methods surveyed by Dobrica and Niemelä [49]) help assess whether the chosen decomposition supports the desired quality attributes before implementation lock-in. At the code/design level, quantitative indicators such as coupling, cohesion, and complexity metrics (including CK metrics) provide a complementary signal on whether architectural intent is being preserved in implementation [50]. Empirical evidence also shows that architectural structure influences defect proneness and software evolution outcomes, reinforcing the practical value of architecture-aware design and analysis [51].

This monolith-centric view remains relevant today, especially with the rise of *modular monoliths* as an intentional architecture strategy in cloud settings [52]. Notably, recent industrial experience also suggests a non-trivial *reverse trend*: some organizations are consolidating overly fine-grained or operationally costly microservice landscapes back into modular monoliths to reduce distributed complexity while preserving clear internal boundaries. However, at scale, team autonomy and independent deployability often remain dominant concerns, and software engineering progressively shifted from "quality through internal modularization" toward "quality through distributed architectural boundaries," thereby motivating the transition to component-based systems and, later on, to microservice applications.

4.2   Architecture Design and Analysis for Quality in Componentized Enterprise Systems

Between monolithic applications and microservices, many industrial systems evolved through *componentized* paradigms such as client–server and multi-tier architectures, Component-Based Software Engineering (CBSE), and Service Oriented Architectures (SOA). This period did not replace quality concerns; it *reallocated* them across components, tiers, and integration mechanisms. Architecture design focused on establishing stable component boundaries and well-defined interfaces, while architectural analysis increasingly accounted for deployment topologies, middleware interactions, and the dependencies that span components.

In CBSE, quality was pursued through encapsulation and interface-driven composition: components were treated as independently developed units with explicit provided/required interfaces, promoting reuse and modifiability while enabling more systematic reasoning about compatibility and substitution [53]. In parallel, enterprise architecture patterns consolidated around layered and tiered structures (e.g., presentation, domain, data access), which made certain quality tactics easier to implement via central control points (e.g., caching layers, connection pooling, centralized authentication, transaction management) [54]. However, these same structures introduced integration and performance sensitivities at tier boundaries, so architecture analysis had to address communication costs, concurrency, and resource contention across tiers.

SOA further externalized component boundaries into network-addressable services and emphasized service contracts, composition, and governance. This introduced new quality trade-offs: while service orientation improved organizational alignment and integration flexibility, it also increased the importance of contract stability, versioning, message mediation, and end-to-end latency across service compositions [55,56]. Compared to monoliths, emergent behavior became more frequent due to distributed interactions and middleware effects, yet systems were often governed through stricter standardization and centralized deployment/release practices than in microservices.

This componentized era established much of the technical and conceptual groundwork later amplified by microservices: explicit interface/contract thinking, decomposition aligned to organizational boundaries, and quality achieved through a combination of design-time structure and runtime coordination. Microservices intensified these principles by pushing toward finer-grained services, independent deployment, and decentralized governance, which increases the need for continuous architectural verification and operational feedback.

4.3   Architecture Design and Analysis for Quality in Microservice Applications

Microservice architectures inherit the quality concerns of earlier monolithic *and componentized enterprise* systems, but intensify them in a more decentralized and independently deployable setting. As a result, software architecture design and analysis become even more central: architects must define not only module/component boundaries, but also *service boundaries*, interaction styles, data ownership, deployment topology, and operational controls suited to frequent change and partial failures. The literature consistently reports that the shift toward microservices is motivated by quality goals such as scalability, deployability, team autonomy, and evolvability, while simultaneously introducing new risks and trade-offs in performance, reliability, observability, and operational complexity [57–60].

From a design perspective, quality in microservices depends on the quality of decomposition decisions: service granularity, bounded contexts, API contracts, and data partitioning directly shape latency, fault propagation, and maintainability. Comparative studies and reviews show that microservices are not universally superior to monoliths; rather, they trade local simplicity for distributed flexibility, making architecture decisions highly context-dependent [57,61,62]. This is why architecture design in microservices must remain explicitly *quality-attribute-driven*, with clear prioritization of scalability, resilience, consistency, and operability constraints before migration or decomposition.

Architecture analysis and verification are equally important *after design*. In microservices, many critical failures emerge from runtime interactions rather than isolated component defects. Workload characterization, for example, is essential to understand inter-service communication patterns, skew, and bottlenecks that directly affect performance and scalability [63]. Similarly, continuous software engineering in microservices highlights that architecture quality cannot be treated as a one-time artifact: frequent releases, independent deployments, and evolving APIs require recurring architecture checks and operational feedback loops [64]. In practice, this motivates architecture conformance checks, contract testing, compatibility validation, and continuous monitoring as part of the development pipeline.

Another important lesson from monolith to componentized and microservice-based systems is that migration itself is a *quality engineering process*, not merely a structural refactoring. Migration studies emphasize the need to define target quality attributes up front and use them to guide decomposition and sequencing decisions; otherwise, organizations risk replacing monolithic complexity with distributed fragility [58,65,66]. Recent work on modular monoliths also suggests that in some contexts, improving architectural modularity inside a monolith may yield better quality/cost trade-offs than premature service decomposition [52].

This progression—from monoliths through componentized and, in many cases, microservice-based systems—also reflects a broader change in software engineering practice: architectural quality is increasingly sustained not only through design-time structure but also through the combined effects of design, runtime monitoring/analysis, and continuous verification. This shift is especially driven by the rise of highly dynamic, self-adaptive, and cloud-hosted systems that must cope with variable load and partial failures, supported by virtualization (and later containers) and automated delivery pipelines.

4.4   Architecture Design and Analysis for Quality in ML-Enabled Systems and Agentic AI

ML-enabled and agentic applications further expand the scope of software architecture quality assurance. In these systems, architecture must coordinate heterogeneous elements—traditional software services, data pipelines, models, feature stores, prompt/tool orchestration, memory components, and human oversight workflows—whose interactions determine system quality. Consequently, software architecture design, analysis, and verification remain essential, but must be extended beyond classical code-centric concerns to include *data quality, model behavior, monitoring and retraining processes*, and *trustworthiness controls* [67–70].

A foundational insight from ML systems engineering is that many failures are architectural rather than purely algorithmic. Sculley et al. [68] describe how ML systems accumulate hidden technical debt through entanglement, undeclared consumers, feedback loops, and pipeline dependencies. This directly supports an architectural viewpoint: quality depends on explicit boundaries, dependency management, and observability across the full ML pipeline, not just model accuracy. Amershi et al. [67] further show that industrial ML development spans a multi-stage workflow involving data collection, labeling, training, deployment, and monitoring, requiring architectural coordination across roles and tools. In other words, *architecture becomes the mechanism that integrates software engineering and data science practices into a quality-governed system lifecycle.*

Design-time architectural decisions in ML-enabled systems should therefore explicitly address: (i) separation of online inference from offline training; (ii) reproducible data/model pipelines; (iii) feature and schema governance; (iv) fallback and degradation strategies; and (v) monitoring hooks for drift, performance, and safety. Operationally, production readiness depends on systematic verification practices such as the ML Test Score and continuous data validation, which convert tacit engineering expectations into repeatable checks [71,72]. These mechanisms play a role analogous to architecture fitness functions in conventional systems, but target ML-specific failure modes (e.g., schema drift, distribution shift, stale features, training-serving skew).

MLOps research reinforces this architectural perspective by framing *quality as a socio-technical pipeline problem*: successful ML systems require coordinated automation, CI/CD processes, continuous testing, metadata management, and runtime feedback loops [70]. Surveys of deployment case studies likewise show that challenges arise across all stages, from problem framing and data pipelines to integration and maintenance, implying that architecture analysis must consider lifecycle dependencies and operational uncertainty from the outset [69]. Domain-specific QA literature (e.g., in radiation therapy) adds a critical lesson for high-stakes contexts: acceptable uncertainty must be bounded through validation protocols, monitoring, and human-in-the-loop controls [73]. More general QA guidance for ML-based AI also emphasizes structured assurance dimensions beyond raw predictive performance [74].

For *agentic* applications (e.g., LLM-based agents and multi-agent systems), these concerns intensify because system behavior emerges from iterative reasoning, tool use, memory, and environment interaction. The architecture must define guardrails for tool permissions, state management, recovery, observability, and escalation to humans. Recent surveys highlight common architectural building blocks (planning, memory, tools, reflection) and evaluation challenges for LLM-based autonomous agents [75,76]. From a software architecture viewpoint, this means quality assurance should be framed at multiple levels: component quality (e.g., LLM, reasoners, planners, retrievers), orchestration quality (workflow correctness, latency, robustness), and mission-level quality (task success, safety, compliance, controllability).

Finally, trustworthy AI assurance provides the governance layer that links architectural decisions to organizational risk management. Frameworks such as the NIST AI RMF position trustworthiness as a lifecycle property that must be designed, measured, and monitored across development and operation [77]. For ML-enabled and agentic applications, architecture is therefore the primary vehicle for operationalizing assurance: it allocates responsibilities, embeds checks, structures feedback loops, and makes quality attributes auditable in systems whose behavior is partly learned and partly programmed.

5   Future Horizons: AI-Enhanced Architecture Quality

Rather than viewing AI as an end in itself, we position it as a *supportive mechanism* for strengthening architecture design, analysis, and verification in future-quality systems. The central idea is that AI can help turn architectural intent (e.g., quality-attribute scenarios, tactics, constraints, and policies) into *continuously enforced* and *measurable* properties, reducing the gap between design-time decisions and run-time reality. This goal may be achieved through different evolution paths, as presented below.

AI-Enhanced Architectures as Autonomous Guardrails: we envision AI-enhanced architectures as a means to implement *autonomous guardrails*. As systems increasingly incorporate ML components and agentic AI, system behavior becomes more probabilistic and context-dependent, and quality assurance must move beyond static design compliance. In this setting, *architecture should encode guardrails that constrain and shape autonomy:* permissions for tool use, data access boundaries, escalation paths to humans, termination and recovery rules, and acceptable operational envelopes (e.g., latency, cost, energy, privacy, and safety constraints). AI then acts as an enforcement and adaptation layer, monitoring whether the system remains within these envelopes and triggering corrective actions when it does not.

From Passive Monitoring to Self-Healing Quality Control: AI-enhanced architectures also enable a shift from passive observability to *self-healing quality control.* By combining architectural knowledge (views, ADRs, service dependencies, policies) with telemetry (logs, traces, metrics, model/prompt signals), AI can support anomaly detection, causal diagnosis, and targeted remediation recommendations. Crucially, this should not be interpreted as unrestricted autonomy: architectural guardrails define what actions are allowed (e.g., safe rollback, configuration adjustment, resource reallocation, circuit breaking, failover, or model fallback), and AI selects or sequences actions within these constraints. The outcome is a self-guarded architecture in which corrective behavior is both automated and auditable.

AI-Assisted Implementation Synthesis and Continuous Verification: a further horizon is *AI-assisted implementation synthesis* guided by architectural intent. Instead of using AI solely to generate code, the architecture can provide explicit constraints and quality goals that steer generation (e.g., dependency rules, interface contracts, performance budgets, security baselines). Candidate implementations (or architectural refactorings) can then be automatically verified against architecture-level quality checks, such as conformance rules, contract tests, policy checks, and fitness functions. This supports an iterative loop in which multiple candidate solutions are generated, executed, and evaluated under realistic workloads and operational conditions, converging toward implementations that best satisfy architectural constraints. This perspective also suggests a practical refinement over purely model-based exploration. While modeling and simulation remain valuable for early reasoning, AI-enhanced architectures can additionally support *execution-based* evaluation: alternative implementations are exercised in controlled environments (e.g., canary releases, shadow traffic, sandboxed agent workflows), with automated assessment of quality objectives. Software engineers remain responsible for final decisions and accountability, but AI can reduce the exploration cost and increase the evidence available for selecting among competing solutions.

Governance and Accountability: finally, AI-enhanced architecture quality must be aligned with governance and trustworthiness requirements. Guardrails should be defined as enforceable policies and accompanied by evidence-producing mechanisms (e.g., audit logs, provenance tracking, decision traces, and compliance checks). In this sense, architectural quality becomes inseparable from organizational risk management: the architecture does not only prescribe structure, but also embeds the constraints, verification hooks, and accountability mechanisms needed to operate AI-enabled and agentic systems safely over time.

6 Conclusion

This paper has argued that software quality is not a post-hoc discovery achieved through testing, but an emergent property of intentional architectural decisions. By adopting a "shift-left" imperative, software architecture serves as the system's structural backbone, defining the non-functional boundaries and structural constraints within which implementation resides.

As systems have evolved from monolithic units with centralized control to the current frontier of agentic AI, the strategic role of architectural design has only intensified. In the contemporary probabilistic era, the architectural backbone must evolve to act as a set of sophisticated guardrails that ensure system reliability and trustworthiness amidst autonomous reasoning and stochastic model behavior.

Ultimately, while technologies and computational paradigms shift, architecture remains the singular constant and the primary vehicle for engineering and sustaining software excellence.

Acknowledgment. The author would like to thank Rick Kazman, Patricia Lago, and Ralf Reussner for their feedback on a preliminary version of this paper.

References

1. Jansen, A., Bosch, J.: Software architecture as a set of architectural design decisions. In: 5th Working IEEE/IFIP Conference on Software Architecture (WICSA 2005), pp. 109–120 (2005). https://doi.org/10.1109/WICSA.2005.61
2. Babar, M.A., Dingsøyr, T., Lago, P., Van Vliet, H. (eds.): Software Architecture Knowledge Management. Springer (2009). https://doi.org/10.1007/978-3-642-02374-3
3. Fowler, M.: Design - who needs an architect? IEEE Softw. **20**(5), 11–13 (2003). https://doi.org/10.1109/MS.2003.1231144
4. Bass, L., Clements, P., Kazman, R.: Software Architecture in Practice, 4th edn. Addison-Wesley Professional (2021)
5. Kazman, R., Klein, M., Clements, P.: ATAM: method for architecture evaluation (CMU/SEI-2000-TR-004). Available from SEI Library (2000)
6. Abowd, G., Bass, L., Kazman, R., Webb, M.: SAAM: a method for analyzing the properties of software architectures (1996). https://www.sei.cmu.edu/library/saam-a-method-for-analyzing-the-properties-of-software-architectures/.   SEI Library entry (reposted by SEI)

7. Asundi, J., Kazman, R., Klein, M.H.: Using economic considerations to choose among architecture design alternatives. Technical report, CMU/SEI-2001-TR-035, Software Engineering Institute, Carnegie Mellon University (2001). https://www.sei.cmu.edu/library/using-economic-considerations-to-choose-among-architecture-design-alternatives/. SEI Library entry
8. ISO/IEC/IEEE 42010:2011 systems and software engineering—architecture description (2011). Architecture description standard defining concepts such as stakeholders, concerns, viewpoints, and views
9. ISO/IEC/IEEE 42010:2022 software, systems and enterprise—architecture description (2022). Updated edition of the architecture description standard
10. Nygard, M.: Documenting Architecture Decisions. Blog post, Cognitect (2011). https://www.cognitect.com/blog/2011/11/15/documenting-architecture-decisions
11. Ahmeti, B., Linder, M., Groner, R., Wohlrab, R.: Architecture decision records in practice: an action research study. In: Proceedings of the 18th European Conference on Software Architecture (ECSA). Springer (2024). https://doi.org/10.5281/zenodo.11635100. See also accompanying Zenodo material
12. Tofan, D., Galster, M., Avgeriou, P., Schuitema, W.: Past and future of software architectural decisions – a systematic mapping study. Inf. Softw. Technol. **56**(8), 850–872 (2014). https://doi.org/10.1016/j.infsof.2014.03.009
13. Keeling, M.: The psychology of architecture decision records. IEEE Softw. **39**(6), 114–117 (2022). https://doi.org/10.1109/MS.2022.3198195
14. Javed, M.A., Zdun, U.: A systematic literature review of traceability approaches between software architecture and source code. In: Proceedings of the 18th International Conference on Evaluation and Assessment in Software Engineering (EASE), pp. 1–10. ACM (2014)
15. Tang, A., Jin, Y., Han, J.: A rationale-based architecture model for design traceability and reasoning. J. Syst. Softw. **80**(6), 918–934 (2007). https://doi.org/10.1016/j.jss.2006.10.009
16. Angelov, S., Grefen, P., Greefhorst, D.: A classification of software reference architectures: analyzing their success and effectiveness. In: 2009 Joint Working IEEE/IFIP Conference on Software Architecture & European Conference on Software Architecture (WICSA/ECSA), pp. 141–150. IEEE (2009). https://doi.org/10.1109/WICSA.2009.5290800
17. Angelov, S.A., Grefen, P.W.P.J., Greefhorst, D.: A framework for analysis and design of software reference architectures. Inf. Softw. Technol. **54**(4), 417–431 (2012). https://doi.org/10.1016/j.infsof.2011.11.009
18. Garcés, L., et al.: Three decades of software reference architectures: a systematic mapping study. J. Syst. Softw. **179**, 111004 (2021). https://doi.org/10.1016/j.jss.2021.111004
19. Buschmann, F., Meunier, R., Rohnert, H., Sommerlad, P., Stal, M.: Pattern-Oriented Software Architecture, Volume 1: A System of Patterns. Wiley (1996)
20. Buschmann, F., Henney, K., Schmidt, D.C.: Pattern-Oriented Software Architecture, Volume 5: On Patterns and Pattern Languages. Wiley (2007)
21. Richards, M., Ford, N.: Fundamentals of Software Architecture: An Engineering Approach. O'Reilly Media (2020)
22. Bachmann, F., Bass, L., Klein, M.: Deriving architectural tactics: a step toward methodical architectural design. Technical report, CMU/SEI-2003-TR-004, Software Engineering Institute, Carnegie Mellon University (2003)

23. Alebrahim, A., Faßbender, S., Filipczyk, M., Goedicke, M., Heisel, M.: Towards systematic selection of architectural patterns with respect to quality requirements. In: Proceedings of the 20th European Conference on Pattern Languages of Programs (EuroPLoP 2015), pp. 1–20. ACM (2015). https://doi.org/10.1145/2855321.2855362

24. Mirakhorli, M., Cleland-Huang, J.: Detecting, tracing, and monitoring architectural tactics in code. IEEE Trans. Software Eng. **42**(3), 205–220 (2016). https://doi.org/10.1109/TSE.2015.2479217

25. Zhang, P., Muccini, H., Li, B.: A classification and comparison of model checking software architecture techniques. J. Syst. Softw. **83**(5), 723–744 (2010). https://doi.org/10.1016/j.jss.2009.11.709

26. Uzun, B., Tekinerdogan, B.: Model-driven architecture based testing: a systematic literature review. Inf. Softw. Technol. (2018). https://doi.org/10.1016/j.infsof.2018.05.014

27. Muccini, H., Inverardi, P., Bertolino, A.: Using software architecture for code testing. IEEE Trans. Software Eng. **30**(3), 160–171 (2004). https://doi.org/10.1109/TSE.2004.1271170

28. El Murabet, A., Abtoy, A.: Methodologies of the validation of software architectures. J. Comput. Theories Appl. **1**(2), 78–85 (2023). https://doi.org/10.33633/jcta.v1i2.9332

29. Balsamo, S., Marzolla, M.: Simulation modeling of UML software architectures. In: Proceedings of the 17th European Simulation Multiconference (ESM 2003), pp. 562–567. SCS European Publishing House (2003). Best Paper Award, Complex Systems Modeling Track

30. Bogado, V., Gonnet, S., Leone, H.P.: Modeling and simulation of software architecture in discrete event system specification for quality evaluation. SIMULATION **90**(3), 290–319 (2014). https://doi.org/10.1177/0037549713518586

31. Sarjoughian, H.S., Zeigler, B.P., Hall, S.B.: A layered modeling and simulation architecture for agent-based system development. Proc. IEEE **89**(2), 201–213 (2001). https://doi.org/10.1109/5.910855

32. Sharaf, M., Abughazala, M., Muccini, H., Abusair, M.: Software Architecture. Lecture Notes in Computer Science, vol. 10475, pp. 95–111. Springer, Cham (2017). https://doi.org/10.1007/978-3-319-65831-5_7

33. Sharaf, M., Abughazala, M., Muccini, H., Abusair, M.: CAPSim: simulation and code generation based on the CAPS. In: Proceedings of the 11th European Conference on Software Architecture: Companion Proceedings (ECSA Companion 2017), pp. 56–60. ACM (2017). https://doi.org/10.1145/3129790.3129820

34. Sharaf, M., Abughazala, M., Muccini, H., Abusair, M.: Simulating architectures of situational-aware cyber-physical space. In: Proceedings of the 11th European Conference on Software Architecture: Companion Proceedings (ECSA Companion 2017), pp. 66–67. ACM (2017). https://doi.org/10.1145/3129790.3129807

35. Williams, L.G., Smith, C.U.: Performance evaluation of software architectures. In: Proceedings of the 1st International Workshop on Software and Performance (WOSP), pp. 164–177. ACM (1998). https://doi.org/10.1145/287318.287353

36. Balsamo, S., Bernardo, M., Simeoni, M.: Formal Methods for Software Architectures. Lecture Notes in Computer Science, vol. 2804, pp. 207–258. Springer (2003). https://doi.org/10.1007/978-3-540-39800-4_10

37. Cortellessa, V., Di Marco, A., Inverardi, P.: Software performance model-driven architecture. In: Proceedings of the 2006 ACM Symposium on Applied Computing (SAC), pp. 1218–1223. ACM (2006)

38. Becker, S., Koziolek, H., Reussner, R.H.: The palladio component model for model-driven performance prediction. J. Syst. Softw. **82**(1), 3–22 (2009). https://doi.org/10.1016/j.jss.2008.03.066
39. Heinrich, R., Happe, J., Reussner, R.H., Becker, S., Koziolek, A.: Modeling and Simulating Software Architectures: The Palladio Approach. MIT Press (2016)
40. Koziolek, H., Reussner, R.H., Happe, J., Becker, S.: Quality of Software Architectures: Models and Architectures. IGI Global (2008)
41. Cortellessa, V., Di Pompeo, D., Eramo, R., Tucci, M.: A model-driven approach for continuous performance engineering in microservice-based systems (2022). https://doi.org/10.1016/j.jss.2021.111204
42. Erder, M., Pureur, P., Woods, E.: Continuous Architecture in Practice: Software Architecture in the Age of Agility and DevOps. Addison-Wesley (2021)
43. Taibi, D., Lenarduzzi, V., Pahl, C.: Cloud Computing and Services Science. Communications in Computer and Information Science. Springer (2019). https://doi.org/10.1007/978-3-030-29193-8_7
44. Buchgeher, G., Weinreich, R.: In: Babar, M.A., Brown, A.W., Mistrik, I. (eds.) Agile Software Architecture: Aligning Agile Processes and Software Architectures, pp. 161–188. Morgan Kaufmann/Elsevier (2014). https://doi.org/10.1016/B978-0-12-407772-0.00006-X
45. Ford, N., Parsons, R., Kua, P.: Building Evolutionary Architectures: Support Constant Change. O'Reilly Media (2017). https://books.google.it/books?id=pYI2DwAAQBAJ
46. Sobhy, D., Bahsoon, R., Minku, L.L., Kazman, R.: Evaluation of software architectures under uncertainty: a systematic literature review. ACM Trans. Software Eng. Methodol. **30**(4), 51:1–51:50 (2021). https://doi.org/10.1145/3464305
47. Ågren, S.M., et al.: Architecture evaluation in continuous development. J. Syst. Softw. **184**, 111111 (2022). https://doi.org/10.1016/j.jss.2021.111111
48. Bass, L., Clements, P., Kazman, R.: Software Architecture in Practice, 4th edn. Addison-Wesley (2021)
49. Dobrica, L., Niemelä, E.: A survey on software architecture analysis methods. IEEE Trans. Software Eng. **28**(7), 638–653 (2002). https://doi.org/10.1109/TSE.2002.1019479
50. Chidamber, S.R., Kemerer, C.F.: A metrics suite for object oriented design. IEEE Trans. Software Eng. **20**(6), 476–493 (1994). https://doi.org/10.1109/32.295895
51. Kouroshfar, E., Mirakhorli, M., Bagheri, H., Xiao, L., Malek, S., Cai, Y.: A study on the role of software architecture in the evolution and quality of software. In: Proceedings of the 12th Working Conference on Mining Software Repositories (MSR), pp. 246–257. IEEE/ACM (2015). https://doi.org/10.1109/MSR.2015.30
52. Al-Qora'n, L.F., Ahmad, M.O., et al.: Modular monolith architecture in cloud environments: a systematic literature review. Future Internet **17**(11), 496 (2025). https://doi.org/10.3390/fi17110496
53. Szyperski, C.: Component Software: Beyond Object-Oriented Programming, 2nd edn. Addison-Wesley Professional (2002)
54. Fowler, M.: Patterns of Enterprise Application Architecture. Addison-Wesley Professional (2002)
55. Papazoglou, M.P., Georgakopoulos, D.: Introduction to a special issue on service oriented computing. Commun. ACM **46**(10), 25–28 (2003). https://doi.org/10.1145/944217.944233
56. Erl, T.: Service-Oriented Architecture: Concepts, Technology, and Design. Prentice Hall PTR (2005)

57. Hussein, S., et al.: Assessing the quality of microservice and monolithic-based architectures: a systematic literature review. ORESTA (2024). Use with caution if your venue prefers only indexed sources
58. Koch, D.: Migrating monolithic architectures to microservices: a study on software quality attributes. Master's thesis, University of Stuttgart (2022)
59. Razzaq, A., et al.: A systematic mapping study: the new age of software architecture from monolithic to microservice architecture–awareness and challenges. Comput. Appl. Eng. Educ. (2023). https://doi.org/10.1002/cae.22586
60. Li, S., et al.: Understanding and addressing quality attributes of microservices architecture: a systematic literature review. Inf. Softw. Technol. **131**, 106449 (2021). https://doi.org/10.1016/j.infsof.2020.106449
61. Blinowski, G., Ojdowska, A., Przybylek, A.: Monolithic vs. microservice architecture: a performance and scalability evaluation. IEEE Access **10**, 20357–20374 (2022). https://doi.org/10.1109/ACCESS.2022.3152803
62. Bakshi, K.: Microservices-based software architecture and approaches. In: 2017 IEEE Aerospace Conference, pp. 1–8. IEEE (2017). https://doi.org/10.1109/AERO.2017.7943959
63. Ueda, T., Nakaike, T., Ohara, M.: Workload characterization for microservices. In: 2016 IEEE International Symposium on Workload Characterization (IISWC), pp. 1–10. IEEE (2016). https://doi.org/10.1109/IISWC.2016.7581269
64. O'Connor, R.V., Elger, P., Clarke, P.M.: Continuous software engineering–a microservices architecture perspective. J. Softw.: Evol. Process **29**(11), e1866 (2017). https://doi.org/10.1002/smr.1866
65. Martínez Saucedo, A.M., et al.: Migration of monolithic systems to microservices: a systematic mapping study. Inf. Softw. Technol. **178**, 107590 (2025). https://doi.org/10.1016/j.infsof.2024.107590
66. Capuano, R., Muccini, H., Vaccaro, F.: From refactoring to migration: a quality-driven strategy for microservices adoption. In: IEEE International Conference on Software Analysis, Evolution and Reengineering, SANER 2024, Rovaniemi, Finland, 12–15 March 2024, pp. 840–848. IEEE (2024). https://doi.org/10.1109/SANER60148.2024.00092
67. Amershi, S., et al.: Software engineering for machine learning: a case study. In: 2019 IEEE/ACM 41st International Conference on Software Engineering: Software Engineering in Practice (ICSE-SEIP), pp. 291–300. IEEE/ACM (2019). https://doi.org/10.1109/ICSE-SEIP.2019.00042
68. Sculley, D., et al.: Hidden technical debt in machine learning systems. In: Advances in Neural Information Processing Systems (NeurIPS), vol. 28, pp. 2503–2511 (2015)
69. Paleyes, A., Urma, R.G., Lawrence, N.D.: Challenges in deploying machine learning: a survey of case studies. ACM Comput. Surv. **55**(6), 1–29 (2022). https://doi.org/10.1145/3533378
70. Kreuzberger, D., Kühl, N., Hirschl, S.: Machine learning operations (MLOps): overview, definition, and architecture. IEEE Access **11**, 31866–31879 (2023). https://doi.org/10.1109/ACCESS.2023.3262138
71. Breck, E., Cai, S., Nielsen, E., Salib, M., Sculley, D.: The ML test score: a rubric for ML production readiness and technical debt reduction. In: 2017 IEEE International Conference on Big Data (Big Data), pp. 1123–1132. IEEE (2017). https://doi.org/10.1109/BigData.2017.8258038
72. Breck, E., Polyzotis, N., Roy, S., Whang, S.E., Zinkevich, M.: Data validation for machine learning. In: Proceedings of Machine Learning and Systems (MLSys) (2019)

73. Claessens, M., SellerOria, C., Brouwer, C.L., Ziemer, B.P., et al.: Quality assurance for ai-based applications in radiation therapy. Seminars Radiat. Oncol. **32**(4), 421–431 (2022). https://doi.org/10.1016/j.semradonc.2022.06.011

74. Fujii, G., Hamada, K., Ishikawa, F., Masuda, S., Matsuya, M.: Guidelines for quality assurance of machine learning-based artificial intelligence. Int. J. Software Eng. Knowl. Eng. **30**(11–12), 1583–1607 (2021). https://doi.org/10.1142/S0218194020400227

75. Wang, L., Ma, C., Feng, X., et al.: A survey on large language model based autonomous agents. Front. Comp. Sci. (2024). https://doi.org/10.1007/s11704-024-40231-1

76. Jin, H., et al.: From LLMs to LLM-based agents for software engineering: a survey of current, challenges and future. arXiv preprint arXiv:2408.02479 (2024)

77. National Institute of Standards and Technology, Artificial intelligence risk management framework (AI RMF 1.0). Technical report NIST AI 100-1, NIST (2023). https://doi.org/10.6028/NIST.AI.100-1

Process Quality and Quality Assurance

On Effort Awareness for Just-In-Time Defect Prediction

Peter Bludau[1]($\boxtimes$) iD and Alexander Pretschner[1,2] iD

[1] fortiss, Research Institute of the Free State of Bavaria, Munich, Germany
{peter.bludau,alexander.pretschner}@tum.de
[2] Technical University of Munich, Munich, Germany

Abstract. Reviewing software changes is a critical activity that helps prevent the introduction of defects, ultimately saving development time and reducing costs. Just-in-time defect prediction has emerged as a promising approach to support this process by estimating the likelihood of defects in newly submitted commits. Effort-aware evaluations were proposed to better manage developers' limited time and to analyze the applicability of defect prediction approaches. However, current effort-aware approaches neglect the time-dependent nature of software engineering when evaluating the performance and rank commits to find most defective commits with limited effort. This reveals a gap between the evaluation of models in research and their application in practice, where a timely decision for every single commit is needed. To assess the impact of effort-aware evaluations on the applicability of defect prediction approaches, we quantify their limitations and provide insights into the implications for future research. Our findings show that effort-aware metrics can overestimate the proportion of defects identified within a limited inspection budget by up to 55% when accounting for realistic, time-sensitive review processes.

Keywords: JIT Defect Prediction · Effort Awareness · Case Study

1 Introduction

During software development, it is essential to review and test code changes in order to discuss emerging issues and detect defects early. To support this process, just-in-time (JIT) defect prediction assigns a risk value to each new commit in the version control system. This risk value can be used by developers to decide if a review is needed or additional testing activities should be performed [26]. JIT defect prediction naturally integrates with modern software development practices, where every change triggers continuous integration pipelines and undergoes mandatory code review [9].

In recent years, research has increasingly focused on effort awareness to evaluate the practical applicability of JIT defect prediction approaches. The primary objective of effort-aware methods is to identify as many defective commits as possible within a limited inspection budget. This is typically achieved by ranking

© The Author(s), under exclusive license to Springer Nature Switzerland AG 2026
M. Dorner et al. (Eds.): SWQD 2026, LNBIP 581, pp. 25–41, 2026.
https://doi.org/10.1007/978-3-032-24216-7_2

commits according to their likelihood of introducing defects and the estimated effort required to inspect these changes [19]. Based on this ranking, commits are investigated until the predefined inspection budget is fully exhausted. Most studies evaluate their approaches by reporting the proportion of all defective commits that can be identified using 20% of the total inspection effort (e.g., [4,13,14,41]).

Although we acknowledge the importance of considering effort in state-of-the-art JIT defect prediction, several assumptions of effort-aware approaches undermine their practical application. First, effort-aware approaches rank changes to identify a large number of defective commits with limited effort, ignoring the chronological order and postponing reviews until multiple changes are committed. Second, the predefined inspection budget used in the evaluation can only be determined after the development has ended, conflicting with the goal of JIT defect prediction to evaluate new commits promptly. This renders current effort-aware approaches impractical [44].

Evaluating and selecting models based on such criteria can introduce bias and misrepresent the actual effort-saving potential of JIT defect prediction approaches in industrial contexts. In this study, we investigate how current effort-aware evaluation practices influence reported performance results and quantify the gap between research-oriented retrospective evaluations and industry-oriented real-time evaluations.

Our findings show that effort-aware metrics substantially overestimate the proportion of defects that can be identified with limited effort when compared to timely, chronological evaluation methods. Across six open-source projects, we find that effort-aware evaluations overstates defect detection performance by up to 53% in supervised and 45% in unsupervised scenarios relative to real-time, chronological evaluations. This misalignment may lead to overly optimistic deployment expectations, unnecessary integration efforts, and misplaced confidence in predictive models.

2   Background and Related Work

In this section, we describe the background and related work regarding JIT defect prediction approaches and their effort awareness as the foundation for this work.

2.1   Just-in-Time Defect Prediction

JIT defect prediction, introduced by Mockus et al. [26], aims to support developers by predicting defective changes before their investigation. Unlike traditional defect prediction, which targets entire modules or releases, it operates at the change level, offering key advantages. Reviews can be conducted shortly after the change, while still being tangible [35], and defect prediction focuses only on modified lines, enabling more targeted reviews [19]. These benefits align with modern code review practices used in contemporary software development [33,34].

Most JIT defect prediction approaches are based on supervised machine learning models trained on datasets containing defect-fixing and defect-inducing commits. These labels are commonly obtained using variants of the SZZ algorithm [36]. Defect-fixing commits correspond to changes that resolve a documented bug, typically identified via commit messages or links to issue reports. For each defect-fixing commit, SZZ traces the modified lines back through the version history to identify the commits that last introduced those lines; such commits are labeled as defect-inducing. This labeling strategy is widely used in defect prediction research.

The simplest decision strategy marks a new change as defective when the predicted defect probability exceeds a predefined threshold. Various modeling techniques, such as Logistic Regression [18,19,26], Support Vector Machines [21], Naïve Bayes [15], Decision Trees and Random Forests [8,18,31], and Neural Networks [10,11,40,43], as well as evaluation strategies such as effort-aware prediction [1,19], have been proposed to assess their practical applicability.

2.2 Effort Awareness

In an industrial context with limited time, tracking spent effort is essential for quality assurance and verification [1,19]. Thus, Kamei et al. [19] proposed to evaluate JIT defect prediction performance while considering developers' review effort. The goal of effort-aware JIT defect prediction is to optimize the review process by identifying the majority of defects while conserving effort. Most recent studies [44] and various case studies (e.g., [39]) have reported such evaluations.

To quantify the effort needed to inspect a change, Kamei et al. [19] used the total number of changed lines, assuming larger commits take more time to review. This measure is widely adopted, and we denote it as *effort(c)*, where c is the commit.

Effort-aware evaluation approaches assign a risk score to each commit c (Eq. 1). The score represents the perceived need to review a particular commit, factoring in its potential for defects and the effort required to review it. Subsequently, all commits (C) are ranked according to the score to determine the order of investigation (Eq. 2).

$$risk(c) = \text{risk score of } c \text{ where } c \in C \tag{1}$$

$$rank(c_i) = \sum_{j \neq i} [\![risk(c_j) < risk(c_i)]\!] \tag{2}$$

Most risk scores utilize the effort needed to investigate an commit directly. Different approaches propose various risk scores to rank commits [7,13,14,19,23,40], considering factors such as defect likelihood [40], defect density [19] (defect likelihood divided by effort), or a combination of these [14]. Unsupervised methods leverage the observation that small commits require minimal effort and can be reviewed with little impact and use the effort directly to rank commits without the involvement of a defect prediction model [24,41]. These approaches often perform similarly to supervised techniques, as effort-aware evaluations tend to penalize large commits. The described risk scores represent the state-of-the-art in effort-aware JIT defect prediction, where commits are ranked, and the review process stops once an inspection budget is reached.

2.3   Evaluation

When applied in practice, timely defect prediction follows an online learning approach, predicting defects at commit time and updating models once labels become available [37]. In research, however, JIT defect prediction is typically assessed retrospectively, where changes from the software development history are collected and used to assess simulated performance. While online evaluation tracks real-time performance, retrospective evaluation helps practitioners select suitable modeling approaches. In this study, we are concerned with the retrospective evaluation of models and its need to reflect real-world model usage.

The goal of JIT defect prediction is to identify all defective commits while minimizing the practitioners effort. Missing defects can lead to increased costs for debugging and fixing issues over time. As a result, recall (R) is commonly used in most studies to assess the model's ability to identify defects. The widely reported F-Score, which is the harmonic mean of precision and recall, incorporates the number of false positive predictions as a measure of unnecessarily reviewed commits (e.g., [4,14,38,40]). Furthermore, the Matthews Correlation Coefficient (MCC) is gaining prominence as a more balanced metric, particularly in imbalanced datasets [42].

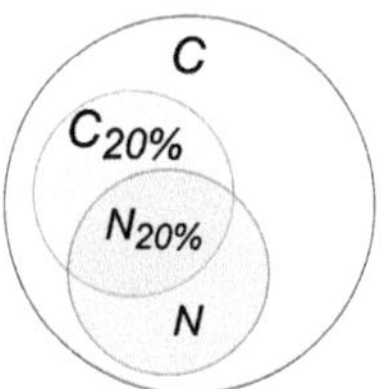

Fig. 1. Set of commits and its effort budget-constrained subsets in an exemplary defect prediction evaluation setting.

To consider effort, several additional evaluation metrics were introduced focused on scenarios with limited inspection budgets. These metrics often explicitly account for the budget by halting the inspection process once the budget is fully consumed. Given that developers have limited time and about 20% of the code contains 80% of defects [29], a budget of 20% of the total effort required to inspect all changes was introduced by Kamei et al. [19]. This threshold has been subsequently adopted (e.g., [4,13,32,41]) as a principal component of effort-aware performance metrics. In this context, let N denote the set of defective commits within the complete set of commits C, as shown in Fig. 1. After expending the effort budget, we define the set of investigated commits as $C_{20\%}$ and the set of defect-inducing commits within these investigated commits as $N_{20\%}$.

$$R@20\% = \frac{|N_{20\%}|}{|N|}$$

The most prominent effort-aware metric is the recall at 20% of spent effort ($R@20\%$) that represents the fraction of found defective commits when only 20% of all changed lines are investigated (Eq. 2.3) [19]. A higher $R@20\%$ indicates efficiency in saving developer effort. Similarly, studies also report the corresponding precision and F-Score applying this budget constraint (e.g., [39]).

Studies occasionally use P_{opt} to assess cost-effectiveness [19] without a fixed budget. It quantifies the area between a model's effort-recall curve ranking changes by its risk score and one that is based on the datasets actual defect density. A higher P_{opt} indicates a smaller gap from the optimal case, reflecting greater efficiency in defect detection per effort spent.

Huang et al. [14] proposed two additional effort-aware metrics. The first, PCI, measures the proportion of reviewed commits within a 20% budget, with lower values preferred due to reduced context switching. The second, IFA, counts false positives before the first correctly identified defective commit, where high values waste effort and frustrate developers [22].

3 Limitations of Effort Awareness

Effort-aware evaluations focus on optimizing risk scores while minimizing early effort. As detailed in Sect. 2.2, commits are ranked by risk score, and investigations proceed until the effort budget is reached. While generally sound, this approach has limitations and contradictions in real-world scenarios. The following section outlines two main issues.

3.1 Delaying Decisions and Re-Ranking Commits

The most pressing issue of effort-aware evaluations is the missing time sensitivity. As pointed out by Çarka et al. [44], an immediate evaluation for new commits is essential in JIT defect prediction. The ranking of commits, a step that naturally delays investigations, is neither practical nor realistic.

In effort-aware evaluations, commits from a certain time span are ordered by label and then by effort, resulting in two distinct sections with increasing commit size. In a more realistic just-in-time evaluation, however, large commits will be reviewed early after they are committed. Thus, *rank-based evaluation* approaches give an illusion of efficient effort awareness, prioritizing commits that are easy to investigate. While this may reduce effort in the initial stages, it potentially leads to a delayed detection of potentially defective commits and skews the applicability of evaluation results.

Case studies on the application of JIT defect prediction in the industry echo the disconnect and focus on the integration and timeliness of approaches to deliver predictions for every new change steering reviewing and testing efforts [20,22,27,28]. This prompts us to question the suitability of effort-aware rankings in the context of applicable JIT defect prediction. If models are optimized or selected based on these evaluations, they must align with the application context. Otherwise, one cannot assume that effort-aware approaches that perform well in research settings will translate effectively into practical usage.

3.2   Limited Effort Budget

With a fixed budget of 20% of the total effort not all defective commits can be investigated. Due to the re-ranking and delay of the investigation described above smaller commits can be investigated first. In a *just-in-time evaluation* setting more effort must be invested early and distributed more evenly, as large commits can happen at any time and need to be investigated directly after they are commited. By ranking commits based on size, there is an overestimation of the number of defective commits that can be identified with minimal effort and the number of defects found using the fixed inspection budget is significantly lower. The potentially inflated performance can also be seen in unsupervised approaches reporting very compelling results, where low-effort commits are inspected first (e.g., [24, 41]). Although this strategy identifies numerous defects, it neglects many defective commits in the early stages of development. Since the R@20% is the most used effort-aware metric in JIT defect prediction studies [14] and is often the only applied effort-aware metric [44], we find that the limitations may have a significant impact on the validity and applicability of such approaches.

Furthermore, in a continuous and chronological evaluation scenario, it is not possible to determine an appropriate budget in advance, as the total effort required within the given time-frame is unknown. This uncertainty makes it unclear how to interpret and set a fixed budget percentage, such as 20%, in real-world scenarios.

4   Case Study

In Sect. 3, we outlined the limitations of effort awareness in JIT defect prediction. This study examines how different risk-based ranking mechanisms impact the validity of performance results and applicability of approaches. Our focus is on implications of effort-aware evaluations on reported performance, particularly the recall at 20% of spent effort. We benchmark the top-performing supervised and unsupervised effort-aware scoring mechanisms in a chronological evaluation setting. For the supervised approach, we use *CBS+* [14], identified as the most effective method, including in industry [39]. *CBS+* ranks commits by defect density, prioritizing high-risk, low-effort changes. For the unsupervised approach, we use *CHURN* [24], which ranks commits by total changed lines, aligning with the effort notion used in supervised methods.

Rather than improving JIT defect prediction models, we assess current effort-aware strategies and their practical applicability. Thus, we use an already published defect dataset [5] and its associated features [4], covering the development in six open-source projects from January 2015 to January 2021, as detailed in

Table 1. Overview of used defect data sets

Project	Commits	Inducing commits	Fixing commits
Airflow	7,311	1,582 (21.64%)	1,396 (19.09%)
Angular	16,050	2,545 (15.86%)	2,013 (12.54%)
Calcite	2,463	774 (31.43%)	1,182 (47.99%)
Jenkins	8,784	380 (4.33%)	750 (8.54%)
Kafka	5,812	1,377 (23.69%)	1,722 (29.63%)
Pulsar	4,127	1,016 (24.62%)	903 (21.88%)

Table 1. Each commit in this dataset is labeled to indicate whether it was defect-inducing and includes state-of-the-art predictive features.

For simplicity, graphs and illustrations presented henceforth are based on evaluations of the Kafka project. All detailed evaluations are available, in the replication package of this work [6].

5   Results

5.1   Impact of Effort-Awareness on Timely Evaluations

The major issue of effort-aware evaluations is the missing time sensitivity. In this section, we illustrate the natural impact of the delayed and ranked investigation of commits in effort-aware methods compared to a timely JIT defect prediction scenario.

We consider an oracle prediction model that predicts the correct label for every commit. Figure 2 shows three subplots. In each, the x-axis lists the first 500 commits of the Kafka project as an exemplary except of the development history of a project. The y-axis shows the size of each commit, used as a proxy for review effort. The black bars indicate defective commits, while the gray bars represent non-defective commits according to the defect data set. The upper graph chronologically orders the commits, with large commits (high bars) are scattered across the whole commit history, while some are defective and some are not. The center graph represents a perfect *rank-based evaluation*—where commits are sorted by label and then by effort, which produces two clearly separated regions with increasing commit size. This is the outcome that a perfect oracle version of the state-of-the-art effort-aware method CBS+ [14] would produce. The bottom subplot shows a perfect approach that keeps the chronological order of commits (*just-in-time evaluation*)—where commits are only sorted by label but the commit time is preserved, which again produces two distinct regions but within them large commits can occur at any time.

The dashed vertical line at 44.97% of effort depicts the total effort required to identify all defective commits, in a perfect oracle setting. This is consistent in both the center and bottom subplot indicating that both approaches would detect all defects investing 44.97% of the total effort. Committing effort beyond

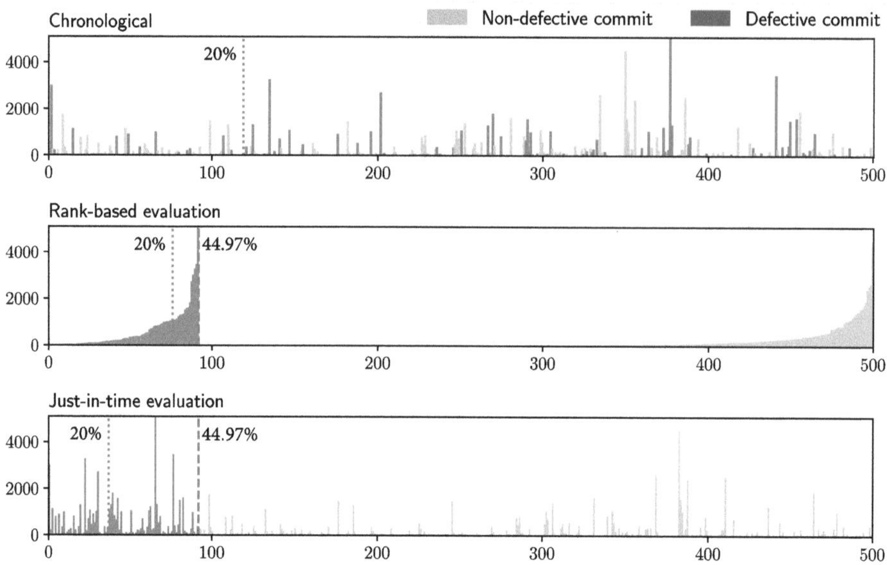

Fig. 2. Defect and effort distribution of the first 500 commits in Kafka project. Each bar represents one commit with the height indicating the number of changed lines in different evaluation settings.

this line becomes unnecessary as all subsequent commits are non-defective and can be disregarded. In the *just-in-time evaluation*, however, large commits will be reviewed early. Thus, *rank-based evaluation* approaches give an illusion of efficient effort awareness, prioritizing commits that are easy to investigate. While this may reduce effort in the initial stages, it potentially leads to a delayed detection of potentially defective commits and skews the applicability of evaluation results.

With a fixed budget of 20% of the total effort not all defective commits can be investigated. Applying a *just-in-time evaluation*, the number of defects found using the budget is significantly lower. Figure 3 illustrates the effort-aware recall curve, represented by a gray line for the *rank-based evaluation* and a black line for the chronological *just-in-time evaluation*. The y-axis shows the percentage of found defects, and the x-axis shows the total effort percentage, indicating defects found per effort spent. The effort at 20% is indicated by the vertical orange dotted line. The *just-in-time evaluation* curve rises more slowly, requiring more effort early on, and meets the *rank-based evaluation* curve at 44.97% of effort. However, the area under the recall curve in the *just-in-time evaluation* setting is 14.3% smaller than in the *rank-based evaluation* setting, illustrating that more effort is invested early and distributed more evenly, as large commits can happen at any time and need to be investigated directly after they are commited. This phenomena is true in every project and is a natural consequence of the ranking in toady's effort-aware methodologies.

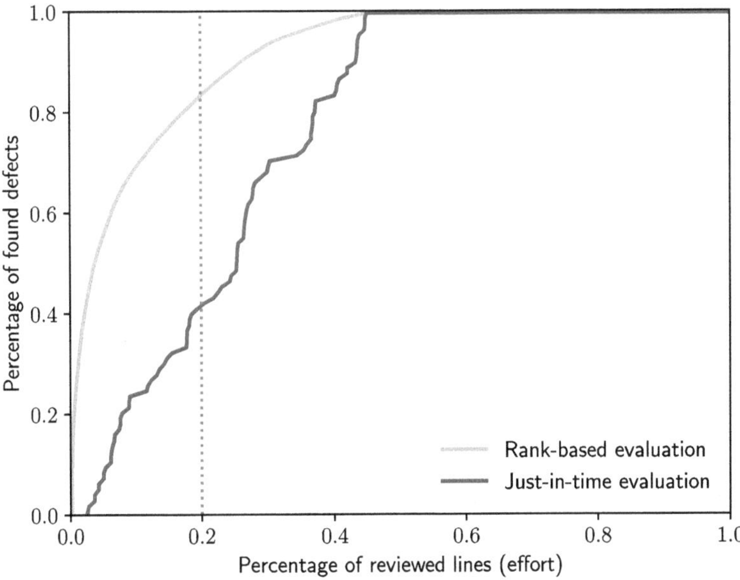

Fig. 3. Direct comparison of the effort-aware recall curve for both the *rank-based evaluation* and *just-in-time evaluation* setting in the Kafka project.

5.2 Impact of Effort-Awareness on Reported Performance

In Sect. 5.1, we demonstrated that the ordering of commits substantially influences reported model performance when evaluation is performed under a limited effort budget. We now extend that analysis by examining the effect of chronological ordering on effort-aware performance metrics, namely $R@20\%$ and P_{opt}.

To quantify this impact, we train defect prediction models using the described dataset, treating it as the ground truth for defect-inducing commits. To capture the temporal dynamics of software development, we adopt a short-term, six-month modeling strategy as proposed by McIntosh et al. [25]. Specifically, we partition each project's development history into consecutive six-month intervals using a time-wise cross-validation scheme, yielding nine evaluation periods per project. For each time frame, we train a JIT defect prediction model based on the extracted features and evaluate it on the subsequent interval. Random Forest classifiers are used, as this algorithm has shown consistently strong performance on the employed dataset [4].

Consequently, we compare three evaluation settings: the supervised effort-aware approach (*CBS+*), the unsupervised baseline (*CHURN*), and a realistic, time-ordered evaluation (*CHRON*). For each configuration, we compute the recall (R), recall at 20% inspection effort ($R@20\%$), and the P_{opt} metric. Table 2 reports the mean results averaged across all time periods for each project.

Overall, the results reveal a consistent and substantial decline in both $R@20\%$ and P_{opt} when evaluations are conducted in a chronological manner. For instance,

Table 2. Mean recall and effort-aware performance metrics across time periods and selected projects.

Project	R	$R_{@20\%}^{CBS+}$	$R_{@20\%}^{CHURN}$	$R_{@20\%}^{CHRON}$	P_{opt}^{CBS+}	P_{opt}^{CHURN}	P_{opt}^{CHRON}
Airflow	0.72	0.74	0.70	0.25	0.92	0.90	0.58
Angular	0.78	0.66	0.62	0.20	0.87	0.85	0.53
Calcite	0.77	0.61	0.56	0.26	0.89	0.87	0.62
Jenkins	0.68	0.79	0.71	0.26	0.89	0.85	0.53
Kafka	0.84	0.67	0.58	0.21	0.91	0.85	0.55
Pulsar	0.81	0.68	0.63	0.22	0.92	0.89	0.58

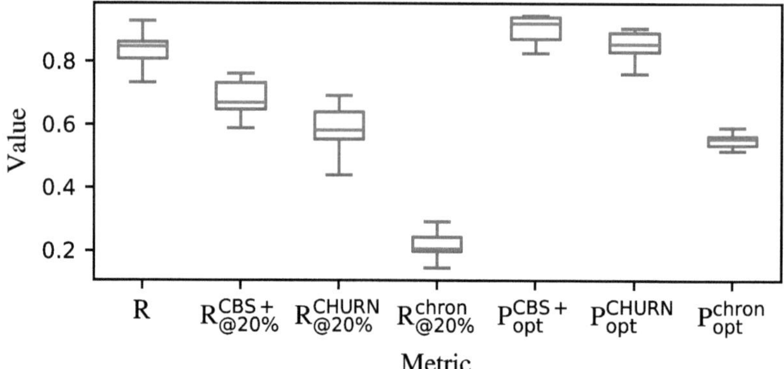

Fig. 4. Performance boxplot for the different metrics in the Kafka project.

across all six projects, $R@20\%$ values under the *CHRON* setting are markedly lower (ranging between 0.20 and 0.26) compared to those obtained using *CBS+* and *CHURN*, which typically range between 0.56 and 0.79. Similarly, P_{opt} drops from values above 0.85 in effort-aware evaluations to values ranging from 0.53–0.62 under chronological evaluation. This pattern indicates that traditional effort-aware evaluations—by neglecting the temporal order of commits, significantly overstate the proportion of defects that can be detected within a fixed inspection budget. In other words, once realistic time constraints are imposed, models appear less effective at identifying defective commits early. On average, the performance decline corresponds to an overestimation of up to 53% in reported $R@20\%$ and 36% in P_{opt} compared to their chronologically ordered counterparts.

To further analyze temporal effects, we evaluate model performance separately for each six-month time frame. Figure 4 presents the distribution of performance metrics for the Kafka project, while corresponding figures for all other projects are available in the supplementary material. Overall, the trends are consistent across all projects.

The datasets exhibit substantial class imbalance, with defective commits forming a clear minority in all projects. However, these defective commits tend to be larger on average and are dispersed across all examined time frames, which substantially affects the reported performance of effort-aware metrics.

Across projects, the average overall recall (R) ranges from 0.68 (Jenkins) to 0.84 (Kafka). Effort-aware recall ($R@20\%$) under the $CBS+$ setting varies between 0.61 (Calcite) and 0.82 (Jenkins), occasionally exceeding the standard recall. This can be attributed to the integration of both model predictions and commit size in the review prioritization process, which inherently favors smaller commits and may inflate recall scores under limited effort. The unsupervised baseline ($CHURN$), which ranks commits solely by size, achieves comparable recall in some cases (e.g., Jenkins) but generally performs worse on other projects. This indicates that although larger commits are statistically more defect-prone, unsupervised heuristics that emphasize commit size tend to overlook them, leading to diminished defect detection performance overall.

In contrast, the chronological evaluation ($CHRON$) consistently yields lower recall values, ranging from 0.20 (Angular) to 0.26 (Calcite and Jenkins). This drop highlights the limited applicability of effort-aware ranking once realistic temporal constraints are imposed and models cannot reorder commits across time and thus face a narrower window for effective defect detection. A similar trend is observed for P_{opt}, which is consistently lower under the $CHRON$ evaluation compared to both $CBS+$ and $CHURN$. This discrepancy arises because P_{opt} quantifies effort savings relative to an idealized oracle that disregards commit chronology (as discussed in Sect. 5.1). Consequently, effort-aware evaluations tend to overestimate the achievable effort reduction, resulting in a substantial performance gap when models are assessed under a temporally constrained, real-world perspective.

In summary, our results reveal several key insights regarding the impact of effort-awareness and temporal constraints on JIT defect prediction performance. First, effort-aware approaches ($CBS+$) generally achieve recall values comparable to standard defect prediction, while requiring only around 20% of the total inspection effort—indicating that, in principle, effort-awareness can yield efficient defect detection. Second, unsupervised baselines such as $CHURN$ can reach competitive performance levels but tend to prioritize smaller commits, thereby overlooking larger and more defect-prone changes. However, once temporal realism is introduced through chronological evaluation, the effectiveness of effort-aware methods declines substantially. Under these time-constrained conditions, recall values drop by up to 53% compared to conventional (non-chronological) effort-aware evaluation. Moreover, existing effort-aware metrics systematically overestimate the potential effort savings by maximizing the area under the effort curve, leading to an inflation of reported performance by up to 36%.

Overall, these findings challenge the feasibility of selecting or comparing JIT defect prediction models based on traditional effort-aware evaluation results. Current metrics tend to overstate the proportion of defective commits that can realistically be identified within a limited inspection budget, thereby misrepresenting the practical effort-saving potential of JIT defect prediction in real-world, time-sensitive development settings.

6   Discussion

Our findings have significant implications for the practical adoption of JIT defect prediction in industry. Although JIT approaches aim to guide code reviews and reduce the introduction of defects, our results show that current effort-aware evaluation methods substantially overestimate their real-world effectiveness. By retrospectively ranking commits and assuming fixed inspection budgets, these evaluations fail to capture the continuous and time-sensitive nature of modern software development. In practice, predictions must be generated immediately for each commit and must support developers in making timely and actionable review decisions.

For industrial application, this implies that JIT defect prediction tools should shift focus from post-hoc ranking to real-time risk estimation that integrates seamlessly into CI/CD pipelines and modern code review workflows [20,27]. The goal should not be to minimize review effort indiscriminately, but rather to prioritize high-risk changes while maintaining developer trust and sustainable workloads. Models optimized for retrospective, effort-aware metrics may perform well in controlled experiments yet struggle to deliver meaningful support when deployed in live environments. Bridging this gap requires evaluation methods that respect commit chronology and measure the *decision-support value* of predictions in practice. Complementary, developer-centered evaluations, such as tracking review behavior, defect discovery rates, and perceived usefulness—could provide richer insights into the true industrial impact of JIT defect prediction.

Recent advances in Large Language Models introduce new opportunities for enhancing JIT defect prediction [3,12,30]. Unlike traditional approaches that rely on handcrafted features, LLMs can directly analyze code diffs and commit messages, capturing semantic cues that are often missed by metric-based models. Moreover, they can provide natural-language explanations for their predictions, improving interpretability and developer acceptance. However, several challenges remain. LLM-based models must address concerns around data privacy, fine-tuning costs, and domain adaptation, as codebases differ widely across organizations. While LLMs excel at understanding code semantics, they may overfit to stylistic patterns or fail to capture project-specific defect characteristics without sufficient adaptation. Hybrid approaches that combine traditional software metrics with LLM-derived embeddings may therefore offer a balanced path forward—retaining interpretability and generalizability while improving predictive accuracy.

7   Threats to Validity

Threats to **internal validity** may arise due to faulty assumptions in the evaluation process. We carefully evaluated the data set and its characteristics to ensure that the shown limitations are valid for all projects. We calculate well-established metrics and use standard libraries to compute them. We publish all code and evaluations in the supplementary material [6] to provide reproducible results and to mitigate this risk. Threats to **external validity** relate to the generalizability of the study results. We used six open-source projects, covering five years of development and varying in size. The projects belong to different application domains and contain different programming languages. Nonetheless, the data set may be incomplete. This may affect the accuracy of our experimental results. However, the case study in this paper is often used as a visualization of inherent limitations. The general nature of the observations should generalize for a large number of projects.

8   Conclusion

This study highlights critical limitations in current effort-aware evaluations of JIT defect prediction and their impact on reported performance. Our findings emphasize the need for evaluation strategies that align more closely with development workflows to ensure a fair representation of their practical applicability.

We systematically quantify the discrepancy between retrospective and timely effort-aware evaluations of JIT defect prediction. By introducing a chronological evaluation protocol across six open-source projects, we show that traditional metrics, such as $R@20\%$ and P_{opt}, inflate the perceived effort-saving potential due to their disregard for commit chronology. We demonstrate that effort-aware metrics overestimate real-world defect detection performance by up to 53% in supervised and 45% in unsupervised scenarios. These findings provide a foundation for rethinking how JIT defect prediction models are evaluated and compared in both research and practice.

In practice, JIT models must deliver timely predictions for individual commits rather than rely on post-hoc ranking under fixed inspection budgets. Software development is inherently asynchronous, and commits must be reviewed and merged promptly rather than accumulated over long evaluation windows. Since code reviews are already an integral part of software development [2], the challenge lies in prioritizing high-risk changes rather than minimizing review effort [17]. Developers' reluctance to adopt JIT tools, often due to high false-negative rates and limited interpretability [10,16], further underscores the need for realistic, developer-centered evaluations.

Practitioners should exercise caution when selecting models based on retrospective effort-aware metrics, as these may overstate real-world effectiveness. We argue that effort-aware performance evaluations must preserve the chronological order of commits and avoid dependence on fixed, post-hoc inspection budgets. We note, however, that this requirement applies to evaluation design rather than to practical deployment. Consequently, a more practical use of JIT defect prediction is to prioritize high-risk commits within short, rolling review windows. Such an approach better reflects real-world development workflows, where predictions are consumed continuously as changes arrive, and allows JIT defect prediction to guide review effort efficiently without imposing unrealistic delays. Supporting these operational constraints while ensuring fair evaluation methodologies remains an important direction for future work.

References

1. Arisholm, E., Briand, L.C., Johannessen, E.B.: A systematic and comprehensive investigation of methods to build and evaluate fault prediction models. J. Syst. Softw. **83**(1), 2–17 (2010)
2. Bacchelli, A., Bird, C.: Expectations, outcomes, and challenges of modern code review. In: Proceedings of the 2013 International Conference on Software Engineering, ICSE 2013, pp. 712–721. IEEE Press (2013)
3. Bhutamapuram, U.S., Chonari, F., Anilkumar, G.K., Konchada, S.K.: LLMs for defect prediction in evolving datasets: emerging results and future directions. In: Proceedings of the 33rd ACM International Conference on the Foundations of Software Engineering, FSE Companion 2025, pp. 520–524. Association for Computing Machinery, New York (2025). https://doi.org/10.1145/3696630.3728491
4. Bludau, P., Pretschner, A.: Feature sets in just-in-time defect prediction: an empirical evaluation. In: Proceedings of the 18th International Conference on Predictive Models and Data Analytics in Software Engineering, PROMISE 2022, pp. 22–31. Association for Computing Machinery, New York (2022). https://doi.org/10.1145/3558489.3559068
5. Bludau, P., Pretschner, A.: PR-SZZ: how pull requests can support the tracing of defects in software repositories. In: 2022 IEEE International Conference on Software Analysis, Evolution and Reengineering (SANER), pp. 1–12 (2022). https://doi.org/10.1109/SANER53432.2022.00012
6. Bludau, P., Pretschner, A.: Supplementary code for: on effort awareness for just-in-time defect prediction (2025). https://doi.org/10.6084/m9.figshare.28519349
7. Fu, W., Menzies, T.: Revisiting unsupervised learning for defect prediction. In: Proceedings of the 2017 11th Joint Meeting on Foundations of Software Engineering. ACM (2017). https://doi.org/10.1145/3106237.3106257
8. Fukushima, T., Kamei, Y., McIntosh, S., Yamashita, K., Ubayashi, N.: An empirical study of just-in-time defect prediction using cross-project models. In: Proceedings of the 11th Working Conference on Mining Software Repositories, MSR 2014, pp. 172–181. Association for Computing Machinery, New York (2014). https://doi.org/10.1145/2597073.2597075
9. Gousios, G., Storey, M.A., Bacchelli, A.: Work practices and challenges in pull-based development: the contributor's perspective. In: 2016 IEEE/ACM 38th International Conference on Software Engineering (ICSE), pp. 285–296 (2016). https://doi.org/10.1145/2884781.2884826
10. Hoang, T., Dam, H.K., Kamei, Y., Lo, D., Ubayashi, N.: DeepJIT: an end-to-end deep learning framework for just-in-time defect prediction. In: 2019 IEEE/ACM 16th International Conference on Mining Software Repositories (MSR). IEEE (2019). https://doi.org/10.1109/msr.2019.00016
11. Hoang, T., Kang, H.J., Lo, D., Lawall, J.: CC2Vec: distributed representations of code changes. In: Proceedings of the ACM/IEEE 42nd International Conference on Software Engineering, ICSE 2020, pp. 518–529. Association for Computing Machinery, New York (2020). https://doi.org/10.1145/3377811.3380361

12. Hou, X., et al.: Large language models for software engineering: a systematic literature review. ACM Trans. Softw. Eng. Methodol. **33**(8) (2024). https://doi.org/10.1145/3695988
13. Huang, Q., Xia, X., Lo, D.: Supervised vs unsupervised models: a holistic look at effort-aware just-in-time defect prediction. In: 2017 IEEE International Conference on Software Maintenance and Evolution (ICSME). IEEE (2017)
14. Huang, Q., Xia, X., Lo, D.: Revisiting supervised and unsupervised models for effort-aware just-in-time defect prediction. Empir. Softw. Eng. **24**(5), 2823–2862 (2019). https://doi.org/10.1007/s10664-018-9661-2
15. Jiang, T., Tan, L., Kim, S.: Personalized defect prediction. In: Proceedings of the 28th IEEE/ACM International Conference on Automated Software Engineering, ASE 2013, pp. 279–289. IEEE Press (2013). https://doi.org/10.1109/ASE.2013.6693087
16. Johnson, B., Song, Y., Murphy-Hill, E., Bowdidge, R.: Why don't software developers use static analysis tools to find bugs? In: International Conference on Software Engineering, pp. 672–681 (2013)
17. Jureczko, M., Kajda, L., Górecki, P.: Code review effectiveness: an empirical study on selected factors influence. IET Softw. **14**(7), 794–805 (2020). https://doi.org/10.1049/iet-sen.2020.0134
18. Kamei, Y., Fukushima, T., McIntosh, S., Yamashita, K., Ubayashi, N., Hassan, A.E.: Studying just-in-time defect prediction using cross-project models. Empir. Softw. Eng. **21**, 2072–2106 (2016). https://doi.org/10.1007/s10664-015-9400-x
19. Kamei, Y., et al.: A large-scale empirical study of just-in-time quality assurance. IEEE Trans. Softw. Eng. **39**(6), 757–773 (2013). https://doi.org/10.1109/tse.2012.70
20. Khanan, C., et al.: JITBot: an explainable just-in-time defect prediction bot. In: 2020 35th IEEE/ACM International Conference on Automated Software Engineering (ASE), pp. 1336–1339 (2020)
21. Kim, S., Whitehead, E.J., Zhang, Y.: Classifying software changes: clean or buggy? IEEE Trans. Software Eng. **34**(2), 181–196 (2008). https://doi.org/10.1109/tse.2007.70773
22. Kochhar, P.S., Xia, X., Lo, D., Li, S.: Practitioners' expectations on automated fault localization. In: Proceedings of the 25th International Symposium on Software Testing and Analysis, ISSTA 2016, pp. 165–176. Association for Computing Machinery, New York (2016). https://doi.org/10.1145/2931037.2931051
23. Li, W., Zhang, W., Jia, X., Huang, Z.: Effort-aware semi-supervised just-in-time defect prediction. Inf. Softw. Technol. **126**, 106364 (2020). https://doi.org/10.1016/j.infsof.2020.106364
24. Lin, J., Zhou, Y., Yang, Y., Lu, H., Xu, B.: Code churn: a neglected metric in effort-aware just-in-time defect prediction. In: 2017 ACM/IEEE International Symposium on Empirical Software Engineering and Measurement (ESEM). IEEE (2017). https://doi.org/10.1109/esem.2017.8
25. McIntosh, S., Kamei, Y.: Are fix-inducing changes a moving target? A longitudinal case study of just-in-time defect prediction. IEEE Trans. Softw. Eng. **44**(5), 412–428 (2018)
26. Mockus, A., Weiss, D.M.: Predicting risk of software changes. Bell Labs Tech. J. **5**(2), 169–180 (2002). https://doi.org/10.1002/bltj.2229
27. Nayrolles, M., Hamou-Lhadj, A.: CLEVER: combining code metrics with clone detection for just-in-time fault prevention and resolution in large industrial projects. In: Proceedings of the 15th International Conference on Mining Software Repositories. ACM (2018). https://doi.org/10.1145/3196398.3196438

28. Oishie, N.Z.Z., Roy, B.: Commit-checker: a human-centric approach for adopting bug inducing commit detection using machine learning models. In: Proceedings of the 15th Innovations in Software Engineering Conference, ISEC 2022. Association for Computing Machinery, New York (2022). https://doi.org/10.1145/3511430.3511463
29. Ostrand, T., Weyuker, E., Bell, R.: Predicting the location and number of faults in large software systems. IEEE Trans. Softw. Eng. **31**(4), 340–355 (2005). https://doi.org/10.1109/tse.2005.49
30. Pan, C., Gu, A., Gao, Y.: Unveiling insights in source code defect prediction using ChatGPT: moving beyond predictive metrics. In: Nayyar, A., Kolivand, H. (eds.) Fourth International Conference on Signal Processing and Computer Science (SPCS 2023), vol. 12970, p. 129702R. International Society for Optics and Photonics, SPIE (2023). https://doi.org/10.1117/12.3012284
31. Pornprasit, C., Tantithamthavorn, C., Jiarpakdee, J., Fu, M., Thongtanunam, P.: PyExplainer: explaining the predictions of just-in-time defect models. In: 2021 36th IEEE/ACM International Conference on Automated Software Engineering (ASE), pp. 407–418 (2021). https://doi.org/10.1109/ASE51524.2021.9678763
32. Qiao, L., Wang, Y.: Effort-aware and just-in-time defect prediction with neural network. PLOS ONE **14**(2), 1–19 (2019). https://doi.org/10.1371/journal.pone.0211359
33. Rigby, P.C., Bird, C.: Convergent contemporary software peer review practices. In: Proceedings of the 2013 9th Joint Meeting on Foundations of Software Engineering, ESEC/FSE 2013, pp. 202–212. Association for Computing Machinery, New York (2013). https://doi.org/10.1145/2491411.2491444
34. Sadowski, C., Söderberg, E., Church, L., Sipko, M., Bacchelli, A.: Modern code review: a case study at google. In: International Conference on Software Engineering, Software Engineering in Practice track (ICSE SEIP) (2018)
35. Shihab, E., Hassan, A.E., Adams, B., Jiang, Z.M.: An industrial study on the risk of software changes. In: Proceedings of the ACM SIGSOFT 20th International Symposium on the Foundations of Software Engineering - FSE 2012. ACM Press (2012). https://doi.org/10.1145/2393596.2393670
36. Śliwerski, J., Zimmermann, T., Zeller, A.: When do changes induce fixes? In: Proceedings of the 2005 International Workshop on Mining Software Repositories, MSR 2005, pp. 1–5. Association for Computing Machinery, New York (2005). https://doi.org/10.1145/1082983.1083147
37. Song, L., Minku, L.L., Yao, X.: On the validity of retrospective predictive performance evaluation procedures in just-in-time software defect prediction. Empir. Softw. Eng. **28**(5), 124 (2023). https://doi.org/10.1007/s10664-023-10341-8
38. Tessema, H.D., Abebe, S.L.: Enhancing just-in-time defect prediction using change request-based metrics. In: 2021 IEEE International Conference on Software Analysis, Evolution and Reengineering (SANER). IEEE (2021). https://doi.org/10.1109/saner50967.2021.00056
39. Yan, M., Xia, X., Fan, Y., Lo, D., Hassan, A.E., Zhang, X.: Effort-aware just-in-time defect identification in practice: a case study at Alibaba. In: Proceedings of the 28th ACM Joint Meeting on European Software Engineering Conference and Symposium on the Foundations of Software Engineering. ACM (2020). https://doi.org/10.1145/3368089.3417048
40. Yang, X., Lo, D., Xia, X., Zhang, Y., Sun, J.: Deep learning for just-in-time defect prediction. In: 2015 IEEE International Conference on Software Quality, Reliability and Security. IEEE (2015)

41. Yang, Y., et al.: Effort-aware just-in-time defect prediction: simple unsupervised models could be better than supervised models. In: Proceedings of the 2016 24th ACM SIGSOFT International Symposium on Foundations of Software Engineering. ACM (2016). https://doi.org/10.1145/2950290.2950353

42. Yao, J., Shepperd, M.: Assessing software defection prediction performance: why using the Matthews correlation coefficient matters. In: Proceedings of the 24th International Conference on Evaluation and Assessment in Software Engineering, EASE 2020, pp. 120–129. Association for Computing Machinery, New York (2020). https://doi.org/10.1145/3383219.3383232

43. Zeng, Z., Zhang, Y., Zhang, H., Zhang, L.: Deep just-in-time defect prediction: how far are we? In: Proceedings of the 30th ACM SIGSOFT International Symposium on Software Testing and Analysis. ACM (2021)

44. Çarka, J., Esposito, M., Falessi, D.: On effort-aware metrics for defect prediction. Empir. Softw. Eng. **27**, 1–38 (2022). https://doi.org/10.1007/S10664-022-10186-7

Business Intelligence Architecture for Process Quality Monitoring with BDD

Stefan Biffl[1,2,3]($\boxtimes$) (iD), Matteo Martinelli[4] (iD), Hossein Rahmani[1] (iD),
and Marco Picone[4] (iD)

[1] Institute of Information Systems Engineering, Technische Universität Wien,
Vienna, Austria
{stefan.biffl,hossein.rahmani}@tuwien.ac.at
[2] Secure Business Austria, TU Wien, Vienna, Austria
[3] Austrian Center for Digital Production, TU Wien, Vienna, Austria
[4] Distributed and Pervasive Intelligence (DIPI) Group, Department of Sciences and
Methods for Engineering (DISMI), University of Modena and Reggio Emilia,
Modena, Italy
{matteo.martinelli,marco.picone}@unimore.it

Abstract. The Industry 4.0 vision aims for high-quality and flexible production processes that are automated with Cyber-Physical Production Systems (CPPSs) to address changes in demand and the environment. Process Quality Monitoring (PQM) shall ensure the desired process quality and low delay in reacting to deviations towards undesired process outcomes. Digital Twin (DT) functions mend CPPS limitations to monitor conditions in a multi-domain environment, including the physical system. However, it remains unclear how to elicit the tacit and scattered knowledge required to specify conditions for effective PQM under uncertainty. This paper introduces the approach *Process Quality Monitoring with Behavior-Driven Development (PQM+BDD)* to (i) represent the business intelligence architecture, i.e., cause-effect knowledge and data, required for PQM of a valuable process outcome and (ii) leverage capabilities of Behavior-Driven Development scenarios to specify key conditions as input to design a PQM information system with DT functions. We evaluated PQM+BDD on the design of a CPPS to explore its feasibility, effectiveness, and efficiency. The results indicate PQM+BDD to be feasible, and effective in comparison to a best-practice approach.

Keywords: Industry 4.0 · Cyber-Physical Production System · Multi-domain Modeling · Behavior-Driven Development

1 Introduction

Industrial digitalization has become an established reality across manufacturing sectors, with significant expectations regarding its capacity to enhance system performance and operational outcomes [12]. Digital Twin (DT) functions provide

© The Author(s), under exclusive license to Springer Nature Switzerland AG 2026
M. Dorner et al. (Eds.): SWQD 2026, LNBIP 581, pp. 42–62, 2026.
https://doi.org/10.1007/978-3-032-24216-7_3

a bridge between the physical and digital domains to facilitate real-time monitoring, analysis, and control of production systems [12,13]. To address operational challenges, such as unplanned downtime and issues with process traceability and adaptability, producers aim at improving Process Quality Monitoring through emerging digital technologies [21]. For example, workpiece drops during transfer in automated logistics material handling (cf. Fig. 1, Sect. 3) lead to unplanned downtime and compromised production outcomes.

Process Quality Monitoring (PQM) shall ensure the desired process quality by collecting and processing diverse production data for operations, maintenance, quality, and planning [21]. To realize this goal and answer stakeholders' questions, PQM requires input on what data to gather and analyze from various sources related to Product, Process, and Resource assets [23]. Engineering models define cross-disciplinary dependencies [10] that provide a foundation for capturing cause-effect relations that inform PQM. However, traditional PQM often builds on Total Quality Management, Total Productive Maintenance, and Lean Manufacturing [21], which support operational execution and continuous improvement but fall short in two key aspects: (i) leveraging the multi-domain knowledge in Cyber-Physical Production System (CPPS) engineering models, and (ii) addressing the interplay of the digital and physical domains at the heart of modern CPPSs. These limitations reduce the traceability of undesired outcomes to their causes and adaptability after deployment. Even recent proposals [17,20] do not bridge the physical details and digital systems, neither consider digitalization in the context of improvement with PQM. To specify conditions for effective PQM under uncertainty, a key challenge is insufficient elicitation of the required business intelligence from the tacit and scattered domain knowledge.

To address these limitations, this paper proposes a model-based approach to consistently define PQM specifications in CPPS engineering and operations. We investigate the following research question: *"What is an effective model-based approach to support a quality manager in* (i) *eliciting and representing the Business Intelligence architecture–encompassing cause-effect knowledge and data–required for PQM of a valuable process outcome,* and (ii) *deriving from this knowledge actionable specifications (e.g., Behavior-Driven Development scenarios) as input to design a PQM Information System, such as a Digital Twin, in a multi-domain production environment?"* To address this research question, we follow design science [24] to explore foundations for a meta-model for *Process Quality Monitoring with Behavior-Driven Development (PQM+BDD)* and propose a systematic method for answering stakeholder questions on valuable process outcomes. The method shall facilitate: (i) design and validation of a Business Intelligence architecture that captures cause-effect dependencies from multi-domain stakeholders' views and data sources, and (ii) leveraging Behavior-Driven Development scenarios to specify process conditions as actionable input to configure a PQM system for valid data collection.

The PQM+BDD approach focuses on stakeholder questions regarding the debugging of production processes while considering dependencies across concerns for business, production process, and data acquisition and analysis [23] to collect and integrate the required domain knowledge. We simplify process debugging by applying principles of conditioned production process slicing [3] using multi-domain CPPS knowledge models.

This generates a targeted knowledge graph containing the data required for evaluating the main causal factors influencing production outcomes. We employ Behavior-Driven Development to elicit and formalize domain knowledge on processes and systems, as scenarios and conditions that both stakeholders–from diverse Industry 4.0 domains– and computer systems can interpret [6]. This approach shall foster interdisciplinary collaboration and enable rigorous validation of process conditions [13]. We demonstrate PQM+BDD through a proof of concept on the design of a lab-scale physical CPPS with industry-grade controllers, focusing on a scenario for *Workpiece Transfer* (cf. Sect. 3) that requires the integration of data from heterogeneous sources including Internet of Things sensors and DTs.

The remainder of this work is structured as follows. Section 2 reviews related work. Section 3 presents an illustrative use case. Section 4 introduces PQM+BDD. Section 5 reports on a feasibility study of PQM+BDD. Sections 6 and 7 discuss findings and limitations, conclude, and outline future work.

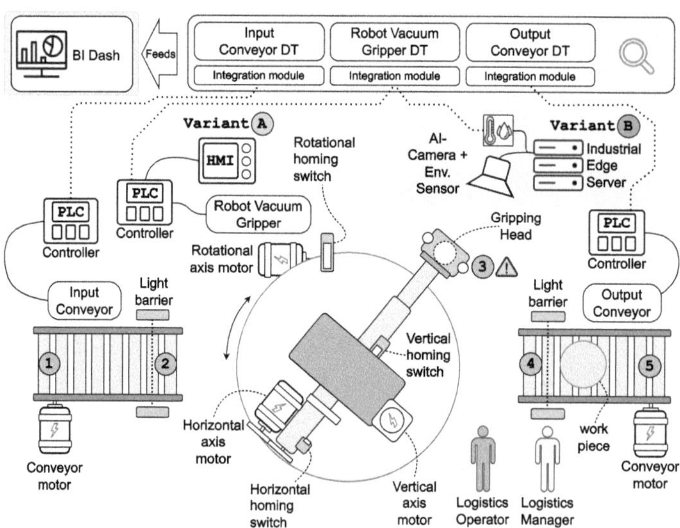

Fig. 1. CPPS of the use case *Workpiece Transfer*, from (1) to (5), with potential loss of the workpiece at (3), with three variants: baseline: *no sensor* for loss; A: *human sensor* reporting loss through an Human-Machine Interface (HMI); B: *camera and environmental sensor* feeding loss event data to a DT system.

2   Related Work

This section summarizes related work on process improvement and quality monitoring, Digital Twin concepts for Process Quality Monitoring, and multi-domain modeling for Business Intelligence.

2.1   Process Improvement and Quality Monitoring

Process Improvement and Quality Monitoring are essential in both industrial and software domains [14,19,21]. Industrial systems depend on complex, expensive assets that must run efficiently to justify their cost, leading to the development of management systems focused on product and process quality, and continuous improvement activities [21]. However, classical Lean methods, built for offline, manual data tracking, do not fully use sensor data or digital models for comprehensive analysis [21]. Therefore, digitalization in industry demands advanced PQM methods to leverage connected equipment to overcome these limitations.

Industry 4.0 aims at exploiting the best of physical and digital worlds, e.g., by integrating Behavior-Driven Development in industrial Virtual Commissioning [7]. This study exemplifies how physical and digital aspects of Cyber-Physical Systems can be synthesized by modeling physical components and their relationships as Product-Process-Resource graphs, mapping behaviors with Behavior Diagrams, as input to *Gherkin* tests for Programmable Logic Controller code development. While this is a promising approach, the case study does not take advantage from existing input, such as industrial PQM modeling of faults that smart CPPSs should detect and manage. In this work, we consider DTs to support integration and monitoring of CPPSs for continuous knowledge extraction from production data and adaptive responses. Further, we consider Business Intelligence to bridge critical gaps in representing and eliciting domain knowledge–especially regarding multi-domain cause-effect chains in production.

2.2   Digital Twin Concepts for Process Quality Monitoring

The Digital Twin (DT) concept centers on creating a digital counterpart that mirrors and influences a physical system. Originating from Grieves' work within Product Life-cycle Management [9], it relies on bidirectional data flows to address fragmented product information [22]. Subsequent research clarified distinctions between digital models, shadows, and twins [12], and introduced Internet of Things-enabled DTs [16]. The research community is aligned in considering DTs foundational for industrial Cyber-Physical Systems (CPSs) [11], as they decouple the complexity of the physical layer from higher-level modeling and reasoning layers [13]. By providing a consistent flow of context-aware, real-time data, DTs ensure accurate visibility and synchronization across the CPS, thus supporting advanced data analysis and knowledge extraction towards effective PQM.

Newrzella et al. [17] introduce a process to manage digitalization projects involving DTs by prioritizing value for stakeholders and the availability of the required data. However, this method lacks technical detail and structured quality checks, making it difficult to verify system quality at the physical process level.

Recent contributions aim at bridging theoretical and practical aspects of DTs along the CPS lifecycle. Qamsane et al. [20] propose iterative planning, design, and updates for CPS, while Wortmann et al. [14] stress the need for continuous improvement. Despite clarifying digitalization requirements, both works lack practical testing strategies and descriptions of physical system behavior.

Picone et al. [19] emphasize considering the perspectives of physical objects and stakeholders in DT development. They propose involving relevant actors at each stage and introduce the Mock Physical Twin to simulate missing physical entities during development. The proposal enables novel integration evaluations, but does not discuss practical guidelines for testing or monitoring.

For improving quality monitoring of physical assets, such as products, processes, and systems, DTs build on Grieves' vision [9] to overcome challenges of dispersed data and fragmented systems [1,18]. However, most DT approaches lack clear models of physical system structure and behavior, which are core parts for a Business Intelligence architecture to answer questions on asset quality and DT validation. In this paper, we explore a sufficiently complete set of models for PQM,, which is a foundation for defining targeted quality tests for DT systems in Industry 4.0, which shall provide validated input to PQM.

2.3   Multi-domain Modeling for Business Intelligence

Business Intelligence shall provide the knowledge and data required for data analysis to inform decision making [4], e.g., the quality manager in monitoring and improving production process quality. Process improvement approaches, such as Total Quality Management or Lean Management [21], assume sufficient knowledge of the scope for work. However, this knowledge is often implicit and scattered among stakeholders and heterogeneous artifacts in several domains. Often, it is limited to the system's physical aspects, neglecting CPPS variants.

For providing the multi-domain knowledge from CPPS engineering for operation, this work shall build on the models in [4]: (i) the value proposition canvas [4] to understand business pain points of a client as undesired conditions to improve, (ii) Cause + Effect Networks [3,5] to represent main causes of undesired conditions, and (iii) a Production Asset Network [3] to represent CPPS and production dependencies. Together, these models provide contributions to design the Business Intelligence for answering questions on process outcomes.

While these models are already useful for reasoning, they require solution elements to turn the knowledge into actionable advice to guide human-machine teams for monitoring and improvement. Behavior-Driven Development (BDD) scenarios [6] provide the capabilities to (i) elicit the concepts required for PQM from diverse domain experts and (ii) map the concepts to a PQM software architecture for implementation. Therefore, we build on multi-domain knowledge from CPPS engineering to design the Business Intelligence architecture required to derive BDD scenarios that specify conditions for PQM of causes that contribute to valuable process outcomes, as input to PQM implementation.

3   Illustrative Use Case for Evaluation

This section introduces the use case *Workpiece Transfer* to illustrate requirements for PQM during CPPS engineering, ramp-up, and operation. We abstracted the use case from a domain analysis of a typical logistics process [15] in a discrete manufacturing line. Core stakeholders in production logistics are the Logistics Manager, the Quality Manager, and the operator, supported by the maintenance engineer and process and specific technology experts. Logistics Managers are interested in economically operating the CPPS to fulfill customer orders on time with sufficient throughput and quality. The Quality Manager ensures product quality based on CPPS functions. Process/technology experts provide knowledge to ensure process and CPPS functionality and stability.

For instance, in a complex workpiece transfer process (cf. Fig. 1), which involves a robot with a gripper interfacing to partner systems and a workpiece, the design combination of workpiece, system interfaces, processes and system control programs shall ensure process quality.PQM shall check correct and timely closure of process steps to collect data on key performance indicators and notify the operator on issues. The operator shall relate the notification message to plan the resolution of the issue, often concerning several systems that depend on each other. For each system, there is an operation manual, also an operating procedure for their combination, to guide the operator. However, in case of an unexpected issue, the operator has to debug the process or escalate the issue to the Quality Manager for causes beyond the knowledge of the operator, which grows over time. Due to changes in the environment – such as different material characteristics of the workpiece surface, a new version of the robot control program, and new personnel in operation and maintenance – process quality may deteriorate. For example, the effectiveness of *Workpiece Transfer* may decline due to increasing failure rate, even when isolated causal contributions are small. Hence, multiple stakeholders' knowledge is required to (i) identify the source of issues and (ii) plan effective improvements to minimize their impact.

Figure 1 illustrates the industrial setup of a CPPS for transferring a workpiece from an input conveyor to an output conveyor, which senses the workpiece at the interface with a light barrier. The robot shall pick up the workpiece at the input conveyor and safely transfer the workpiece to place it at an output interface. For simplicity, this use case considers only one output interface. Recently, PQM reported more production delay due to workpieces not arriving on time or getting lost and damaged. Unfortunately, the traditional CPPS was designed with limited sensor equipment, to monitor handover at interfaces but not the transfer process. To represent the knowledge on valid CPPS configuration structures with improvement options, Fig. 1 illustrates CPPS and architecture variants for improved PQM capabilities: (i) *baseline* traditional CPPS; (ii) *variant A*: CPPS improvement with a human sensor; and (iii) *variant B*: CPPS improvement with physical augmentation via a camera and environmental sensor, and digital augmentation [16] with an Artificial Intelligence classification system [11] integrated via DTs feeding the PQM information system consumed by the operator.

This work focuses on stakeholder questions to a PQM Information System on causes of effects towards production condition monitoring on CPPS engineering and operation data. Specifically, it has been motivated by questions of the Logistics Manager to improve throughput: *Q1: Why is the workpiece transfer failure rate high?* and *Q2: When is the failure rate of the workpiece transfer system high?* The result shall be a PQM Information System dashboard based on data analysis of selected machine parameters to assess the risk level of production quality conditions with an impact on production throughput.

Traditional best-practice approach to design PQM knowledge for issue analysis and improvement is *PQM of process post-conditions.* In the use case, PQM mainly focused on controls preserving the system's minimal operational capabilities, tied to the Programmable Logic Controller program and workpiece detection timeouts. Despite system connectivity, the system was severely limited in data collection for technical monitoring and business reporting. Consequently, data on process pre-conditions were missing, weakening the system's ability to track the impact of changes and uncertainty in production.

Under an improvement perspective, the Quality Manager and the domain experts applied the DIN EN 60812 [5] and collected cause-and-effect conditions in natural language [3]. These conditions were useful for understanding the logistics process, but were (i) not sufficiently complete due to tacit operator knowledge and isolated partial expert knowledge, (ii) not well connected to the technical reality of the CPPS and (iii) not validated with data sources as input to PQM Information System design. Therefore, the knowledge architecture for PQM suffered from semantic mismatches, did not represent important cause concepts, and contained superfluous data that cluttered data analysis and impeded process improvement. This hindered PQM to analyze the contributions coming from main cause conditions that concerned processes in different parts of the CPPS.

From these limitations we derive the following requirements for (R1) representing and (R2) designing a Business Intelligence architecture for PQM with BDD to validate knowledge and answer questions with diverse stakeholders.

R1. Representation of Business Intelligence Architecture for PQM with BDD. PQM+BDD shall facilitate the translation from stakeholder questions on process outcomes to required technical contributions, as input to actionable BDD scenarios that inform PQM to answer the questions. PQM+BDD shall facilitate representing: *R11. Business Intelligence architecture views* concerning (i) knowledge on value creation elements, including process conditions regarding desired and undesired outcomes, processes, and contributions to a process outcome and (ii) knowledge on PQM elements, including conditions that refer to assets and data sources required for monitoring. *R12. BDD scenarios that specify PQM capabilities* for a process condition, e.g., an undesired outcome, consisting of (i) process pre-conditions (GIVEN), (ii) process start and end events (WHEN), and (iii) process post-conditions (THEN).

R2. Method for eliciting Business Intelligence architecture for PQM with BDD scenarios. PQM+BDD shall facilitate eliciting: *R21. Business Intelligence architecture views* on (i) value creation elements in stakeholder questions, concerning business, production, data collection and analysis, linked to PQM elements and (ii) Business Intelligence architecture structure, e.g., modules and interfaces, on a conditional process slice [3] for a valuable outcome. *R22. BDD scenarios for PQM regarding an undesired outcome*, including (i) pre-conditions for a process and (ii) post-conditions for a process to specify the data to monitor and conditions to evaluate as input to answer stakeholder questions.

4   Solution Approach

This section discusses the meta-model and introduces the method for *Process Quality Monitoring with Behavior-Driven Development (PQM+BDD)* to facilitate depicting partial condition and domain asset models as a context for focused data collection and analysis on specific production effects and causes.

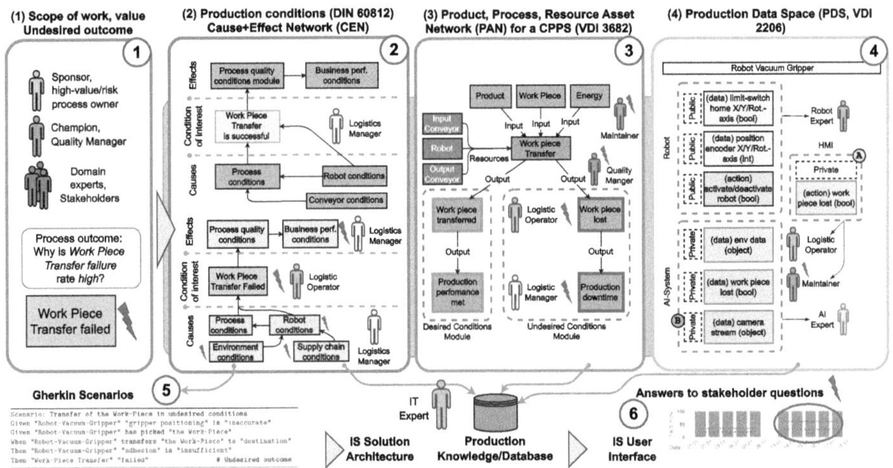

Fig. 2. *Process Quality Monitoring with Behavior-Driven Development* approach with Business Intelligence architecture and information system, based on [3,4]. See details of the solution parts (2) to (6) in Figs. 3 to 7 and Lst. 2 respectively.

Solution overview. Figure 2 provides an overview of the PQM+BDD approach. PQM+BDD aims at linking previously isolated models (1) to (4) into a *Business Intelligence architecture* to inform PQM: (1) *stakeholder questions* regarding production concepts; (2) cause-effect conditions, represented in *Cause + Effect Networks (CENs)* (cf. Figs. 4 and 5); (3) CPPS model data, represented in a *Production Asset Network (PAN)* (cf. Fig. 3) or in engineering artifacts; and (4) data sources in a *Production Data Space (PDS)* (cf. Fig. 6). This way, a Quality Manager can trace production conditions in a production configuration, which considers processes with their CPPS resources and Failure Mode and Effects Analysis (FMEA) concerns, such as logistics issues, to PAN assets and properties and to stakeholder production data views. By integrating these disparate models, Quality Managers can validate (i) production configuration plausibility and correctness against engineering data, and (ii) the availability of data in the PDS to evaluate the production conditions for a PAN scope, which builds the foundation for conditioned production process slicing [3] to identify in a small graph candidate factors that contribute to a specific undesired production outcome. Graph queries on the CEN knowledge graph can efficiently report missing references from production conditions to the PAN or PDS[1] [2].

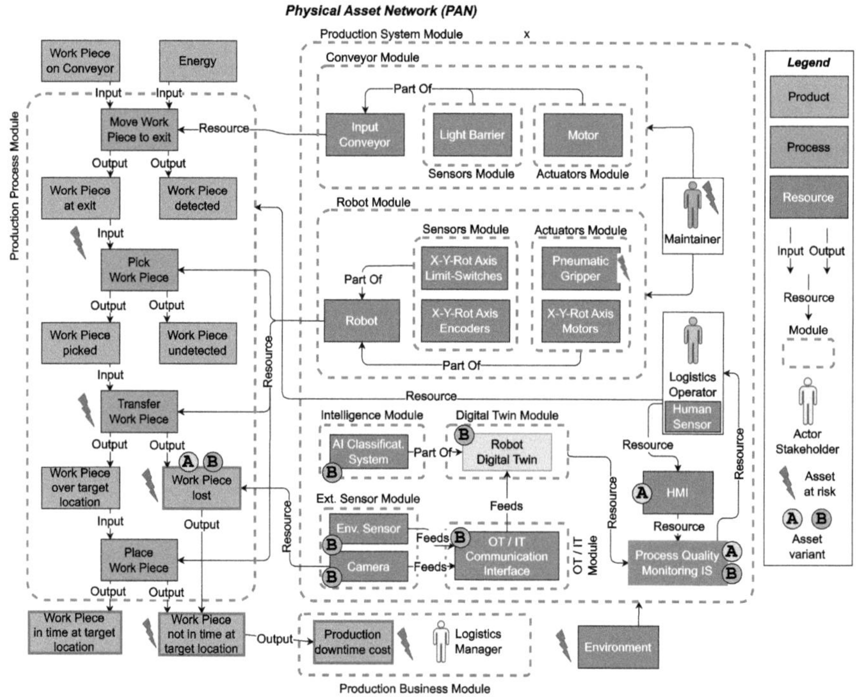

Fig. 3. Detailed production asset network of the process *Workpiece Transfer*, representing the concepts in desired and undesired conditions, based on [3,23].

(5) BDD is well established [6] for specifying software prototypes and tests with diverse domain experts. PQM+BDD applies BDD to (i) elicit process conditions in scenarios (domain view) and (ii) inform the PQM design and validation

---

[1] See online supplementary materials at https://dub.sh/pqm-for-cpps-with-bdd.

(software view). *Gherkin* [6] scenarios facilitate for a domain expert to specify scenarios for PQM in natural language and for a software engineer to transform natural language constructs into executable artifacts to configure a PQM environment for data acquisition, integration, and evaluation. Production conditions, such as *Workpiece Transfer failed* (cf. Fig. 5), shall provide the domain concepts to design BDD scenarios in *Gherkin* to specify concepts for PQM automation.

(6) After a successful validation of a production configuration and the *Gherkin* scenarios, IT experts shall design a PQM information system that builds upon the PQM+BDD knowledge graph and incorporates data from CPPS engineering, operations, and PQM itself. This system shall answer stakeholder questions by, for example, utilizing DTs for system integration to: (i) evaluate production conditions over time; (ii) identify and correlate factors that may strongly influence undesired production outcomes to enable improvements (cf. Fig. 7); and (iii) calculate and report key performance indicators.

4.1 PQM+BDD Meta-Model Concerns

Considering meta-models, which are likely to have considerable overlap with the PQM+BDD scope of the intended Business Intelligence architecture, we explored the meta-models on *Production Test Scenario Validation (PTSV)* [2] and *Multiaspect FMEA Configuration Management (MFCM)* [3] to identify candidates for addressing modeling requirements for PQM+BDD and gaps that require alternative solutions. PTSV focuses on validating conditions of production test scenarios, while MFCM links FMEA risk knowledge in CEN modules to CPPS assets and data sources. Therefore, the combination of these meta-models seems to be promising for PQM+BDD models and facilitate designing the production knowledge base for a PQM Information System.

PTSV supports (i) processes with pre- and post-conditions to describe test cases, comparable to BDD scenarios; (ii) cause-effect networks by linking these conditions, (iii) assets that represent the data in the conditions, and (iv) production data views with artifacts to extract the asset data and evaluate the conditions. MFCM builds on PTSV to add the concept of modules in CENs and PANs to support the definition of model configurations for version control of risk knowledge [5] validated with engineering knowledge.

Therefore, the PTSV meta-model [2], augmented with the MFCM extensions [3], seems to be a sufficient foundation for the application as a PQM+BDD meta-model to represent, in addition to the CPPS engineering and risk knowledge, also the run-time knowledge required for a Business Intelligence architecture to inform PQM. As PTSV concerns production test scenarios, it represents already the knowledge required for specifying the elements of BDD scenarios.

4.2 PQM+BDD Method for Designing Monitoring Solutions

This section describes the method *Process Quality Monitoring with Behavior-Driven Development*, to design the Business Intelligence models (cf. Fig. 2) required to derive BDD scenarios with key conditions that specify input to design a PQM Information System augmented through DT's capabilities. PQM+BDD builds on the method *procan.do Business Intelligence* [4] to identify the knowledge and data required to analyze multi-domain dependencies for production process outcomes of interest. The method PQM+BDD is illustrated with data from the use case *Workpiece Transfer* (cf. Section 3). The method shall be conducted by a moderator and domain experts in the scope of application. The method steps can be conducted in iterations to consider new knowledge.

Step 1: Identify an Undesired Outcome in the Scope of Work. The moderator and domain experts shall define the scope of work, e.g., a production process to monitor, and an undesired process outcome, such as recurring loss of workpieces. The result includes: (i) a definition of scope–processes with inputs and outputs; (ii) at least one undesired outcome with high business impact, prioritized if multiple candidates exist; and (iii) stakeholder questions about the outcome that PQM and data analysis shall address, such as "Why is the Workpiece Transfer Failure rate high?" (cf. Fig. 2).

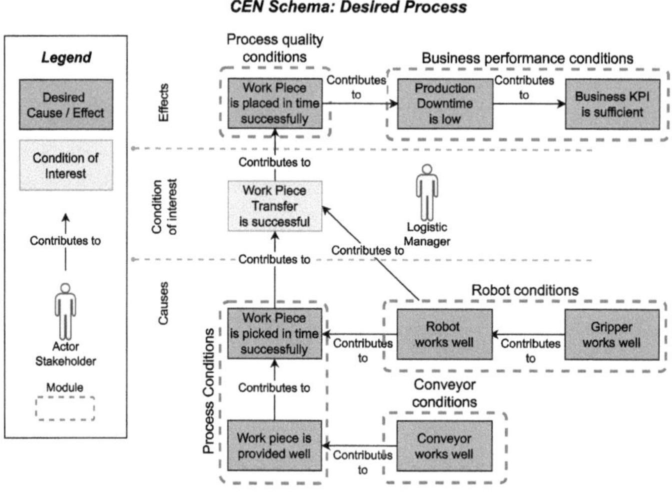

Fig. 4. Simplified CEN contributing to a *desired process outcome* [4].

Step 2: Analyze Production Conditions in Cause-Effect Networks. The domain experts shall focus on the undesired process outcome identified in Step 1. Contextually, the desired process description can be built as well, to identify the corresponding desirable process outcome of the system. Process and domain experts shall design *networks of desired and undesired conditions* [4], which serve as inputs to define normal and special cases in quality risk analysis, Process Quality Monitoring, and data analysis. They shall backtrack from a process outcome–similar to conditioned process slicing [3]–to an appropriate level of detail using methods like FMEA [5], and identify contributing conditions coming from root causes. Each condition shall refer to an asset property, e.g., *Workpiece Transfer was successful.* Condition modules [3] group conditions within stakeholder knowledge to analyze stakeholder interfaces. The result of this step includes: (i) at least one *network of desired conditions* for a *desired outcome* in the normal process flow (cf. Fig. 4), and (ii) at least one *network of undesired conditions* (cf. Fig. 5) that contribute to an *undesired outcome*, possibly impacting business performance severely, e.g., extra cost for unfinished products undelivered due to delays.

Step 3: Validate the Production Conditions with Production Assets. The domain experts shall validate the production conditions from Step 2 and list issues to address before using condition networks for analysis. The process expert shall check each condition with its related asset to design *asset networks* representing the data required to evaluate the condition (cf. Fig. 3). Starting from post-conditions of key processes will result in a minimal set of assets, which can be expanded to include assets related to undesired conditions. Assets and their dependency relations form a network connecting process outcomes to root causes in assets affecting them. Backtracking follows aspects of requirements, exploring domain expert knowledge and interfaces to neighboring knowledge, to validate impact paths within the asset network. Each asset includes a list of properties, (see Footnote 1) e.g., modeled in *Unified Modeling Language.*

The result of this step is (i) at least one *asset network* [3], describing the production domain architecture of products, processes, technical systems, and stakeholders [23] related to desired and undesired process outcomes; (ii) a structured *list of asset properties*, (see Footnote 1) such as engineered or measured values or thresholds like *high*, used to define equivalence classes (e.g., *Workpiece Transfer Failure rate is high*); and (iii) a *list of issues* [3] to address, ensuring the condition/asset networks are sufficiently complete and consistent to explain the process outcomes.

Step 4: Validate the Production Conditions with Production Data Space. The domain and IT experts shall consider the assets and their properties coming from Step 3 to explore and validate technical and semantic access to the data sources required to monitor the data for evaluating the conditions in the condition networks. Each condition shall be possible to evaluate with data that a stakeholder can access in the data space (cf. Fig. 6) (see Footnote 1). The result of this step is (i) a *set of data sources* that provide the data to evaluate conditions, (ii) *a list of stakeholders with technical access to and semantic understanding of the data sources*, and (iii) a *list of issues* to check or improve data source quality.

Step 5: Derive BDD Scenarios for Monitoring the Conditions. The quality manager shall define BDD scenarios that combine conditions to specify normal and special cases as input to design and validate a PQM Information System with the concepts in the conditions identified in Step 2. A goal is to

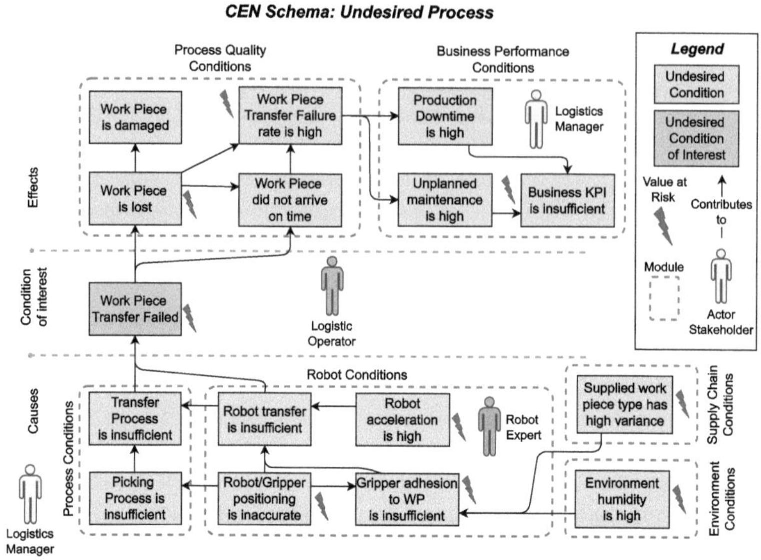

Fig. 5. Simplified CEN contributing to *undesired process outcomes* [4].

```
1  Scenario: Conditions for a production process
2  Given <direct or indirect process pre-condition> # cf. condition network
3  When <process>                                   # cf. asset network
4  Then <direct process post-condition>             # cf. condition network
```

Listing 1: BDD template to specify conditions for monitoring (cf. Lst 2).

identify scenarios that limit production performance, or provide early warnings towards an undesired production outcome. The result of this step is a *set of BDD scenarios* (cf. Listings 1 and 2) that specify asset data to monitor for evaluating the conditions, as input to data analysis and process improvement (cf. Fig. 2).

PQM Implementation. The IT expert shall map the data specified in each BDD scenario to DT functions that collect this data and make PQM operational.

5   Evaluation in a Feasibility Study

The feasibility study [8] aimed to demonstrate the PQM+BDD method in a multi-domain production architecture with production process slicing [3]. The target was to derive the knowledge, data, and BDD scenarios required to design a PQM Information System with data analysis for answering stakeholder questions. The study followed the PQM+BDD method with three practitioners for the use case *Workpiece Transfer* [8]. Reflection with the practitioners evaluated their traditional approach compared to PQM+BDD. The practitioners provided the use case and model content while a facilitator ensured adherence to PQM+BDD, answered questions, and collected data on model content and effort. The practitioners, i.e., a quality manager, a process expert, and a production expert received initial training on PQM+BDD. The domain experts conducted the PQM+BDD method, supported by two researchers acting as PQM+BDD facilitators and tool experts. They designed *PQM+BDD models* for *Workpiece Transfer*, aiming at the logistics of semi-finished workpieces (cf. Figs. 3 to 6), including the improvement of the CPPS design with added sensor and augmented data processing functions through DTs [16] to improve the PQM capabilities of the CPPS design. They conducted the PQM+BDD steps in iterations to consider and validate new knowledge on target production effects and their causes.

Step 1: Identify an Undesired Outcome in the Scope of Work. The lead expert defined the scope of work (see Footnote 1) focused on monitoring the logistic transfer process of a workpiece (cf. Sect. 3). They specified the undesired outcome as *Recurring loss of Workpieces* and the stakeholder question as *Why is the Workpiece Transfer Failure rate high?* where *high* refers to a threshold, e.g., 20%. They designed a process model comprising the production workflow steps, including workpiece arriving at the input conveyor, robot gripping, lifting, transporting, and placing (cf. Fig. 1), along with desired and undesired outcomes (cf. Fig. 3). The stakeholders formulated 5 questions and 6 process steps with 15 inputs and outputs on a shared whiteboard, which took the experts 4 person hours.

Step 2: Analyze Production Conditions in a Cause-Effect Network. The domain experts followed the normal production steps, recording a sequence of desired conditions based on process step post-conditions (cf. Fig. 4). Then they backtracked from the undesired outcome *Workpiece Transfer failed* through functional causes to identify key cause conditions contributing directly or indirectly to this outcome (cf. Fig. 5). This condition network, similar to exploring CEN modules with slices of stakeholder effect and cause knowledge [2,3], revealed important stakeholders, their roles and interfaces. They grouped cause conditions into modules by domain views: (i) production process, (ii) production system, (iii) supply chain (via input products), and (iv) environment/issues. The experts identified 11 CEN modules with 32 production conditions and 36 contribution relations, requiring 17 person-hours in three validation iterations.

Step 3: Validate Production Conditions with Production Assets. The domain experts validated the concepts in the condition networks with assets in the PAN (cf. Fig. 3) and properties, (see Footnote 1) in three refinement iterations to address models with diminishing validation issues. They validated

```
1   Scenario: Transfer of the Work-Piece in undesired conditions
2   Given "Robot-Vacuum-Gripper" "gripper positioning" is "inaccurate"
3   Given "Robot-Vacuum-Gripper" has picked "the Work-Piece"
4   When "Robot-Vacuum-Gripper" transfers "the Work-Piece" to "destination"
5   Then "Robot-Vacuum-Gripper" "adhesion" is "insufficient"
6   Then "Work-Piece Transfer" "failed"                      # Undesired outcome
```

Listing 2: BDD scenario to specify undesired conditions for monitoring (cf. Fig 5).

the completeness of asset dependencies from impact back to main causes, and condition network relations [2,3]. The domain experts identified 21 PAN modules with 34 assets, and 38 asset dependency relations. This step took around 23 person hours.

Step 4: Validate Production Conditions with Production Data Space. The domain experts reviewed artifacts in the PDS (see Footnote 1) (cf. Fig. 6) that provided the data required to evaluate conditions for Process Quality Monitoring. They found five PDS artifacts. However they also identified three conditions that could not be evaluated with the available data. To collect data for these conditions, they considered advanced PQM architecture variants (cf. Figs. 1 and 3): (A) a human sensor with a custom HMI to facilitate reporting states, e.g., the loss of a workpiece to PQM; (B) an additional camera and environmental sensor that feed data on loss events to a DT system, which extends the data collection and validation capabilities of PQM. This step took about 5 person-hours.

Step 5: Derive BDD Scenarios for Monitoring the Conditions. The quality expert defined BDD scenarios (see Footnote 1) in *Gherkin* to specify the conditions and data for monitoring (cf. Lst. 2). These scenarios were built from validated condition concepts to cover desired and undesired cases. The domain experts created 12 BDD scenarios grouped into four features–one desired, three undesired–with 32 conditions. This step took about 5 person-hours.

CPPS Improvement for Advanced PQM. To overcome limitations of the legacy CPPS in tracking workpiece losses during transfer, domain and IT experts considered advanced PQM functions (cf. options (A) and (B) described in Step 4, cf. Figs. 1 and 3). The BDD scenarios were found useful to specify DT and PQM behavior for exploring the solution variants A and B, first enacted by a human, then a machine taking over one task a time, for trustworthy automation. The IT expert estimated the effort to operationalize monitoring these conditions and associated data to around 40 person-hours.

PQM Information System Prototype. Using stakeholder questions, validated production configuration, BDD scenarios, and test data, the IT and domain experts designed a PQM Information System with user interface prototypes, data access, and analysis of the production knowledge graph to explore system effects and causes. The result was a PQM Information System design and prototypes for interfaces, logic, and data. To answer stakeholder questions, a researcher and IT expert exported a knowledge graph to a *Neo4J* database, enabling queries and data access in *MS Power BI*. The BDD scenarios in the *Gherkin* DSL [6] provided structured concepts that were easy to transfer to the PQM system for data collection, given suitable data source access.

Figure 7 shows an example prototype PQM Information System dashboard with data analysis highlighting the Quality Manager view using multi-domain production knowledge. The dashboard displays selected production conditions and real-time data on processes and CPPS parameters, facilitating the evaluation of condition states for production process slicing [3]. Condition parameters, such as temperature, humidity, or maintenance state, support detailed time series analysis to trace variable change impacts, such as environment shifts followed by increased loss rates (cf. Figure 7, highlight), to facilitate identifying likely causes of undesired process outcomes for improvement. The evaluation showed the design, validation, and use of Business Intelligence required to collect and analyze PQM data and conditions, with BDD scenarios that (i) facilitated PQM data specification and (ii) informed the design and validation of PQM implementation.

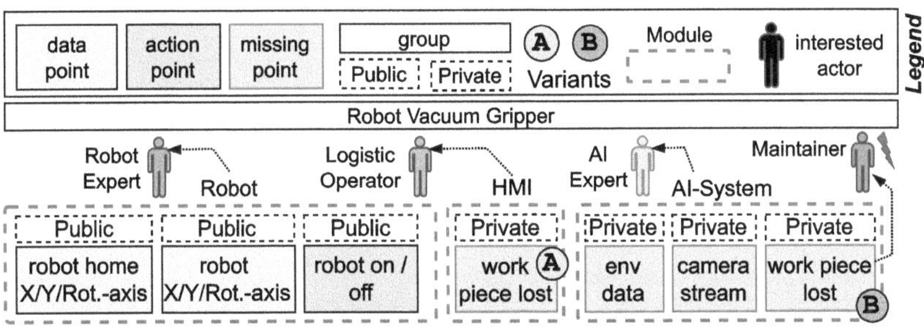

Fig. 6. Simplified PDS including conditions not assessable with baseline data.

Comparison of PQM+BDD to traditional best-practice PQM regarding the requirements introduced in Sect. 3. The practitioners' approach involved in the feasibility study was PQM from the perspective of the quality manager (cf. Section 3), but (i) with isolated partial knowledge, e.g., regarding tacit operator knowledge or gripper issues and where workpieces typically get lost, and (ii) with a focus on process post-conditions, without considering relevant process pre-conditions, in particular indirect pre-conditions, possibly due to the organizational distance of the QM from stakeholders with this knowledge.

The PQM+BDD CEN and PAN addressed by design *R11* by modeling (i) value creation elements: conditions that refer to processes that result in outcomes and contributions to processes; and (ii) assets and data sources required for PQM to evaluate these conditions; and *R12* by adopting BDD scenarios as a technology-agnostic representation of the conditions and data to monitor as (i) process start/end events; and (ii) process pre-/post-conditions.

The PQM+BDD method to design Business Intelligence architecture views on CEN modules [3] addressed *R21* by (i) designing for an undesired outcome a conditional process slice [3] on cause conditions linked to assets and data sources and (ii) designing stakeholder modules in the CEN and PAN to identify interfaces between stakeholders' spheres of knowledge and influence; and *R22* by designing for an undesired outcome BDD scenarios for PQM that specified for a process condition (i) desired and undesired pre-conditions and (ii) post-conditions to evaluate the frequency of process outcomes and to answer stakeholder questions.

The traditional PQM approach ignored prioritizing valuable technical data collection and processing (*R11/R21*), therefore, spreading limited resources over a wide range of unclear data, and missing risky areas. Moreover, the traditional approach relied on technology-specific configurations that failed to link monitoring results to actionable stakeholder advice (*R12/R22*). Stakeholders focused on CPPS aspects lacked awareness of production dependencies, such as resource and stakeholder interactions across modules. This made defining and validating a PQM production configuration difficult. Changes in CPPS configurations caused inconsistencies in traditional PQM setups and reports.

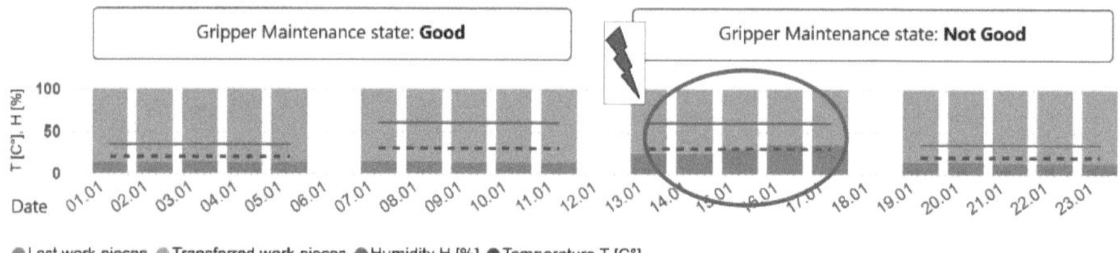

Fig. 7. Prototype of a PQM Information System dashboard: undesired outcome.

6   Discussion

This section discusses the results concerning the Research Question (RQ): *What is an effective model-based approach to support a quality manager in (i) eliciting and representing the Business Intelligence architecture–encompassing cause-effect knowledge and data–required for PQM of a valuable process outcome, and (ii) deriving from this knowledge actionable specifications (e.g., Behavior-Driven Development scenarios) as input to design a PQM Information System in a multi-domain production environment?*

Therefore, we explored meta-model concerns for *Process Quality Monitoring with Behavior-Driven Development (PQM+BDD)* by building on preliminary work in Production Test Scenario Validation [2] and Multi-aspect FMEA Configuration Management [3], which provided the Business Intelligence for testing and debugging a production process and provided a good foundation for the cause-effect knowledge and data required to design PQM solution variants.

Further, we introduced the PQM+BDD method to elicit and validate the knowledge from stakeholders regarding the Business Intelligence architecture, a modular process condition model with cause-effect dependencies (cf. Figs. 3 to 5), which represent multi-domain expert views and data sources, as input to define process contexts that require monitoring. The validation of the conditions in the Business Intelligence architecture ensured the connection of the condition to the data required to evaluate the condition or resulted in an issue on data quality that required resolution as a pre-condition for monitoring.

The process conditions informed BDD scenarios on the processes to monitor, by defining (i) process pre-conditions that influence its own course, (ii) process post-conditions on desired and undesired process outcomes, and (iii) process variants and parameters to address and document the operation of normal and special cases. Therefore, the BDD scenarios specified validated concepts for data collection and informed the design and testing of the PQM system. Further, these process scenarios and conditions provided the vocabulary for designing an Information System building on input from data analysis (cf. Lst. 2 and Fig. 7).

We reported on a proof of concept [8] for applying PQM+BDD on the design of a CPPS, focusing on a process for *Workpiece Transfer* (cf. Fig. 1). PQM+BDD represented multi-domain Business Intelligence on undesired process outcomes by combining CENs into a system-level Business Intelligence configuration that described business and technology causes of undesired outcomes (cf. Fig. 5). This Business Intelligence configuration can be effectively validated with PANs and data sources for completeness and sufficient data quality.

The PQM+BDD method overcomes limitations by addressing PQM issues covered by traditional industrial approaches [21] while also considering the increased pervasiveness and potential of CPPSs. We advance the state of the art with a structured, technology-agnostic way to model a CPPS and its behavior, supporting improvements in both physical and digital components [1,18].

Practitioners can build on the concept of *undesired outcomes* to design Digital Twin-enabled CPPS solutions that identify and manage undesired states through collected data, overcoming CPPS interface limitations. They can use *Gherkin* scenarios to condense this knowledge into a clear, human-readable format, usable across system areas–from physical debugging to DT model design, implementation, and testing.

Lessons Learned. The idea of validating Business Intelligence concerns with engineering domain concepts as input to actionable guidance for PQM with BDD scenarios was found useful and seems to be applicable to a wide range of problems, where experts coming from several disciplines cooperate based on mature domain-specific models of technical impact and dependencies that concern natural laws and engineering models or functions, e.g., general CPS engineering.

PQM+BDD models can aid in negotiating and defining agreements at stakeholder interfaces. Analyzing a condition network reveals where one stakeholder's knowledge ends and connects to another. This marks an interface that may involve exchange, value, and risk. Domain experts sharing these interfaces often negotiate contributions, such as transformations of information, energy, or materials, and may adjust quality or risk assumptions accordingly.

PQM+BDD modules can help link solution detail levels to better understand and solve issues. Modules in an asset network may represent production system elements like mechanical parts, electrical and IT/OT components, or the environment that contributes and causes disturbances. The IT expert must ensure adequate quality of data access for analysis functions, such as monitoring data changes in normal and special process cases, which may lead to data refinery needs. Data quality problems can hinder quality analysis, including risk indicator assessments.

Limitations. The proof of concept focused on a use case derived from a standard production process in discrete manufacturing as a specific design of a CPPS. This may introduce bias due to the specific selection of requirements for production effects, Business Intelligence concerns, and their validation, and of the alternative approaches considered, as well as the roles or individual preferences of the domain experts. To overcome these limitations, we plan empirical studies in a wider variety of application contexts.

7   Conclusion and Future Work

This paper introduced the approach *Process Quality Monitoring with Behavior-Driven Development* to (i) represent the *Business Intelligence architecture*, i.e., knowledge modules on assets and cause-effect conditions, and data sources required to monitor and evaluate conditions for with PQM and (ii) derive from these model views *actionable BDD scenarios* with Gherkin as input to specify and validate a PQM information system that facilitates for a quality manager improving and augmenting CPPS capabilities, e.g., with a Digital Twin, in a flexible production environment.

The Business Intelligence and BDD scenarios facilitate specifying and validating stakeholder knowledge, which may come from several domains, on conditions that contribute to undesired process outcomes, similar to a production process slice [3]. These conditions concern direct and indirect contributions, which can provide early warning signs before the undesired process outcome will result. Therefore, this production Business Intelligence provides a common language for these stakeholders to express and negotiate their input to operational guidance and to process and monitoring improvement during CPPS engineering, ramp-up, and operation.

In a proof of concept study, we evaluated PQM+BDD on the design of a real-world production process and system to explore the method feasibility, effectiveness and efficiency. During the feasibility study, industrial data coming from heterogeneous resources has been considered and combined to understand how the PQM activities can be improved by the analyzed approach. In the empirical study, PQM+BDD was found to be feasible, and effective overcoming limitations of traditional approaches. The application of the method significantly improved the PQM capabilities of the system design, also providing valuable input for the Test-Driven Development of Industrial DTs. PQM+BDD seems to be applicable to a wide range of processes executed by technical systems, supporting their digitalization through the emerging technology of DTs.

Practitioners can build on PQM+BDD to make implicit production knowledge of domain experts explicit for interpretation by human and computer agents. They can use this knowledge to guide the design of Information Systems for answering multi-domain questions on production engineering and operation, and to design advanced computer functions, e.g., AI-based CPPS engineering.

Future Work. We plan to investigate the efficient *reuse of PQM+BDD knowledge* in PQM+BDD models for monitoring solution variants on work lines that require similar capabilities, e.g., logistics systems. We plan case studies on the applicability and scalability of PQM+BDD for a production family to reduce recurring risks. These studies shall clarify the adaptation effort of PQM+BDD configurations for flexible CPPSs and the effort required to adapt and validate the PQM+BDD models and the associated PQM Information Systems.

We envision the *application of PQM+BDD beyond the CPPS domain*. Therefore, we plan to investigate PQM+BDD in socio-technical systems with various stakeholder concerns, such as business process improvement or DTs [2]. A scenario of our interest involves bridging the concerns of security analysts about the relationship between product quality and production resources against silent cyber-physical attacks, in order to improve security monitoring.

References

1. Acharya, S., Khan, A.A., Päivärinta, T.: Interoperability levels and challenges of digital twins in cyber-physical systems. J. Ind. Inf. Integr. **42**, 100714 (2024)
2. Biffl, S., Hoffmann, D., Kiesling, E., Meixner, K., Lüder, A., Winkler, D.: Validating production test scenarios with cyber-physical system design models. In: International Conference on Business Information. IEEE (2023)
3. Biffl, S., Kropatschek, S., Meixner, K., Hoffmann, D., Lüder, A.: Configuring and validating multi-aspect risk knowledge for industry 4.0 information systems. In: International Proceedings on Advanced Information Systems Engineering, pp. 492–508. Springer, Heidelberg (2024)
4. Biffl, S., Marhold, K., Musil, J., Meixner, K.: Business intelligence for value-based process and systems engineering and operation with procan.do. In: Business Intelligence for Multi-domain Systems Engineering and Operation. Springer, Heidelberg (2026)
5. International Electrotechnical Commission. IEC 60812: Failure Mode and Effects analysis (FMEA). IEC (2018)

6. Farooq, M.S., Omer, U., Ramzan, A., Rasheed, M.A., Atal, Z.: Behavior driven development: a systematic literature review. IEEE Access **11**, 88008–88024 (2023)
7. Garg, I., Hoffmann, D., Lüder, A., Rudolph, M.: Integrating domain expertise into dynamic digital models: A methodology for behaviour-driven production modelling. In: 2024 IEEE International Conference on Emerging Technologies and Factory Automation (ETFA), vol. 28, pp. 1–8. IEEE (2024)
8. Gregor, S., Hevner, A.R.: Positioning and presenting design science research for maximum impact. MIS Q. 337–355 (2013)
9. Grieves, M., Vickers, J.: Digital twin: mitigating unpredictable, undesirable emergent behavior in complex systems. In: Transdisciplinary Perspectives on Complex Systems: New Findings and Approaches, pp. 85–113 (2017)
10. Verein Deutscher Ingenieure. VDI 2206: Development of mechatronic and cyber-physical systems. Beuth (2021)
11. Jan, Z., et al.: Artificial intelligence for industry 4.0: systematic review of applications, challenges, and opportunities. Expert Syst. Appl. **216**, 119456 (2023)
12. Kritzinger, W., Karner, M., Traar, G., Henjes, J., Sihn, W.: Digital twin in manufacturing: a categorical literature review and classification. IFAC-PapersOnLine **51**(11), 1016–1022 (2018)
13. Martinelli, M., Zhang, J., Splettstoßer, A.K., Picone, M., Lippi, M., Wortmann, A.: Hierarchical digital twin ecosystem for industrial manufacturing scenarios. In: 2024 50th Euromicro inproceedings on Software Engineering and Advanced Applications (SEAA), pp. 56–63. IEEE (2024)
14. Michael, J., et al.: Model-driven engineering for digital twins: opportunities and challenges. Syst. Eng. (2025)
15. Mikušová, N., Čujan, Z., Tomková, E.: Robotization of logistics processes. In: MATEC web of conferences, vol. 134, pp. 00038 (2017)
16. Minerva, R., Lee, G.M., Crespi, N.: Digital twin in the IoT context: a survey on technical features, scenarios, and architectural models. Proc. IEEE **108**(10), 1785–1824 (2020)
17. Newrzella, S.R., Franklin, D.W., Haider, S.: Methodology for digital twin use cases: definition, prioritization, and implementation. IEEE Access **10**, 75444–75457 (2022)
18. Picone, M., Martinelli, M., Burattini, S., Giulianelli, A., Ricci, A.: The two faces of interoperability: Bridging cyber and physical spaces with digital twins. In: International Conference on Distributed Computing in Smart Systems and the Internet of Things (DCOSS-IoT), pp. 1–8. IEEE (2025)
19. Picone, M., Talasila, P., Bicocchi, N., Larsen, P.G.: Exploring devops practices for lifecycle management of physical and digital twins in cyber-physical systems. In: International Conference on Industrial Cyber-Physical Systems, pp. 1–6. IEEE (2025)
20. Qamsane, Y., et al.: A methodology to develop digital twin solutions for manufacturing systems. IEEE Access **9**, 44247–44265 (2021)
21. Rosin, F., Forget, P., Lamouri, S., Pellerin, R.: Impacts of industry 4.0 technologies on lean principles. Int. J. Prod. Res. **58**(6), 1644–1661 (2020)
22. Tao, F., Cheng, J., Qi, Q., Zhang, M., Zhang, H., Sui, F.: Digital twin-driven product design, manufacturing and service with big data. Int. J. Adv. Manuf. Technol. **94**, 3563–3576 (2018)
23. VDI. VDI Guideline 3682 Formalised Process Descriptions. Beuth Verlag (2015)
24. Wieringa, R.J.: Design Science Methodology for Information Systems and Software Engineering. Springer, Heidelberg (2014)

Software Architecture and Design

Using LLMs to Evaluate Architecture Documents – Results from a Digital Marketplace Environment

Frank Elberzhager[✉] ⓘ, Matthias Gerbershagen, and Joshua Ginkel

Fraunhofer IESE, Fraunhofer Platz 1, Kaiserslautern, Germany
`{frank.elberzhager,matthias.gerbershagen,`
`joshua.ginkel}@iese.fraunhofer.de`

Abstract. Generative AI plays an increasing role during software engineering activities to make them, e.g., more efficient or provide better quality. However, it is often unclear how much benefit LLMs really provide. We concentrate on software architects and investigated how an LLM-supported evaluation of architecture documents can support software architects to improve such artefacts. In the context of a research project where a digital marketplace is developed and digital solutions should be analyzed, we used different LLMs to analyze the quality of architecture documents and compared the results with evaluations from software architects. We found out that the quality of the artifact has a strong influence on the quality of the LLM, i.e., the better the quality of the architecture document was, the more consistent were the LLM-based evaluation and the human expert evaluation. While using LLMs in this architecture task is promising, our results showed inconsistencies that need further analyses before generalizing them.

Keywords: Software Architecture · LLMs · generative AI · Evaluation · Automated Feedback

1 Introduction

Software development is at a turning point. A survey by Daigle et al. showed that almost all software developers stated that they had already tried AI coding tools, and about 60% expect them to improve the fulfillment of customer requirements [1]. However, even the most powerful AI systems are subject to a fundamental principle: the quality of their output is largely determined by the quality of the input. While humans implicitly use domain and company knowledge, AI systems only use the knowledge acquired during training and explicit input. This makes documents that are developed early in the software development process, such as specifications or architecture, and which form the basis for later implementation, a critical success factor for dealing with AI. It is important to ensure the best possible quality of these software artefacts, as issues, defects, ambiguities, missing information, and inaccuracies early in the development process lead to potentially expensive correction cycles if they are implemented and then only found late in testing activities or even by the user.

© The Author(s), under exclusive license to Springer Nature Switzerland AG 2026
M. Dorner et al. (Eds.): SWQD 2026, LNBIP 581, pp. 65–81, 2026.
https://doi.org/10.1007/978-3-032-24216-7_4

During software development, there are therefore a variety of methods that support early quality assurance, which is reflected both in constructive support (for example in the form of design and architecture patterns) and analytical support (for example in the form of reviews or static model analyses). Based on the observation that implementation is increasingly being carried out autonomously or at least with support of generative AI, it is even more crucial that the quality of the input is maximized. Typically, different architecture diagrams, architecture drivers and textual descriptions are a major input for coding activities. Analyzing the quality of architecture documents is nothing new and many approaches, from experience-based over tool supported to structured analyses, exist [3]. We were interested in how generative AI can be used in those early software development phases to support architecture tasks.

Before we strive towards higher automation in creating architecture artifacts, for example by using agents that develop certain architecture models, we first wanted to analyze whether generative AI can evaluate different architecture documents and models. We wanted to understand whether generative AI provides adequate results in judging the resulting quality of architecture documents and how this can be compared to architecture experts. As there is usually not ?the one? architecture and there are even discussions among software architects, it is relevant to understand how the AI performs and whether this can become a real support (and, for example, can make software development more efficient or of higher quality) or whether the results are more anecdotal. Therefore, the focus in this article and our main research question is:

Under the assumption that generative AI can be used to evaluate architecture documents, what is the quality of the evaluation compared to human software architects?

In order to start answering this research question, we analyzed software repositories from a digital marketplace[1]. While we develop and operationalize the marketplace, several solution providers can offer their digital solutions, apps and services on that marketplace. The focus is on solutions in the area of smart cities. Municipalities can decide which digital solutions they would like to use and offer their citizens. Because of many solutions provided on the marketplace, municipalities asked for some kind of quality evaluation of the solutions, and defined a set of quality criteria, such as documentation quality, community aspects or architecture. Such criteria are then automatically checked by an AI-based component, and we were able to draw first conclusions about the general applicability of generative AI for analyzing different artifacts. As such quality criteria are, however, typically on a higher abstraction level than what we would think of regarding a detailed evaluation of architecture documents, we performed an additional and more fine-grained analysis of available documents to understand better how good generative AI can do such a task.

The remainder of the paper is structured as follows: Sect. 2 provides related work regarding how generative AI is used in architecture work. Section 3 shows some details about the marketplace in order to better understand our evaluation setting. Section 4 then describes our solution that is able to perform the automated analysis of different

---

[1] https://marktplatz.deutschlanddigital.org/

input documents with generative AI. Section 5 provides details about our evaluation and discusses the results, and Sect. 6 summarizes the paper and gives an outlook on next steps.

2 Related Work

In this section, we concentrate on related work regarding evaluation of software architecture documentation and on how LLMs are used in architecture work.

2.1 Quality Evaluation in Software Architecture and Software Architecture Documentation

As Bass et al. [2] have previously outlined, there are no universally applicable guidelines for good software architectures, as these are always tailored to meet the specific requirements of the project. Consequently, architecture can be considered either suitable or unsuitable, but not necessarily good or bad. To ensure a high standard of quality, several methods and procedures have been established over time.

One of the first established ones is the Architecture Tradeoff Analysis Method (ATAM). The process is divided into four phases. First, teams are assembled, then information is collected. Next, the information is analyzed. Then, risks, quality requirements, and important decisions are documented, and finally presented. The participating groups consist of an external evaluation team, the project decision-makers, and the architecture stakeholders.

The Software Architecture Analysis Method (SAAM) is a systematic approach consisting of five phases. During the first phase, the system is divided into basic functions. Following, these basic functions are mapped to the architecture. The third phase involves specifying quality characteristics and defining benchmarks. The result is an assessment of the degree of fulfilment and difficulties [2].

An approach specifically designed for the evaluation of architecture-related documents can be found in the Documentation Quality Check (DQC) within the framework of Fraunhofer RATE (Rapid ArchiTecture Evaluation). At the outset, all artifacts are collected and knowledge about the target groups of the architecture documentation is gathered. Using surveys or perspective-based reading [4], a model is created for each target group, for example, an instruction manual for the users of the product. An evaluation is based on whether all relevant information was included in the creation process [3].

Furthermore, there are various approaches and tools that combine both manual and automated processes to ensure the quality of software architecture documentation. A common manual approach is to use best practice checklists, which architects use to systematically check documentation for completeness, comprehensibility, and consistency. These checklists are often based on established quality criteria and serve as a tool for identifying typical problems and ambiguities at an early stage.

Beyond purely manual procedures, several automated approaches have been developed that analyze documents for quality aspects. The Automatic Checking of Quality

Best Practices in Software Development Documents tool checks development documents against around 80 rules relating to naming conventions, duplicate detection, and word choice, among other things [5]. The aim is to automatically detect recurring quality defects and thus reduce the effort required for manual checks.

Another example is the Document Quality Checking Tool for Global Software Development, developed by IBM Japan in 2012. This tool was designed specifically for the challenges faced by globally distributed development teams, where differences in time zones, languages, and cultures often lead to inconsistencies in documentation. It uses a comprehensive set of 144 checking rules to identify linguistic and structural quality issues and ensure a consistently high level of documentation quality [7].

In addition to these documentation-specific tools, general automation technologies also contribute to quality assurance. These include the automation of testing, deployment, and debugging, as well as the translation of outdated code into modern programming languages and the generation of test data and are able to improve the efficiency [6].

2.2 LLMs Used for Software Engineering and Software Architecture

Generative AI also plays a strongly growing role in software engineering activities and considers all phases, from requirements engineering to architecture to implementation and testing. Hou et al. [11] provide a large literature review on large languages models for software engineering and sort literature to six phases, with a focus of identified papers for software development, quality assurance and maintenance. Only a very limited number of papers were found to support the design phase. In general, there was an explosion of papers from the year 2022 to 2023, and this trend continued.

Jahic and Sami [12] provide a state-of-the-practice analysis on LLMs in software engineering and software architecture. They conducted an interview-study and performed LLM-assisted architecture design. The authors claimed potential in these activities but also stated reasons that have to be overcome in the future such as copyright issues, low quality and checking efforts of the LLM-based results.

Schmid et al. [13] performed a literature review analyzing which tasks can be supported by LLMs. Based on 18 papers identified, typical tasks such as generating code from architecture models, analyzing or supporting decision making are not a focus until now, but get a growing interest.

With respect to architecture tasks, some solutions also emerge. Cervantes et al. [14] explored how LLMs can assist in designing software architecture by integrating them into the Attribute-Driven Design (ADD) method. An LLM was given a detailed description of ADD, an architect persona as well as a structured plan for iterative design. In collaboration with a human designer the LLM-assisted ADD process created designs that are close to established solutions and partially satisfy key architectural requirements.

Díaz-Pace et al. [15] presented an LLM-based assistant designed to support novice software architects in making higher-quality architectural design decisions by explaining trade-offs, suggesting alternatives and linking decisions to quality attributes. By comparing architectural design decisions of novice architects with and without LLM support, the authors concluded that LLMs are most effective as educational and decision-support tools.

Gustrowsky et al. [16] followed a similar approach by fine-tuning a Llama 2 LLM with a custom dataset of requirement-pattern examples to enable the model to map requirements to architecture pattern suggestions. In experiments, the fine-tuned model correctly suggested the appropriate architecture pattern in about 70% of test cases, also showing that generative AI can assist architects in decision making.

Guerra and Ernst [17] examined how LLMs perform on tasks related to understanding and applying front-end software architecture knowledge. The authors developed an evaluation framework to assess the LLM?s capabilities across different cognitive levels such as remembering, understanding, applying, analyzing, evaluating and creating. Experimental results with ChatGPT-4 Turbo showed the model doing well on higher-order tasks like evaluating and creating architectural structures but struggling with lower-order tasks that required precise recall of architectural details.

It can be concluded that there is a huge and even growing number of papers on almost all relevant software engineering conferences, journals and magazines nowadays and that genAI will play a growing role in software engineering tasks.

3 Use Case and Implementation Insights

To investigate the potential of generative AI when evaluating software architecture documentation, we started our research in the following project setting: Evaluation of the architecture documentation of open-source solutions in the smart city context. The output of our tool should give helpful support for municipalities concerning the quality of the architecture documentation so they can decide on the use of an open-source solution. The results of the evaluation are integrated into ?Deutschland Digital?, a marketplace that has been developed for municipalities. We used the evaluation criteria provided by the German Federal Ministry for Housing, Urban Development and Building. In the domain of software architecture, the main criteria to evaluate are modularity, configurability, code quality and documentation.

For our first prototype we chose a small set of open-source solutions and did the evaluation with the help of LLMs and a static code analysis tool (Sonarqube[2]). We tried to evaluate all criteria given by the ministry to cover a broad range of aspects. Most of the evaluation was done by using an LLM. Due to the small set of solutions under evaluation, it was easy to just use an LLM for almost everything and tune the prompts accordingly. With this approach we covered most aspects and got early adequate results. Of course, such a solution does not scale very well, and the results are hard to reproduce.

To provide meaningful decision support for municipalities, the results of our evaluation needed to be more stable over time. Furthermore, the service needs to be able to evaluate all open-source solutions provided in the marketplace. Currently, there are more than 100 digital solutions, and the number is increasing by about two to five solutions per week. This means we needed to consider scalability of the service and costs for LLM calls. Consequently, for the production-ready service we choose a different approach than for the initial prototype. Most criteria are evaluated using deterministic code and established tools, like for example scorecard [9]. LLM-based evaluations are only done

---

[2] https://www.sonarsource.com/products/sonarqube/

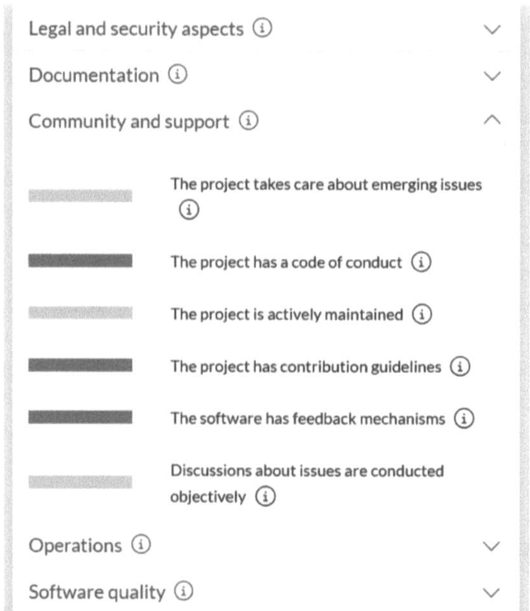

Fig. 1. Excerpt of an Evaluation of a Marketplace Solution

for a handful of sub-criteria, which are hard to evaluate using a deterministic approach, like for example judging whether the language used in the issues in the issue tracker of the project is rude or not. In the final service, the LLM is just another tool in our toolbox. But still some criteria of the prototype are not evaluated in the final service at all, because to evaluate them, we would require additional context information, for example about the execution of certain organizational processes in the municipality. Beyond that, we choose to use weighted quality models [10] to aggregate and structure our evaluation in a deterministic way. Our quality models used for the evaluation are stored in our database and are not part of the source code. This choice also allows us to dynamically adjust the evaluation (for example, to change the weight of certain sub-criteria) without changing the code of our service. In Fig. 1, the aggregated results of such a quality- model based evaluation in the marketplace can be seen.

4   Automated Evaluation of Documents with LLMs

We have developed an MVP of an LLM-based tool called ?Quasar? to support the evaluation of software quality. It uses different software engineering (SE) artifacts as input and generates quality scores as output. These scores are used to evaluate different qualities of software solutions. Figure 2 illustrates the essential building blocks of our solution idea in the marketplace setting.

For each relevant aspect (e.g. architecture documentation, operations, or software qualities such as usability in particular), we have developed a quality model that supports a systematic evaluation. Quality models combine and weight measurements of

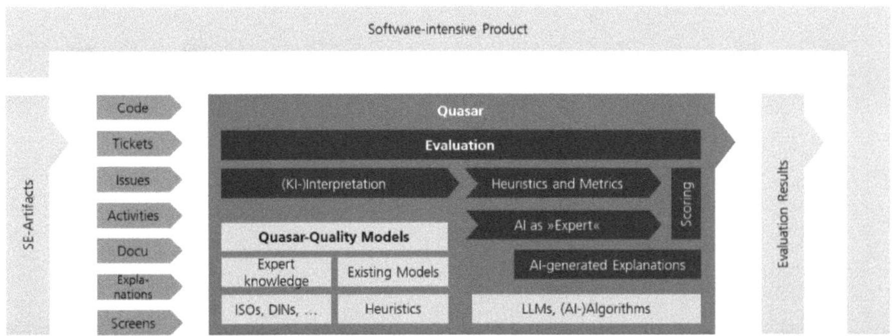

Fig. 2. General Workflow and main Components of the Quasar Solution to Evaluate Architecture Documents from Digital Solutions provided on a Digital Marketplace

different metrics to assess quality in a systematic way [10]. The model defines threshold values that determine whether the desired quality level has been achieved or not. Traditionally, measurements related to the evaluation of architectural documentation are performed manually: human experts analyze the available material, talk about it with relevant stakeholders, understand the system context, and then evaluate the documentation quality based on conclusions. We first wanted to evaluate to what extent we could replace the human expert with an LLM-based expert. The goal was to find out whether our solution would be able to assess the quality of the documentation and provide a rationale for the assessment that is plausible.

Our solution does not expect a specific architecture documentation structure. However, certain predefined content types are expected (in the case of underlying architecture documentation, for example, an introduction, naming of stakeholders, delimitation of the system context, a functional breakdown, explicit design decisions). Various documentation formats are then initially processed by a converter. This uses an external library that can handle many common documentation formats such as PDF, DOCX, Markdown, etc.

Quasar is divided into two layers: the UI and the backend (see Fig. 3). The UI serves as a lightweight way to interact with the MVP through a web browser and to launch requests to analyze development projects. The backend processes the requests, downloads the files of the development project, filters and analyzes suitable files, supplemented by further architecture documentation that can be provided via the UI. Different evaluator components in the backend then take care of analyzing the evaluation criteria. First, it converts data into a format suitable for the LLM using the file or image converter. Then it uses a set of prompts for different LLMs to evaluate the criteria with the help of the LLM client component. As a last step, the evaluation component combines the responses from the LLMs into the evaluation result.

We used different models from different vendors for our prototype. Therefore, we introduced the LLM client component. Its main purpose is to take care of the interaction with different LLMs. With this component, we reduced the coupling of the evaluator components to the concrete LLM. This facilitates subsequent extensions or changes and makes it easy to address other models in the future.

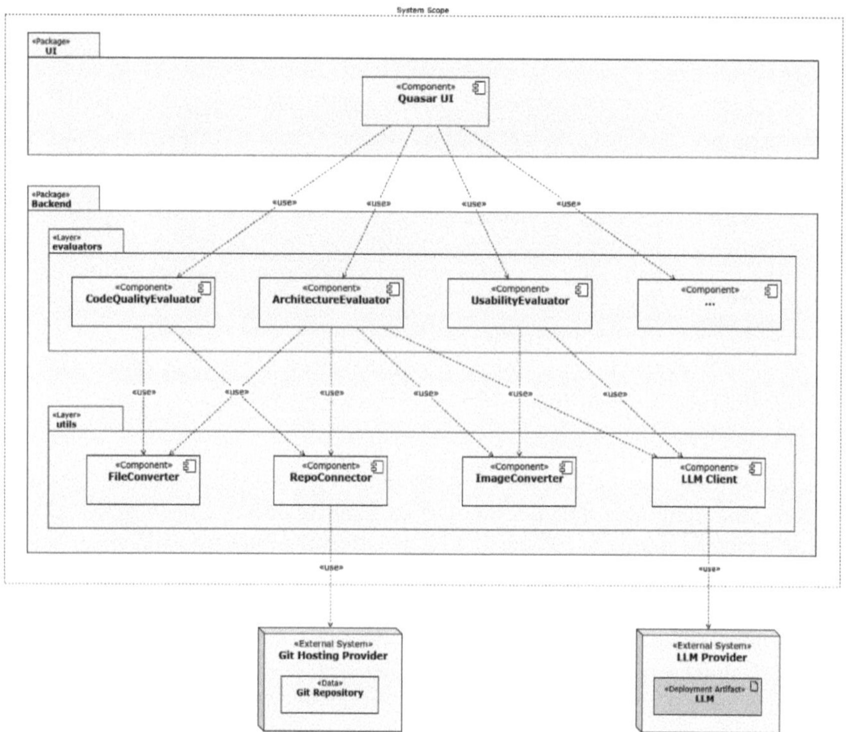

Fig. 3. Architecture of the Quasar Solution

Another important decision was to divide the evaluators according to use cases. For example, there is an evaluator for architectural documentation, but also for qualities such as usability. The main advantage of this is the simplified parallel development of evaluators by different teams, as well as a clear separation of use cases and domains.

5 Evaluation

In this section, we will give details on some kind of initial evaluation before we describe a more systematic procedure and discuss the findings.

5.1 Pre-evaluation of Architecture Documentation

In connection with our digital marketplace, the analysis of architecture documentation was carried out on open-source development projects that are actively used by users in practice (and the publicly accessible architecture documentation). The marketplace was developed to support the improvement of services of general interest in rural regions. The special feature of the marketplace is its nationwide availability as well as the search and mediation of quality-assured and needs-based digital offers. Municipalities, for example, can find and purchase digital solutions for specific challenges in the marketplace. These solutions can be placed on the marketplace by providers and are available after a review. Quality assurance for a scalable marketplace is not possible (or very time-consuming) through manual evaluations by experts alone, which also includes analyzing the architecture documentation. This is where our Quasar solution supports: an initial, lightweight quality assurance of the submitted solutions. With the help of genAI, an evaluation is now carried out to support experts and save time. An example of such an evaluation is shown in Fig. 1 before. There, five criteria can be seen with some more details regarding community and support.

In the use case described, it was sufficient to make a general statement on the quality of the architecture documentation in order to provide a rough orientation and to ensure that such documentation was available at all. However, we realized early on that there are stakeholders who are much more interested in detailed information. Therefore, we shifted more towards software developers and especially software architects to provide information on the quality of the architecture documentation (and other findings). With this, we can directly give feedback to the developers of the solutions on the marketplace so that they can improve their solutions and the documents developed.

5.2 Detailed Evaluation of Architecture Documentation

Goals, Metrics and Procedure

The aim of this evaluation is to gain an impression of the comparability between human and AI-based assessments of software architecture artifacts. We wanted to gain more clarity on the question of whether or how LLMs can support experts in their daily work or even take over parts of it. For this study, we selected two solutions from different solution providers on the marketplace and took a closer look at them. One of the projects provided comprehensive documentation of its architecture, while the second project only offered basic information. For an objective investigation, we compared the agreement of humans with that of Quasar on a scale from 0 (disagree completely) to 4 (agree completely) based on 25 statements.

To achieve this, two software architects were surveyed, and Quasar was applied to each project three times. As there is no official, universally valid evaluation to use as a basis for comparison, the individual runs of Quasar are checked for consistency and completeness, and the average human evaluation is compared and examined for similarity. Both used the same evaluation sheet. An overview of the procedure can be found in Fig. 4.

Dataset Preparation

The basis for evaluating architecture documentation is the collection of all relevant artifacts. To begin with, both the repository of the relevant project and its wiki are downloaded from GitHub. From all files, those that contain potential architecture information are filtered out by first converting the file in question into a readable format using Docling[3] and then comparing its content with a list of keywords. The files found, which include images, diagrams and text, were evaluated using LLMs.

---

[3] https://www.docling.ai/

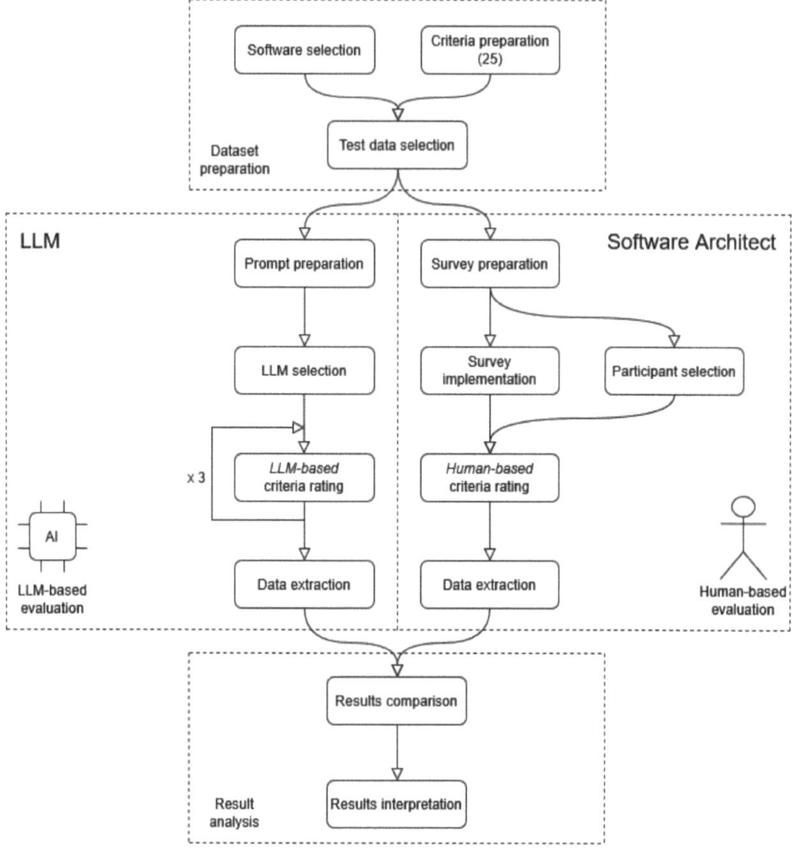

Fig. 4. Evaluation Procedure

The first project utilizes GitHub Pages to present its content. Its documentation folder comprises a total of 266 files, including 95 Markdown files, 23 PDFs, and 126 images. The term ?Architecture? occurs 11 times. The second project employs the GitHub Wiki, which contains only 11 Markdown files with 25 embedded images. The word ?Architecture? was found three times. Projects with varying documentation sizes were deliberately selected to investigate how the extent of documentation influences the results.

Model Selection

The specific models used were Qwen2[4] and Llama3.1[5], which we host locally on a hardware with three NVIDIA Tesla V100 SXM3 32 GB GPUs. While Llama3.1 only processes text, Qwen2 is a multimodal model that can process both text and image inputs, making it possible to analyze diagrams not only in isolation, but also in conjunction with accompanying text.

---

[4] https://huggingface.co/collections/Qwen/qwen2.
[5] https://huggingface.co/collections/meta-llama/llama-31.

Instrumentation and Data Collection

The overall evaluation was based on 25 predefined evaluation criteria. There is a corresponding prompt for each of these criteria. An example of such a prompt is: ?The key design decisions relating to the solution concepts are presented and justified.? All criteria/prompts can be seen in Appendix A.

A file, including any images, is sent to the LLM together with the respective prompt, which returns a score as an evaluation. Each file is evaluated according to the 25 defined criteria, and the overall evaluation is composed of the respective individual evaluations. If a file does not contain any relevant information, this is considered in the overall evaluation by excluding this file from the evaluation for the specific criterion. If a criterion is not found in any file, this results in a poor evaluation of this criterion. The process is controlled by a Python program. The focus is on the evaluation in the form of a score and less on a textual justification for this evaluation, but Quasar still outputs a machine-readable file that contains a score for each evaluation criterion as well as a summary justification generated by the LLM.

Research Questions

The overall research question was already stated as whether generative AI can be used to evaluate architecture documents and what is the quality of the evaluation compared to software architects. We refined this question into three sub-questions for a more detailed analysis:

RQ 1.1: How effort-intensive is the evaluation of the architecture documentation by Quasar compared to human architecture experts?
RQ 1.2: How consistent is the result from Quasar if repeated several times?
RQ 1.3: How is the quality of the evaluation from Quasar compared to human architecture experts?

Results

The results of the evaluations showed significant differences between the projects.

RQ 1.1 (Project 1): In the first project, the processing time was approximately 60 min for humans and 68 min for Quasar.

RQ 1.2 (Project 1): The three automated runs of the model showed a largely consistent evaluation (see Fig. 5).

RQ 1.3 (Project 1): In comparison to the expert, there were almost exact matches for two statements, while 36% of the assessments differed by a maximum of 15%. The average deviation was 27% (see Fig. 6).

RQ 1.1 (Project 2): In the second project, the processing time was significantly shorter at 22 min (human) and 14 min (Quasar). In this instance, the model was unable to provide a result for three statements, while the overall average deviation was 43%, implying that there is virtually no discernible apparent correlation.

RQ 1.2 (Project 2): The three automated runs of the model showed a weak consistency. For three statements, Quasar was unable to produce a result in any run (see Fig. 7).

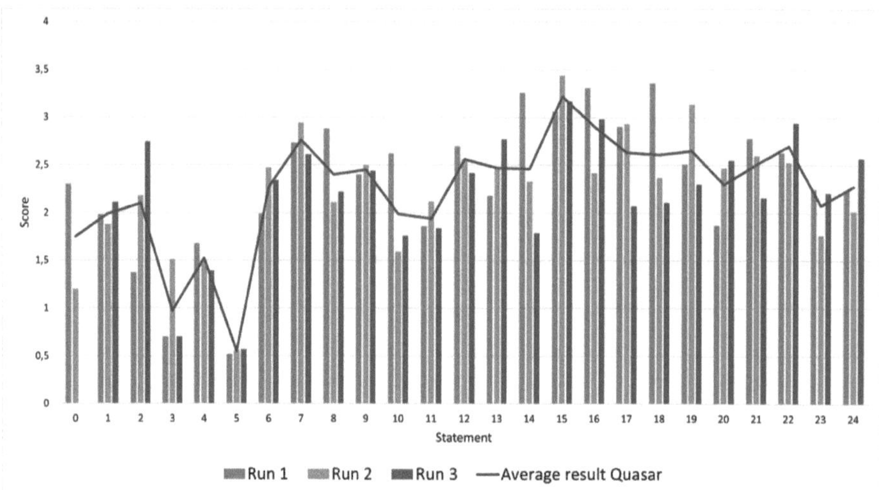

Fig. 5. Overview of the Consistency of the Three Runs (Project 1)

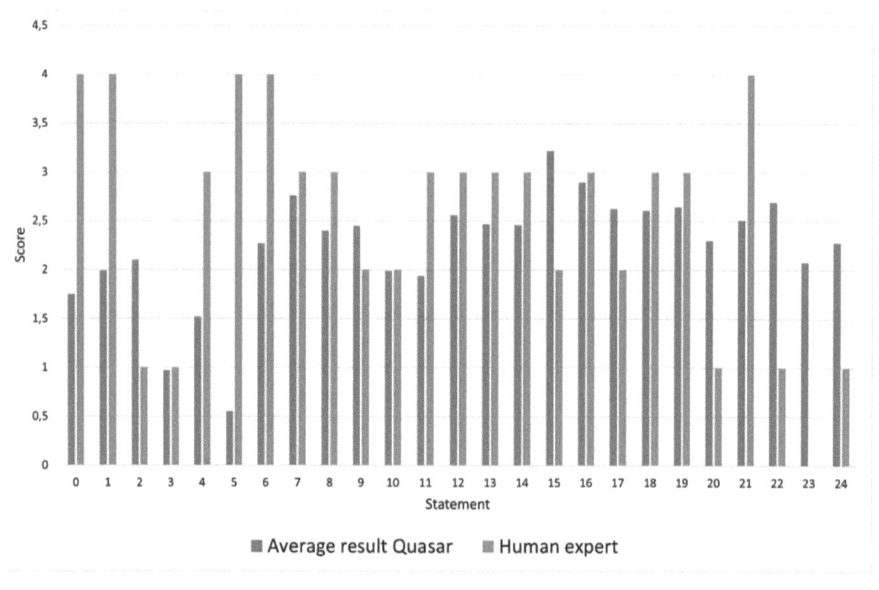

Fig. 6. Comparison of the average Deviation between Quasar and the Human Expert (Project 1)

RQ 1.3 (Project 2): In comparison to the expert, no apparent correlation can be established. All evaluations show a significant difference with an average deviation of 43% (see Fig. 8).

Discussion and Threats to Validity

The results of the evaluation show both the potential and the limitations of using LLMs to

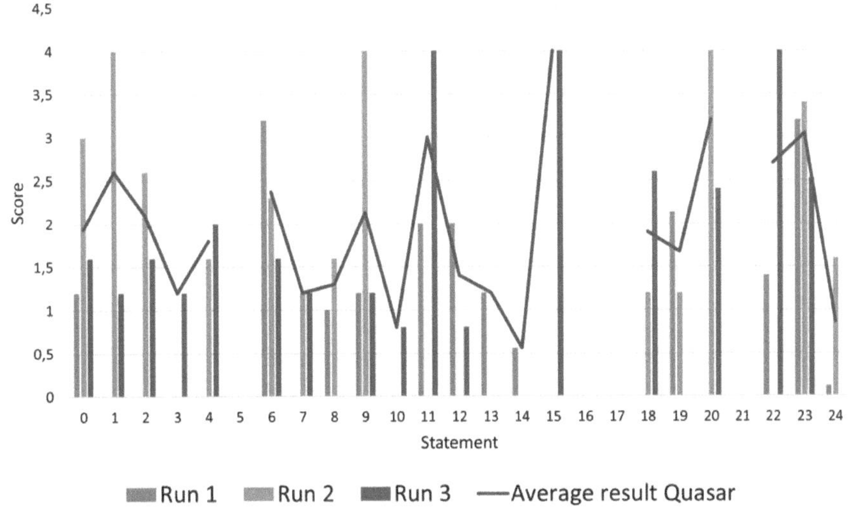

Fig. 7. Overview of the Consistency of the three Runs in Project 2

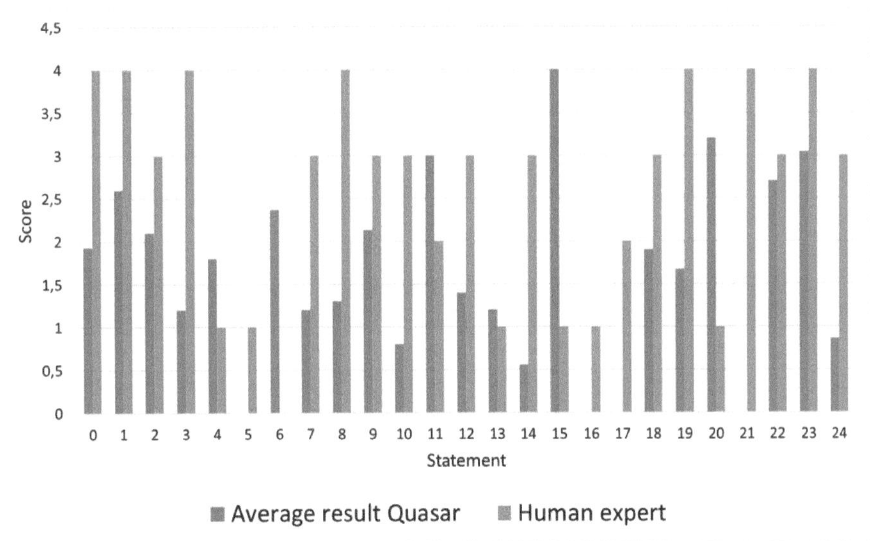

Fig. 8. Comparison of the average Deviation between Quasar and the Human Expert (Project 2)

evaluate architectural documentation. We were able to show that AI models are capable of reliably recognizing simple quality aspects and evaluating them in a structured manner based on statements, while more complex relationships can only be captured to a limited extent at this stage.

By observing that the quality of the input material has a decisive influence on the quality of the LLM outputs, we were able to deepen our assumptions. The more structured and complete the artifacts were, the stronger the apparent correlation between the LLM evaluations and the assessments of the software architects. In contrast, when the information density was low, there were significant deviations.

From a technical perspective, there have been various innovations since the study was conducted, which are described in more detail in Sect. 5.3. Due to the use of smaller models and the decision not to use retrieval-augmented generation, we had to develop our own data management and filtering system, which sorted sections in or out using a list of keywords. This means that some information may have been lost.

The number of projects that we considered, and the number of human experts, was rather low so that generalization is not possible based on the current results. We also had to rely on the accuracy of the experts? assessments. These could never be completely objective, as every person is influenced by their abilities and experiences.

Regarding RQ 1.1, the results fully met our expectations. A larger amount of data requires more time, while a smaller amount requires less. This was reflected both in machine processing and in human evaluation. The time effort between humans and the machine was very similar in our assessment. However, an assumption for future evaluation is that if the document size increases, the automated solution will be faster. In this case, however, quality will also play a major role, i.e. to evaluate whether saved time comes with a drawback in quality or whether the genAI solution provides adequate results one can rely on. Many further detailed questions are reasonable, of course.

For RQ 1.2, an apparent correlation could be observed between the quality and volume of the input data and the consistency of the results. Higher-quality input reduces hallucinations and allows the task to be executed in a more structured manner.

The same relationship is evident for RQ 1.3. With high-quality input, the evaluations of humans and Quasar deviate only slightly, whereas insufficient input leads to greater discrepancies.

Overall, the study shows that LLMs are a useful support for human work and can provide an initial impression of the quality of software documentation, which is a valuable addition, especially for the marketplace use case.

5.3 Evaluation Optimizations for Future Iterations

For future evaluations, several optimizations are possible to obtain a more defined impression of the comparability between human experts and machines.

Firstly, the number of participants to date has been too small to allow for universally valid conclusions to be drawn. The expertise and assessments of individual people are heavily dependent on their experience and education, making it necessary to calculate an average from a larger number of participants. The same applies to the number of projects and (architectural) documentation examined.

From a technical perspective, there have been numerous developments that simplify data processing. In the meantime, the models used have already been replaced, and a switch to a cloud provider was made to achieve better stability and scalability. Current versions of Google's Gemini, for example, offer input lengths of over one million tokens [8], which would be sufficient to process most documentation in its entirety. Another option would be to use Retrieval-Augmented Generation (RAG) to store information in a structured manner and retrieve it as needed. Both variants would guarantee virtually lossless data processing and avoid fragmentation of the input, which would lead to the preservation of contexts across multiple files. By additionally considering the reasoning of humans and LLM, coincidentally similar reasoning could be filtered out, which would strengthen the robustness of the evaluation. Further improvements are hoped for by fine-tuning a model to strengthen domain-specific knowledge.

6 Summary and Outlook

In this paper, we presented an evaluation of architecture documents with support of generative AI. We compared the results of our Quasar solutions with human architecture experts and could show that general support can be provided ? meaning the solution is a promising way to support human architects. The evaluation was based on a small set of participants and documents, so the generalizability has to be shown with further evaluations in the future. Our tool solution Quasar is built in a way to be flexible, i.e. further evaluations of quality can be added easily, and new or alternative LLMs can be considered when better language models are developed or further evolve.

In general, using generative AI to support software engineering roles such as architects is a promising way to, e.g., improve efficiency, provide better quality or give new ideas in designing software systems and digital solutions. We therefore also see potential in developing plugins for tools that software architects use in their daily work, such as Enterprise Architect or draw.io. Such plugins can directly provide feedback during design activities and might provide a smoother working environment compared to a separate tool such as Quasar currently is. In addition, besides evaluation tasks performed or at least supported by a generic AI solution, constructive activities might be a future step, especially when thinking into the direction of agents. We will focus on these two directions basically, i.e., more evaluation and further development to better support software architects.

Acknowledgments. We thank the software architecture experts for supporting us in the evaluation.

Appendix A

Set of questions that were used as prompts in our evaluation of architecture documents.

1. The documentation starts with high level concepts and descriptions (no technical details required).
2. The documentation introduces the basic idea of the system, meaning the system goals are, the motivation for the system existence, the key challenges that the systems should solve, and its business context.
3. In the introductory part of the document, key functional requirements of the system are introduced. (If they are provided explicitly, the rating should be better; if implicitly, less good; if not provided at all, the rating should be 0).

4. In the introductory part of the document, key quality requirements are mentioned. (If they are provided explicitly, the rating should be better; if implicitly, less good; if not provided at all, the rating should be 0).
5. The documentation introduces the system?s constraints. (If they are provided explicitly, the rating should be better; if implicitly, less good; if not provided at all, the rating should be 0).
6. The documentation introduces the system stakeholders. (If they are provided explicitly, the rating should be better; if implicitly, less good; if not provided at all, the rating should be 0).
7. A system context delineation diagram is provided and there is textual explanation for the diagram elements.
8. The list of functions exposed by the system to the external actors (be it humans or external systems) is provided.
9. The data exchange between the system and external actors are described. The description names the data that goes in and the data that goes out of the system.
10. A domain model is provided to illustrate the main entities of the domain and their relationships.
11. The documentation provides the meaning of the key entities of the business domain.
12. The documentation describes the main functional requirements of the system.
13. The documentation provides the quality requirements of the system.
14. The quality requirements are described in a way that the desired behavior of the system can be measured. (and therefore verified) when the solution is implemented.
15. The documentation describes the fundamental solution strategy for the system functional requirements.
16. The documentation describes solution concepts for addressing all the system?s functional requirements.
17. The documentation describes solution concepts for addressing all the system?s quality requirements.
18. The key design decisions related to the solution concepts are presented and justified.
19. The documentation provides a functional decomposition of the system at runtime (i.e., what components and subcomponents the system is composed of).
20. The documentation provides the data flow among different components in the system.
21. The documentation describes the deployment strategy of the system. It includes a deployment diagram. It contains typical elements of a deployment diagram such as the deployment artifacts, the execution environments, the computing nodes, storage systems, etc.
22. The documentation provides information about the key technologies used to implement the system (e.g., programing languages, storage system, libraries, frameworks, etc.).
23. The documentation describes the modules (development time elements) that implement the runtime components.
24. The documentation describes the needed tools and steps to deploy the system.
25. The documentation describes the data model of the system (e.g., class diagram, entity-relationship diagram, etc.).

References

1. Daigle, K., et al.: Survey: the AI wave continues to grow on software development teams (2025). Online abrufbar unter https://github.blog/news-insights/research/survey-ai-wave-grows/
2. Bass, L., Clements, P., Kazman, R.: Software Architecture in Practice, 3rd edn. Addison-Wesley, Boston (2012)
3. Knodel, S., Naab, M.: Pragmatic Evaluation of Software Architectures. Springer, Cham (2016)
4. Basili, V.R., Green, S., Laitenberger, O., et al.: The empirical investigation of perspective-based reading. Empir. Softw. Eng. 1, 133?164 (1996). https://doi.org/10.1007/BF00368702
5. Dautovic, A., Plösch, R., Saft, M.: Automatic checking of quality best practices in software development documents. In: Proceedings of the 11th International Conference on Quality Software (QSIC 2011), pp. 208?217. IEEE, Los Alamitos (2011)
6. Ebert, C., Louridas, P.: Generative AI for software practitioners. IEEE Softw. 40(2), 30?38 (2023)
7. Miyamoto, K., Nerome, T., Nakamura, T.: Document quality checking tool for global software development. In: 2012 Annual SRII Global Conference. IEEE, San Jose (2012)
8. Comanici, G., et al.: Gemini 2.5: Pushing the Frontier with Advanced Reasoning, Multi-modality, Long Context, and Next Generation Agentic Capabilities. arXiv preprint arXiv:2507.06261 (2025)
9. Scorecard HomePage. https://openssf.org/projects/scorecard/. Accessed 28 Oct 2025
10. Wagner, S., et al.: Operationalised product quality models and assessment: the Quamoco approach. Inf. Softw. Technol. 62, 101?123 (2015)
11. Hou, X., et al.: Large language models for software engineering: a systematic literature review. arXiv preprint arXiv:2308.10620 (2024)
12. Jahic, J., Sami, A.: State of practice: LLMs in software engineering and software architecture. In: Proceedings of the ICSA 2024 Workshop on Software Architecture Machine Learning (SAML). Springer, Cham (2024)
13. Schmid, L., et al.: Software architecture meets LLMs: a systematic literature review. arXiv preprint arXiv:2505.16697 (2025)
14. Cervantes, H., Kazman, R., Cai, Y.: An LLM-assisted approach to designing software architectures using ADD. arXiv preprint arXiv:2506.22688 (2025)
15. Díaz-Pace, J.A., Tommasel, A., Capilla, R.: Helping novice architects to make quality design decisions using an LLM-based assistant. In: Galster, M., Scandurra, P., Mikkonen, T., Oliveira Antonino, P., Nakagawa, E.Y., Navarro, E. (eds) Software Architecture. ECSA 2024. Lecture Notes in Computer Science, vol. 14889. Springer, Cham (2024). https://doi.org/10.1007/978-3-031-70797-1_21
16. Gustrowsky, B., Villarreal, J.I., Alférez, G.H.: Using generative artificial intelligence for suggesting software architecture patterns from requirements. In: Arai, K. (ed.) Intelligent Systems and Applications. IntelliSys 2024. Lecture Notes in Networks and Systems, vol. 1068. Springer, Cham (2024). https://doi.org/10.1007/978-3-031-66336-9_19
17. Guerra, L.P.F., Ernst, N.: Assessing LLMs for frontend software architecture knowledge. In: Proceedings of the 2025 IEEE/ACM International Workshop on Designing Software (Designing), pp. 6?10. IEEE (2025)

AI-Assisted REST API Design
with Large Language Models

Jorge Martinez-Gil[1]([✉]), Christoph Daxerer[1], Mario Winterer[1],
Cornelia Neumüller[2], and Matthias Krump[2]

[1] Software Competence Center Hagenberg GmbH, Softwarepark 32a,
4232 Hagenberg, Austria
{jorge.martinez-gil,christoph.daxerer,mario.winterer}@scch.at
[2] Raiffeisen Software GmbH, Goethestraße 80, 4020 Linz, Austria
{cornelia.neumueller,matthias.krump}@r-software.at

Abstract. This work presents an AI-assisted environment that helps
developers design REST APIs using Large Language Models. The system
integrates retrieval-augmented generation with OpenAPI's interface to
deliver a structured, dialogue-based design process. Developers can define
endpoints, describe functionality, and generate specifications, while the
assistant searches for similar existing APIs to promote reuse. The approach is evaluated using complex, domain-specific specifications from a
real-world project to assess its ability to produce valid and complete
API components. The solution has been applied to the needs of a large
financial institution to create compliant APIs for operations processing,
enabling rapid identification of existing internal endpoints and avoiding
duplicated work. The aim is to demonstrate practical value in supporting
developers through faster design cycles and more consistent specifications
in industrial environments.

Keywords: REST API design · Retrieval-augmented generation ·
AI-assisted development

1 Introduction

Designing high-quality RESTful APIs is a critical yet challenging task in modern software engineering. The OpenAPI specification has emerged as a de facto
standard for describing REST APIs in a machine- and human-readable format.
Drafting these specifications by hand before implementation is common to ensure
better-designed services. However, it is error-prone due to the verbose, rigid syn-
tax of `YAML` and `JSON`.

Recent advances in Large Language Models (LLMs) have shown promise in
assisting developers with coding tasks [10]. However, existing LLM-based assistants often struggle with less common formats, such as OpenAPI definitions,
leading to incorrect suggestions [20]. Organizations with large API ecosystems
also face reuse difficulties [1]. With hundreds of internal APIs, developers may

© The Author(s), under exclusive license to Springer Nature Switzerland AG 2026

M. Dorner et al. (Eds.): SWQD 2026, LNBIP 581, pp. 82–97, 2026.
https://doi.org/10.1007/978-3-032-24216-7_5

create duplicate services simply because they are unaware of existing ones. Some companies maintain internal APIs with limited documentation, leaving teams uncertain whether an API for a specific requirement already exists.

The work described in this paper was conducted within a large financial institution that manages an extensive collection of internal APIs to support operations and related services. Designing new APIs in this setting requires strict compliance with security and regulatory requirements. Duplicate functionality can arise when design teams cannot locate relevant endpoints. Rapid identification of existing internal APIs during the design phase reduces redundancy, lowers maintenance effort, and helps maintain consistent adherence to established standards.

To tackle these challenges, we propose an AI-assisted REST API Design framework that uses LLMs to accelerate the creation of new API specifications and promote the reuse of existing APIs. Building on recent advances in LLM-based agents for automation and knowledge-intensive tasks [25], our approach integrates a Retrieval-Augmented Generation (RAG) pipeline with OpenAPI-aware prompting and function-calling capabilities. The system can retrieve relevant API documentation from a knowledge base of API specifications and provide it to an LLM. The model then assists the user in drafting or refining an OpenAPI specification for a new service. The assistant produces structured output to ensure that the generated specifications are syntactically valid and conform to a predefined schema. This approach reduces the risk of creating API descriptions that fail to meet the required standards.

This work also presents an implementation that uses open-source tools and custom modules. A vector database indexes a collection of OpenAPI documents, enabling semantic search to locate relevant APIs. The LLM is configured with OpenAI's function-calling API to generate `JSON` snippets that match the OpenAPI schema; these snippets are then combined into a working specification. Automated validation is applied through linting rules and `JSON Schema` checks to catch errors early in the process. The main contributions of this work are:

- We review the related work in software engineering AI assistants, API documentation and specification tools, automated API reuse, and LLM-powered developer tools, positioning our approach within the state-of-the-art.
- We present a novel combination of RAG, semantic chunking, and structured output prompting for API design. Our framework uses vector-based semantic search over API specifications to inject relevant context. Furthermore, it uses function calls to produce OpenAPI-compliant outputs, with iterative refinement and validation in a loop.
- We demonstrate the implementation of an AI-assisted REST API design approach that combines semantic chunking, retrieval-augmented generation, and OpenAPI function-calling to both accelerate specification drafting and actively promote reuse in a real-world setting in the financial sector with an existing large-scale API ecosystem.
- We evaluate this setting with initial results using quantitative metrics and qualitative developer studies.

The remainder of this work is structured as follows: Section 2 presents the background and related work. Section 3 describes the system architecture and design. Section 4 details the implementation of our prototype. Section 5 discusses evaluation design, developer studies, productivity impact, and limitations. Section 6 concludes the paper.

2 Background and Related Work

This section reviews prior research on AI-driven developer assistants, automated API documentation and specification tools, and techniques for semantic API retrieval.

2.1 LLMs in Software Engineering

The application of LLMs to software engineering tasks has seen rapid growth [5,8,28]. For example, recent studies on the specialization of code models [17] suggest that augmenting pre-trained models can improve developer satisfaction [21] and effectiveness in software engineering tasks [8].

Beyond code completion [6], researchers and practitioners have explored LLMs in testing [2]. For example, LLMs can help generate formal specifications from natural language requirements [14], bridging the gap between high-level needs and implementation. Nonetheless, challenges such as domain-specific language understanding and hallucination persist [7].

Software engineering assistants such as GitHub Copilot have been studied extensively [4]. Recent research evaluated Copilot's code generation and found both benefits and limitations [18]. There are alternative approaches that mined Stack Overflow and GitHub Discussions, reporting that while Copilot often provides useful code and boosts developer satisfaction, integration into existing workflows can be complex [27]. Amazon's CodeWhisperer[1] offers similar AI capabilities. These tools excel at suggesting code in well-known languages but tend to perform poorly on less common tasks. A recent study quantified this gap by benchmarking Copilot on OpenAPI completion and found that it underperforms [20].

2.2 API Documentation and Specification Tools

Documenting and discovering APIs has been a long-standing challenge. Traditional API documentation tools, such as Swagger[2], focus on rendering human-readable documentation from machine-readable specifications [3]. At the same time, code-first frameworks generate OpenAPI specifications from source-code annotations [12]. These approaches help synchronize implementation and specification, but do not alleviate the initial design effort if starting from scratch.

---

[1] https://workshops.aws/categories/CodeWhisperer.
[2] https://swagger.io/.

To improve API quality, organizations often enforce guidelines for their API spec linting tools and perform static analysis on documents to flag guideline violations or inconsistent styles [22]. Some tools offer customizable rules that ensure internal best practices are adhered to. We integrate such linting into our workflow to provide feedback on the AI-generated specs.

Recent research has shown interest in automating the creation of API specifications. One notable work is SpeCrawler [13], which aims to generate OpenAPI specifications from unstructured API documentation by combining rule-based extraction and LLM generation. Prior rule-based methods struggled with the heterogeneity of API docs, but LLMs enable more flexible parsing and generalization. Then, a pipeline uses an LLM to interpret various sections of API documentation and compose a formal specification. Our work involves the interactive creation of new APIs guided by high-level intents rather than generating them from existing documentation.

2.3   API Search and Reuse

Discovering existing APIs that could be reused is a form of information retrieval that historically relied on keyword searches in API directories [15, 16]. API Harmony [23] was an early attempt to facilitate API reuse in large organizations. API Harmony built a graph of APIs and their relations (e.g., data models, functionality overlap) and provided a search interface to find APIs by functionality. The goal was to help developers identify, select, and consume internal or public APIs that fit their needs.

Our approach modernizes API search by using semantic vector search. Instead of manually maintained graphs or simple text matching, we use embeddings of API specifications to capture their functionality. This allows a developer to query in natural language and retrieve relevant API definitions even if exact keywords differ. RAG is a natural fit here since it has been widely applied to knowledge-intensive NLP tasks [24]. It involves fetching documents relevant to the query and feeding them into an LLM's answer generation context [9, 11].

Moreover, treating OpenAPI specs as knowledge documents allows RAG to be applied to the API reuse problem. This finds potentially useful APIs, and the retrieved content can be directly cited or integrated, grounding the assistant's suggestions in real API contracts. RAG has the added benefit of reducing hallucinations and providing traceability for the outputs [26], which is essential in a critical domain like API design, where factual accuracy is important.

2.4   Contribution over the State-of-the-Art

Our work intersects with the broader landscape of LLM-based developer tools. The reason is that LLMs are being integrated into IDEs and DevOps pipelines for various tasks [7], including generating commit messages, providing automated code review comments, and generating test cases from requirements [19]. The idea of constraining the model to produce a `JSON` object that matches a provided schema is to obtain output that is directly parsed and used by programs [2]. We employ this approach by defining a function schema for OpenAPI components and instructing the LLM to invoke this function.

Early experiments required the model to follow a carefully crafted system prompt to generate `YAML` output. When calling functions, our assistant can generate structured data that we then render into valid `YAML`. Recent OpenAI updates even enable strict schema enforcement, ensuring the model's output conforms to the schema.

3   System Architecture

Figure 1 illustrates the architecture of our AI-assisted REST API design tool. Our implementation comprises two key modules: (1) the API Retrieval Module and (2) the API Design Assistant Module, supported by a (3) validation component and (4) two user interfaces.

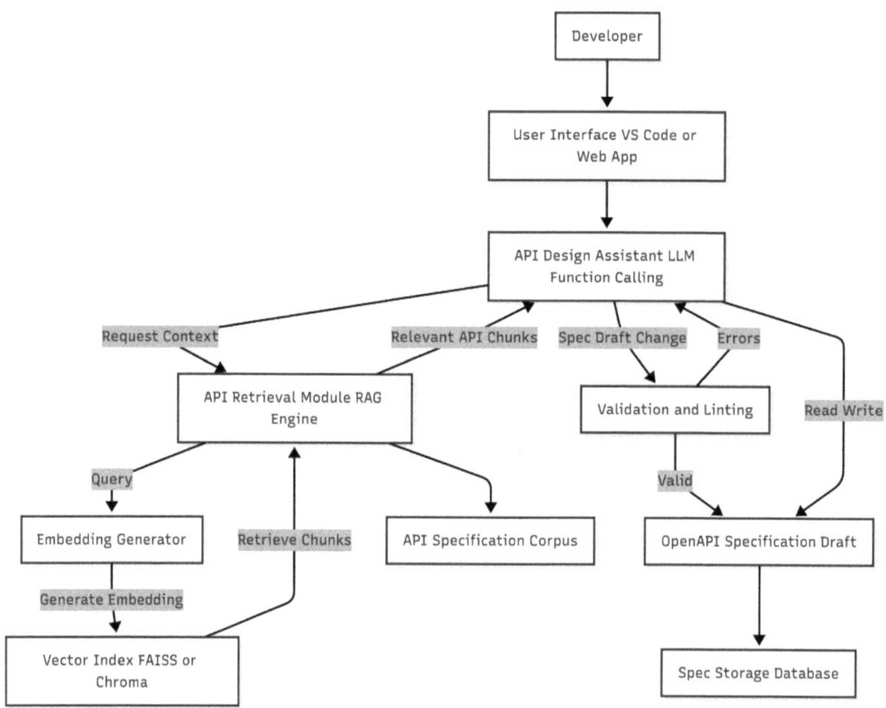

Fig. 1. System architecture of the AI-assisted REST API design tool.

3.1   API Retrieval Module (RAG Engine)

Since a large number of REST APIs already exists and can be reused, this module is responsible for finding relevant existing APIs based on the user's query or design intent. It contains a Vector Index of API specifications: we internally collected an OpenAPI corpus. We embedded them into vector space using OpenAI's text-embedding model. Each document is represented as a high-dimensional vector such that similar APIs are nearby in that space. We use `FAISS` as the backend for efficient k-NN search over these vectors. Given a user's prompt, the query is embedded, and the nearest neighbor specs are retrieved.

A naive approach of chunking by fixed tokens proved suboptimal since many chunks contained only structural information (e.g., a list of parameter names) with little semantic signal, leading to irrelevant retrieval results. Instead, we implement a semantic chunking strategy: each API spec is parsed into logical units (the high-level description, each resource path with all its methods, shared components schema, etc.). For each unit, we generate a concise summary using an LLM (`GPT 4o`). This is a natural language description of what that part of the API does. These summaries are then embedded to populate the vector index.

Figure 2 shows how user queries are matched to relevant parts of `YAML` files using vector embeddings and similarity search. Retrieved chunks are then provided to an LLM assistant for accurate, context-aware responses.

This technique helped to increase retrieval precision. Even specs that lacked explicit documentation could be found because the LLM-generated summary captured the intent of the endpoints. The retrieved results are passed to the next module as contextual knowledge. We limit the number of retrieved documents to avoid overloading the LLM context window; typically, the top-k relevant API specs (or specific endpoints from them) are included.

3.2   API Design Assistant Module

The interactive assistant is powered by an LLM (`GPT-4o`). It operates in a conversational loop with the user, similar to ChatGPT but specialized for API design. We defined a dedicated system prompt to establish the assistant's role:

> *You are an API design assistant helping the user create or modify an OpenAPI specification. You can access documentation snippets of potentially relevant APIs and an editable draft of the user's API spec.*

The assistant is given two forms of context at each turn: (a) the retrieved API snippets and (b) the current draft specification (if one exists). The draft spec context is included by serializing the in-progress `YAML` into the prompt or using function arguments. Hence, the assistant knows the API's context and what is already defined. The assistant decides how to act based on the user's request. We implemented two modes of assistant responses:

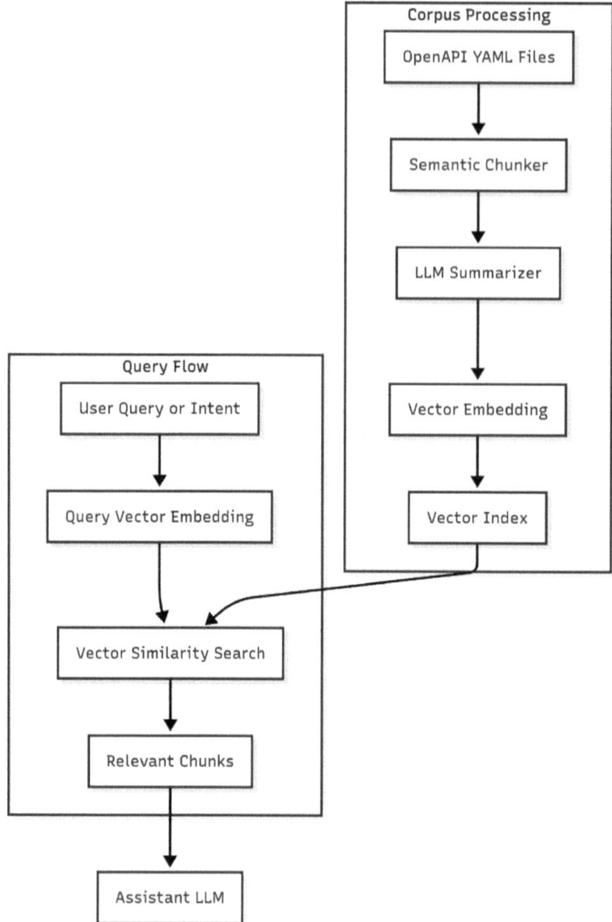

Fig. 2. RAG workflow adopted in our framework.

1. **Natural Language Guidance**: In this mode, the assistant responds with an explanation or suggestion, potentially referencing a retrieved API as inspiration. For instance: *It looks like `ImageService` API has a similar upload endpoint. You might consider a `POST /images` endpoint that takes an image file as form data and returns a URL.*
2. **Spec Generation**: In other cases, the assistant outputs OpenAPI specification snippets (`YAML` or `JSON`) to be merged. This is enabled by function calling[3] that allows models to interface with external systems (tools). When the assistant decides to propose a concrete change, it calls the function with structured arguments.

---

[3] OpenAI function calling: https://platform.openai.com/docs/guides/function-calling.

The chat completion API returns a structured `JSON` object describing the new endpoint. Our system intercepts this response and transforms it into the appropriate internal format. The function output is also shown to the user for transparency. Using function calling with a strict schema guarantees that the model's output is syntactically valid and complete for endpoint generation.

3.3 Iterative Validation

After the assistant proposes changes, the modified OpenAPI spec is run through a validation pipeline. We automatically check JSON schema validity against the OpenAPI 3.1 schema. We also run a linter with a company-specific ruleset. Any errors or warnings are fed back into the conversation.

For example, if the assistant generated a snippet without a response for `HTTP` 400, the linter issues a warning that a default error response is missing. The assistant then suggests adding it, and the improved snippet can be regenerated (the assistant is instructed to explain the issue and correct the spec). This validation loop ensures that each iteration produces a syntactically correct spec that conforms to best practices. The assistant is instructed to apologize and correct the spec if validation finds an issue (this mimics how a human would respond to failing tests).

3.4 User Interface Integration

We integrated this system into two front-ends for evaluation. First, a **Visual Studio Code extension** was developed. It provides a chat sidebar where the developer can converse with the API Design Assistant. The extension syncs the OpenAPI file with the assistant: the user can approve suggestions to apply them to the file, and the assistant can read the current file to inform its following answers. This tight IDE integration aims for a seamless workflow.

The second front-end is a **web application** built with React and Flask backend. This was used to pilot the tool in a team setting. In the web UI, multiple users can collaboratively brainstorm an API design with the assistant. The Flask backend orchestrates calls to the retrieval module and OpenAI API, and the React UI displays the current spec (rendered visually using a Swagger-UI component) alongside the chat interface. This setup is helpful for demonstrations, as it does not require installing an IDE plugin and works in any browser.

4 Implementation Details and Lessons Learned

Our implementation required effort and custom development of (1) an indexed OpenAPI corpus for the RAG, (2) prompt engineering with tailored templates, and (3) a web-based multi-user interface to the AI-based assistant.

4.1 OpenAPI Corpus and Indexing

We collected an initial set of `YAML` files from public repositories, excluding trivial or duplicate entries. We cleaned this dataset by filtering out invalid files and those that were not in the OpenAPI format. To provide high-quality data for retrieval, we linted all specs with OpenAPI ruleset; about 15% were discarded due to significant errors (unparseable or too incomplete). The final corpus spans diverse domains, providing a basis for reuse suggestions. We then constructed embeddings for these documents using OpenAI's `text-embedding-ada-002` model.

After that, we applied the semantic chunking strategy described earlier rather than embedding all specifications (which often exceed token limits). We developed a script to iterate over each spec and break it down into the following components: the info section, each tag group of endpoints, each path (if needed), and each schema component. For each chunk, we prompted `GPT-4o` with a specific instruction to generate a summary documentation.

These summaries and key metadata (such as the API file and section from which they originate) were then embedded in vectors. We used `FAISS` for fast similarity search due to its balance of speed and recall, which is particularly well-suited to our dataset size.

We also experimented with the Chroma vector DB, which wraps `FAISS` and provides persistence and embedding management. Both yielded similar performance, but we opted for `FAISS` for better control over indexing parameters.

4.2 Assistant Prompting and Tools

The design of the system prompt for the assistant went through many iterations. Our latest version that yielded the best results is:

> *You are an expert API designer AI. You will be given: 1. the current API draft or an empty draft, 2. user requests or questions, and 3. snippets from other APIs (as inspiration or reference). Your job is to help the user create a correct OpenAPI specification. You might explain the reasoning, but when appropriate, you should directly provide the spec changes (in YAML) required to implement the request. You have tools to output structured changes (endpoints, schemas, etc.). Do not produce code unrelated to the API spec. Ensure all YAML is valid and complete.*

In addition, we also provided several examples in the system message (few-shot learning) of how the assistant should behave. One example shows the assistant adding a new endpoint, and another shows it suggesting using an existing API instead.

We also maintain the state between user interactions. When the user accepts a suggestion, the spec state updates, and the latest specification must be provided in the conversation if the user requests a follow-up (e.g., if the user requests *Now add an endpoint to delete an image*). Therefore, our implementation stores the current spec in memory and extracts the relevant parts to include in the prompt.

The prompt template uses placeholder tags like `@paths.*.summary` to pull in summaries of all existing paths from the draft, so the assistant is aware of them. To achieve this, we developed a small templating system to map these placeholders to `JSONPath` queries on the spec.

4.3   Integration with Flask and React

The `Flask` backend wraps the retrieval and LLM calls behind a REST API. Key endpoints include: `/query` (for a user question, which triggers retrieval and LLM processing and returns the assistant's answer along with any spec changes), `/validate` (runs the linter and schema validator on the current spec), and `/spec` (to fetch or update the working specification). We also used `Flask-SocketIO` to push real-time updates to the client.

The `React` frontend consists of a chat panel and a preview panel. For the preview, we integrated the *Redoc* and *Swagger-UI* components, which render the OpenAPI document in a visually structured format. This allows the users to view the evolving specification as documentation–users can even try out endpoints if a mock server is configured.

A key implementation detail was supporting multi-user sessions: users were identified by a session `ID`, and we maintained separate spec states per session.

Figure 3 shows the workflow for our assistant to help developers design and validate OpenAPI specifications. User queries are processed through an RAG engine, and proposed spec changes are validated before being saved to the specification database.

5   Evaluation and Discussion

Evaluating an AI-assisted design tool involves assessing both the quality of the artifacts produced and the experience of developers who use it. Our first results from pilot testing in a lab setting indicate that the assistant can reduce the number of validation iterations by about 30–40%, with an expected time saving of 25–35% in producing a complete specification. For the involved company, these gains can help to considerably lower development costs and shorten deployment cycles. However, subsequent evaluation within the company is required to confirm these estimated gains in real-world scenarios.

5.1   Pilot Testing

We are currently performing the first pilot tests in a lab setting in close cooperation with the industry partner. The retrieval module is examined in isolation using a benchmark of query scenarios based on realistic reuse cases, as described in [11]. Each query has a ground truth set of relevant APIs identified by the authors. Standard metrics, such as recall, mean reciprocal rank, and semantic relevance scores from an independent reviewer, are applied.

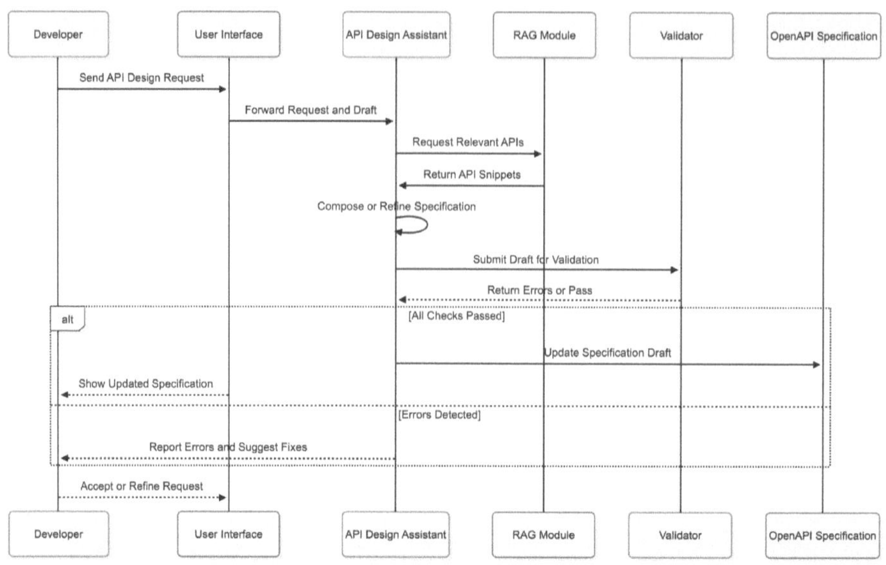

Fig. 3. Architecture for integrating RAG and automated specification validation.

The quality of OpenAPI specifications created with the assistant's support is assessed through correctness and completeness. Correctness is determined by validation checks, recording the number of iterations required for a specification to pass all tests. Completeness is measured against predefined requirements for each task. A set of synthetic API design tasks is used, with reference specifications prepared manually. The assistant processes each task, and the resulting specifications are compared with the references using precision and recall metrics for required endpoints and error case coverage. Text similarity and schema similarity measures are applied to examine how closely the assistant's output matches the reference designs.

Currently, the pilot testing phase is run in a lab setting only, as it is out of scope for the company to use third-party-hosted LLMs for sensitive corporate API data. If our assistant uses proprietary APIs, sending their specs or descriptions to an external API could pose risks. While we use OpenAI's API, one could substitute it with a locally hosted LLM for enhanced privacy. The trade-off would be the cost of running and possibly lower quality for some tasks.

Another aspect is the correctness of the AI's knowledge. Suggesting an insecure design or referencing a deprecated API without warning is considered a blocking issue. We thus plan to incorporate some safety checks. For instance, our corpus could be annotated with deprecation info, and the assistant could be prompted to favor newer APIs. There is also the concern of overdependence: Developers should still be trained in API design fundamentals and not just accept output that they do not fully understand to avoid the propagation of errors.

5.2 User Study Design

As a next step, we plan to migrate the AI-assisted REST API design tool to a company-hosted environment, including an on-premise LLM solution. Based on this setting, we will perform a user study with developers and domain experts in a real-world project context. The design for this study is outlined below.

Developer Experience Evaluation. A key part of the planned evaluation is a user study with developers. It will assess the tool's impact on productivity and satisfaction. Participants will complete an API design task in a controlled setting. A within-subjects design will be used, in which each participant completes one task with the AI assistant and another without it, with the order randomized to reduce learning effects. The tasks will be of similar scope. One scenario will be based on the needs of a large financial institution that develops secure, compliant APIs for operational processing.

The evaluation will record the time taken to complete each task and the quality of the final specification, using either expert review or a checklist of required elements. A usability survey will be given, including questions such as: *Did the assistant help you find useful existing APIs? Did it save time when writing the specifications? How was the quality of its suggestions? Did you trust the suggestions or verify them before use?* Interaction data will also be captured, including the number of prompts, the number of iterations required to correct errors, and other relevant measures.

With the assistant, users are expected to complete tasks more quickly and produce specifications that are at least as complete as those created manually, with greater confidence in meeting format and compliance requirements. The study will also examine potential adverse effects, such as cases in which the assistant produces convincing but inaccurate suggestions. These qualitative aspects will be gathered through interviews conducted after the tasks.

Impact on Developer Productivity. An AI assistant could change how developers approach API design. Instead of navigating through internal wikis or asking, *Does an API for X already exist?* They can get an answer in seconds using our RAG approach. This lowers the barrier to reuse, ultimately reducing duplication across an organization's services.

One interesting side effect is the potential for such an assistant to serve as organizational memory: corporate APIs that have historically been underutilized may gain more adoption if the AI consistently surfaces them when relevant.

From a spec writing perspective, the assistant encourages best practices. However, there is a risk of over-reliance: developers might not learn the ins and outs of OpenAPI if the AI always does it for them, which could be problematic when the AI is unavailable or when debugging an issue. This parallels concerns in code autocomplete tools, where developers may lose some lower-level coding skills. The trade-off is worth it if it frees up time for higher-level design thinking.

Quality of AI Suggestions. Our approach prevents hallucinations by grounding the model with real data and using function constraints. However, subtle issues can still arise. For instance, the assistant might suggest an existing, related API that is not a perfect fit, potentially leading a team down a path of trying to adapt something that is not worth adapting. Final decisions on reuse remain with the developer. For this reason, we see the assistant as augmenting, not replacing, the human in the loop.

In our experience, the best outcomes came when the user operated the framework as if it were a junior assistant, accepting its good suggestions and redirecting it when it was off track. If users accept everything, they might end up with an API that technically works but is not conceptually cohesive. Thus, tooling should encourage a critical review of the AI's output.

Workflow Integration. For real-world integration, this assistant must seamlessly integrate with existing tools and systems. Developers typically use a range of tools, including an IDE, a source control system, and CI/CD pipelines.

Our framework is a step in this direction, but further integration points could be explored for enhanced functionality. For example, a Git pre-commit hook could run the assistant in validation mode. Whenever an OpenAPI file changes, it could automatically suggest improvements or catch mistakes.

Similarly, within API management platforms, an AI assistant can help populate documentation or create initial specifications based on a few inputs. We also consider the possibility of an AI-assisted review process for APIs. When a team submits an API design for review, an AI agent could act as a reviewer, flagging potential issues or asking clarifying questions. Our current assistant already has some of this capability, as it is familiar with best practices.

5.3   Limitations

Our current work focuses on REST APIs using OpenAPI. A natural extension is to consider other interface description language for event-driven systems. The techniques would largely transfer, though the retrieval content and the output schema would differ.

Another limitation is that our framework does not directly integrate with actual code implementation. After designing the API specification, developers implement the service throughout the whole development lifecycle. However, we plan to address this in future work by incorporating tooling that connects the specification to code generation and validation processes.

A future system where the same assistant, having helped write the spec, can also generate skeleton code and possibly even some application logic. There is also room to use the source code when designing an API for an existing system, e.g., parsing code to extract potential API endpoints. Our documentation refinement sub-project attempted something related by linking source code to existing specifications, ensuring documentation and specification completeness. This also enables automated checks that keep the spec, code, and related artifacts aligned during design and maintenance.

6   Conclusions and Future Work

We have presented a novel framework for AI-assisted REST API design using LLMs. Our approach combines the retrieval of existing API knowledge with guided specification generation, addressing two key challenges: allowing developers reuse existing knowledge before reinventing it and easing the burden of writing correct OpenAPI specifications. The rationale for integrating techniques like RAG is to facilitate OpenAPI function calls for structured output and rigorous schema validation. Pilot testing indicates possible gains in speed and quality, with fewer risks of non-compliant or redundant endpoints. The method can be adapted to other sectors with large API ecosystems, offering a practical means to deliver APIs more efficiently in enterprise software engineering. It can even be integrated into enterprise API governance workflows, offering immediate validation and reuse recommendations within CI/CD pipelines.

Our approach helps improve software development practices by assisting teams in drafting consistent API specifications early in the development process. It works with existing developer environments, including editors and validation steps, lowering the chances of missing elements or duplicating prior work. Automated checks and reuse suggestions allow faster progress without reducing quality. This aligns with standard DevOps methods that favor short feedback cycles and repeatable steps. The system also helps teams stay coordinated during API design and implementation. Its structure and components are described in detail, along with related work on software engineering assistants, specification tools, reuse approaches, and the use of LLMs in development.

This work also opens up several lines for future exploration. One is the adaptation of software design to other domains. If LLMs can assist with API specs, they can also help with database schema design or the synthesis of configuration files, especially when there are extensive catalogs of existing artifacts to learn from. Another possible line is deeper IDE integration and even more interactive experiences. From a research perspective, our study contributes to understanding how AI can be effectively incorporated into software design workflows. This area will become increasingly important as AI capabilities continue to advance.

Acknowledgments. We thank the anonymous reviewers for their help in improving the manuscript. The research reported in this paper has been funded by the Federal Ministry for Innovation, Mobility and Infrastructure (BMIMI), the Federal Ministry for Economy, Energy and Tourism (BMWET), and the State of Upper Austria in the frame of the SCCH competence center INTEGRATE (FFG grant no. 892418) in the COMET - Competence Centers for Excellent Technologies Programme managed by Austrian Research Promotion Agency FFG.

References

1. Andreo, S., Bosch, J.: API management challenges in ecosystems. In: International Conference on Software Business, pp. 86–93. Springer, Cham (2019)
2. Austin, J., et al.: Program synthesis with large language models. arXiv preprint arXiv:2108.07732 (2021)
3. Cao, H., Falleri, J., Blanc, X.: Automated generation of rest API specification from plain html documentation. In: Service-Oriented Computing: 15th International Conference, ICSOC 2017, Malaga, Spain, November 13–16, 2017, Proceedings, pp. 453–461. Springer, Cham (2017)
4. Chen, M., et al.: Evaluating large language models trained on code. arXiv preprint arXiv:2107.03374 (2021)
5. Durrani, U.K., Akpinar, M., Adak, M.F., Kabakus, A.T., Ozturk, M.M., Saleh, M.: A decade of progress: a systematic literature review on the integration of AI in software engineering phases and activities (2013–2023). IEEE Access (2024)
6. Feng, Z., et al.: Codebert: a pre-trained model for programming and natural languages. arXiv preprint arXiv:2002.08155 (2020)
7. Hamza, M., Siemon, D., Akbar, M.A., Rahman, T.: Human-ai collaboration in software engineering: lessons learned from a hands-on workshop. In: Proceedings of the 7th ACM/IEEE International Workshop on Software-intensive Business, pp. 7–14 (2024)
8. Hou, X., et al.: Large language models for software engineering: a systematic literature review. ACM Trans. Softw. Eng. Methodol. $33(8)$, 1–79 (2024)
9. Izacard, G., Grave, E.: Leveraging passage retrieval with generative models for open domain question answering. *arXiv preprint* arXiv:2007.01282 (2020)
10. Jiang, J., Wang, F., Shen, J., Kim, S., Kim, S.: A survey on large language models for code generation. arXiv preprint arXiv:2406.00515 (2024)
11. Karpukhin, V., et al.: Dense passage retrieval for open-domain question answering. In: EMNLP (1), pp. 6769–6781 (2020)
12. Koren, I., Klamma, R.: The exploitation of OpenAPI documentation for the generation of web frontends. In: Companion Proceedings of the the Web Conference, vol. 2018, pp. 781–787 (2018)
13. Lazar, K., et al.: Specrawler: generating OpenAPI specifications from API documentation using large language models. arXiv preprintarXiv:2402.11625 (2024)
14. Li, M., et al.: API-bank: a comprehensive benchmark for tool-augmented LLMs. arXiv preprintarXiv:2304.08244 (2023)
15. Ling, C.-Y., Zou, Y.-Z., Lin, Z.-Q., Xie, B.: Graph embedding based API graph search and recommendation. J. Comput. Sci. Technol. 34, 993–1006 (2019)
16. Martinez-Gil, J.: Source code clone detection using unsupervised similarity measures. In: Bludau, P., Ramler, R., Winkler, D., Bergsmann, J., (eds.) Software Quality as a Foundation for Security - 16th International Conference on Software Quality, SWQD 2024, Vienna, Austria, April 23-25, 2024, Proceedings. LNBIP, vol. 505, pp. 21–37. Springer, Cham (2024)
17. Martinez-Gil, J.: Augmenting the interpretability of graphcodebert for code similarity tasks. Int. J. Softw. Eng. Knowl. Eng. $35(5)$, 657–678 (2025)
18. Mastropaolo, A., et al.: On the robustness of code generation techniques: an empirical study on github copilot. In: 45th IEEE/ACM International Conference on Software Engineering, ICSE 2023, Melbourne, Australia, May 14-20, 2023, pp. 2149–2160. IEEE (2023)

19. Mehta, D., Rawool, K., Gujar, S., Xu, B.: Automated devops pipeline generation for code repositories using large language models. arXiv preprint arXiv:2312.13225 (2023)
20. Petryshyn, B., Lukosevicius, M.: Optimizing large language models for OpenAPI code completion. CoRR, abs/2405.15729 (2024)
21. Treude, C., Gerosa, M.A.: How developers interact with AI: a taxonomy of human-AI collaboration in software engineering. In: 2025 IEEE/ACM Second International Conference on AI Foundation Models and Software Engineering (Forge), pp. 236–240. IEEE (2025)
22. Vayadande, K., Mukhopadhyay, K., Chaudhari, V., Manwadkar, S., Mutalik, T., Gawali, I.: Let us lint: a tool for code formatting and code enhancing. In: 2023 14th International Conference on Computing Communication and Networking Technologies (ICCCNT), pp. 1–8. IEEE (2023)
23. Wittern, E., et al.: API harmony: graph-based search and selection of APIs in the cloud. IBM J. Res. Dev. **60**(2–3) (2016)
24. Wu, S., et al.: Retrieval-augmented generation for natural language processing: a survey. arXiv preprint arXiv:2407.13193 (2024)
25. Xi, Z., et al.: The rise and potential of large language model based agents: a survey. SCIENCE CHINA Inf. Sci. **68**(2), 121101 (2025)
26. Yu, H.Q., McQuade, F.: Rag-kg-il: a multi-agent hybrid framework for reducing hallucinations and enhancing LLM reasoning through rag and incremental knowledge graph learning integration. arXiv preprint arXiv:2503.13514 (2025)
27. Zhang, B., Liang, P., Zhou, X., Ahmad, A., Waseem, M.: Practices and challenges of using github copilot: an empirical study. In: Chang, S-K., (ed.) The 35th International Conference on Software Engineering and Knowledge Engineering, SEKE 2023, KSIR Virtual Conference Center, USA, July 1-10, 2023, pp. 124–129. KSI Research Inc (2023)
28. Zheng, Z., et al.: A survey of large language models for code: evolution, benchmarking, and future trends. arXiv preprint arXiv:2311.10372 (2023)

Software Development
and Documentation

Generative AI for Software Development: Study on Current Utilization in Upper Austria

Simon Mairinger[1,2] and Thomas Ziebermayr[1,2(✉)]

[1] University of Applied Sciences Upper Austria - Campus Hagenberg, Hagenberg, Austria
[2] Studyprogram Design of Digital Products, Hagenberg, Austria
thomas.ziebermayr@fh-hagenberg.at

Abstract. The capabilities of generative AI are sweeping across many areas, bringing about lasting and disruptive changes to the world of work. These tools are also widely used in software development. However, due to the relatively short time span, there are still open questions and work required on well-researched procedures and on widely accepted best practices for the application of AI for SE. Our study, based on a questionnaire, provides insight into the current use of these technologies in the daily development and engineering work of 116 people engaged in this domain in Austrian companies. The goal was to create a basis for further measures in research, education, and corporate strategies. The results indicates the current main application of AI for technical tasks and showed that software engineers are aware of possible risks and opportunities when using generative AI for software engineering tasks.

Keywords: Utilization of AI for SE · Generative AI · Software Engineering · Future of SE

1 Introduction

The use of artificial intelligence (AI) in software development has grown significantly in importance in recent years [7]. Especially the emergence of powerful Large Language Models employed for generative AI (gen-AI) such as ChatGPT, GitHub Copilot and Google Gemini provide tools supporting developers in everyday tasks such as writing source code, diagnosing errors and creating technical documentation [2]. But the role in development practice extends beyond technical assistance systems. It also gives rise to new forms of collaboration [10], changed work processes but also raise issues regarding the generated content. Alongside the question of the practical benefits for everyday work, there is also the question of which skills could become more important in the future [12], and how roles and tasks within the team might change.

Despite the increasing use of gen-AI in software engineering, it remains unclear how these developments specifically affect the everyday working lives

© The Author(s), under exclusive license to Springer Nature Switzerland AG 2026
M. Dorner et al. (Eds.): SWQD 2026, LNBIP 581, pp. 101–112, 2026.
https://doi.org/10.1007/978-3-032-24216-7_6

of software developers in Austria. This knowledge gap is the starting point for this work. The aim is to gain structured insights into the actual use and evaluation of generative AI in everyday software development. The focus is on the practical perspective of developers who are already using such tools, as well as the resulting challenges and future development trends. According to that the following questions are formulated as a basis for the study:

1. What role does the use of gen-AI play in the phases of software development?
   a) In which phases of the software development process is gen-AI used?
   b) Which tasks or areas of activity are supported by gen-AI tools?
2. How does the use of gen-AI tools influence the professional practice and role understanding of software developers?
   a) To what extent does gen-AI support change work of developers?
   b) What challenges and skills are required to use AI-supported tools?
3. What are software developer experiences with using gen-AI tools in practice?
   a) Which gen-AI tools are used for what in software development?
   b) How do developers assess the quality and reliability of gen-AI results?
   c) What opportunities and risks are associated with the use of these tools?

Finding answers to those questions is the goal of this research and was also the basis of a bachelor thesis finalized in autumn 2025 and submitted in the study program Design of Digital Products of the University of Applied Sciences - Campus Hagenberg [9]. The presented paper bases on this bachelor thesis.

2   Background and Related Work

Research on the application of AI for software development has increased significantly in recent years. While early work focused on the use of AI in traditional software development processes [3], current research is directed toward generative AI and its potential for everyday development and Human-AI collaboration [13]. This article systematically captures the conditions for the acceptance and introduction of gen-AI in a professional environment and allows us to analyse whether the drivers and barriers identified in the Human-AI Collaboration and Adaptation Framework (HACAF) are also reflected in actual usage practices.

Using GenAI for SE has also impact on the software development process [11]. Productivity, quality, and governance are changing through the use of gen-AI in the software development lifecycle (SDLC). Companies report productivity increases of up to 20% through autocoding tools, but at the same time, new challenges are emerging, for example in terms of code quality, technical debt, and a lack of standard metrics [11].

The role of AI technologies in classical phase models of software development are investigated here [4]. Based on a systematic literature review of more than 60 research papers and supplementary interviews with experts from the field, the authors analyze how different AI methods can be used in specific software development phases. The results show that AI is particularly effective where large amounts of data need to be processed in a structured manner or patterns need to be recognized. AI contributes significantly to increased efficiency although there are differences between "classic" AI approaches (e.g., defect prediction or pattern recognition) and the newer, generative models.

The rise of agentic AI also hits the domain of SE and numerous frameworks are provided to seamlessly support the engineering process. The symbiotic collaboration between software developers and AI systems, which can accompany and partially automate all phases of the software life cycle–from requirements analysis to design, implementation, testing, and maintenance allow further efficiency increasements [6].

Research on generative AI in software development already covers a wide range of topics from acceptance and adoption factors [13], to technical potential in automated frameworks [15], classic applications of AI in the development cycle [3], to security-related issues in software supply chains [1], and future-oriented scenarios for the transformation of roles and processes [6,14]. Nevertheless, there are still open questions e.g.: how developers themselves experience and evaluate the use of generative AI tools in their everyday work. While the existing literature predominantly highlights technical concepts, theoretical models, or organizational frameworks, there is a lack of empirical findings on the subjective experiences, opportunities, and challenges from the perspective of users especially in Austrian companies.

This work addresses this gap and examines the role generative AI tools play in the everyday work of software developers, how they are perceived, and what changes this brings about in their job profiles. The focus is on efficiency gains, risks such as dependency, loss of control, and legal uncertainties. The work thus complements the existing theoretical, technical, and conceptual foundations with a practical empirical perspective and contributes to a holistic understanding of the transformation of development work through generative AI.

3   Study Design and Methodology

To answer the research questions, an approach was chosen that combines quantitative and qualitative survey and evaluation methods to capture the research questions in terms of both breadth and depth. In practice, a combination of both types is often used to ensure comparability and content depth [5]. Empirical data were collected using an online questionnaire.

Participants were selected on the basis of criteria relating to professional practice in software development. Care was taken to include people from different roles, levels of experience, and areas of activity. Participation was voluntary and anonymous. The questionnaire was distributed via personal contacts, institutional distribution lists, and selected companies and educational institutions engaged in software engineering.

Microsoft Forms was chosen as the online tool for the technical implementation of the questionnaire. It was chosen due to its low barrier to entry (participation possible without logging in), user-friendliness, data protection compliance and data export option (data processing in Excel for further evaluation).

When designing the questionnaire, particular attention was paid to clear wording, understandable and neutral. Although a formal pre-test was not carried out, comprehensibility was tested and optimised in advance through an internal review by specialists in the field.

The questionnaire is divided into thematically structured sections that enable a logical progression from general contextual information to specific aspects of gen- AI use in everyday development work. Initial questions about professional role, experience, and area of activity classify the target group, enabling differentiated evaluation by subgroups at a later stage. Next are questions about the specific use of generative AI tools, perceived changes in everyday work, and experienced challenges, potential, and risks. The questionnaire can be found here: Link to Questionaire

3.1   Collecting and Analysing Data

The standardized online survey was the primary empirical method. This format was chosen to reach a large number of people from various business contexts and to preserve a broad range of opinions. The survey included 15 questions aligned with the research questions. Ten of the questions were closed, with single or multiple choice answers, and each was supplemented by an optional free text field ("Other"). Five open-ended questions were designed to provide qualitative insights into experiences, evaluations, and perspectives. This combination allows for a structured yet flexible survey of differentiated perspectives.

Quantitative Analysis: Descriptive statistics are used to analyse the closed

questions. This involves calculating frequencies and distributions to determine the prevalence of certain tools, their areas of application, and perceived changes to everyday working life. This approach enables general trends and patterns in the use of generative AI tools to be identified.

Qualitative Analysis: Open-ended free-text responses are evaluated using

qualitative content analysis. The aim is to identify recurring themes and patterns of argumentation, as well as participants' attitudes. These qualitative findings complement the quantitative results, providing a deeper understanding of the perceived opportunities, challenges, and risks associated with the practical use of AI.

3.2   Limitations

Despite the advantages of questionaries, certain limitations must be considered. The lack of follow-up questions or opportunities for clarification is a limitation. While open interviews would allow in-depth questioning in the event of ambiguities or contradictions, standardised online questions allow for a certain degree of interpretative freedom. This limitation was mitigated by the clear and precise wording of the questions and the inclusion of open response fields. Even for closed questions, an additional answer option of 'Other' was provided, which included a free text field for additional information.

The validity of the information may also be limited as it is not possible to verify the professional position or actual experience of the respondents. Although the questionnaire asked specifically about role, experience, and field of activity, this information is based on self-declaration. To increase plausibility, multiple entries were interpreted using triangulation.

Lastly, the non-random sampling method chosen results in limitations to generalization. The results of this study are not representative but provide an insight in the current state of utilization.

4   Evaluation

The online survey was conducted between mid-May and the end of June 2025. Participants were asked to indicate their current area of activity in software development. The most frequently cited role was full-stack developer (49%). The response option 'Other' (text field for more detailed explanation of own role) was selected by 26 participants (22%). In this context, some indicated that they were students, while others described differentiated or mixed job profiles such as lead developer/architect, Embedded SW Developer, Hardware-related Development or Innovation Manager – AI Innovation. Backend development was also frequently mentioned, with 17 mentions. A complete overview of the distribution is shown in Fig. 1.

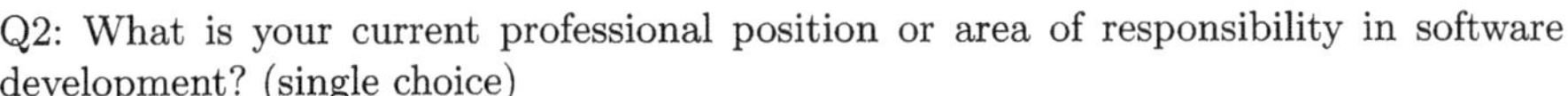

Q2: What is your current professional position or area of responsibility in software development? (single choice)

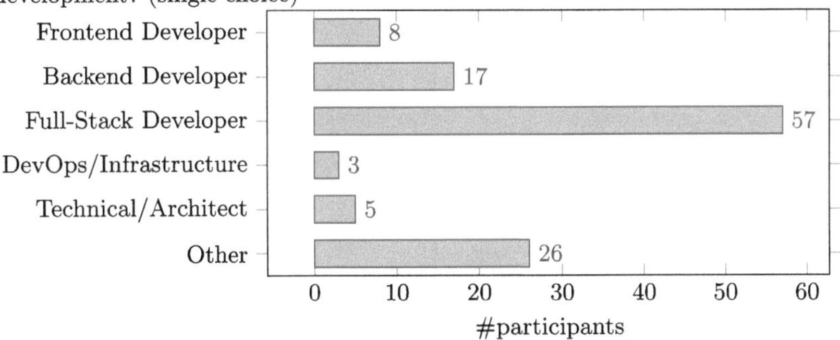

Fig. 1. Participants' professional position

Professional Experience of Participants in Software Development. The majority of participants had several years of experience in software development. The largest group consisted of individuals with 4–6 years of professional experience (n = 41; 35%). There were also participants with 1–3 years of experience (n = 29; 25%) and 7–10 years of experience (n = 19; 16%). The remaining responses were distributed across other experience levels, including individuals with over 20 years' experience. The complete distribution is shown in Fig. 2.

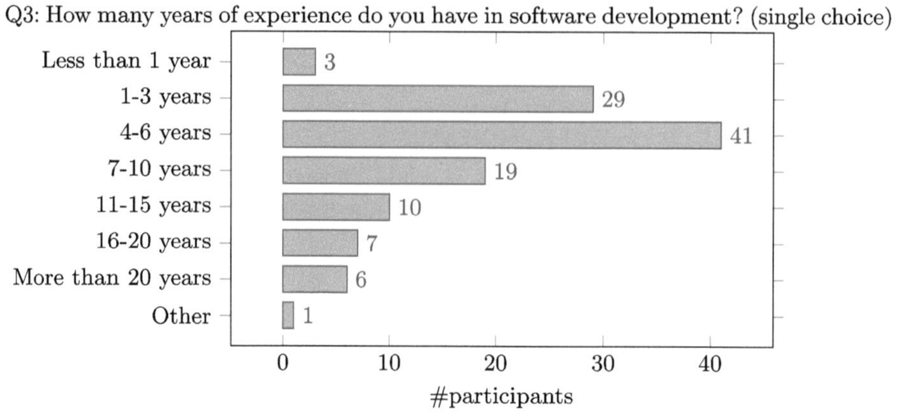

Q3: How many years of experience do you have in software development? (single choice)

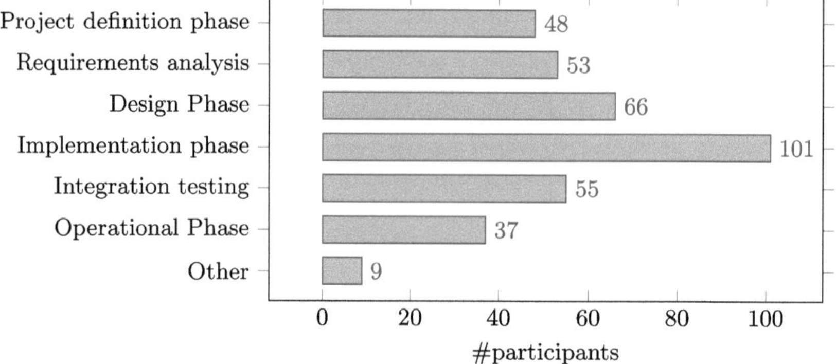

Fig. 2. Details of professional experience in software development.

Areas of Activity of Participants in Software Development. Multiple choices where allowed. The majority of survey participants (n = 80; 37%) stated that they were primarily involved in web development. Other frequently mentioned areas were enterprise software development (n = 43; 20%) and mobile apps (n = 41; 19%). Activities in the fields of AI/ML applications and game development were mentioned less frequently.

Phases of Deployment of AI-Supported Tools. Participants primarily use gen-AI tools during the implementation phase (101 people). The design phase (n = 66) and integration testing (n = 55) were also frequently cited. The remaining phases of the software development process were less frequently associated with AI tools. These phases include e.g. the project definition phase and the operational phase. Figure 3 provides a complete overview of the application phases.

Q6: In which phases of the software development process do you (or your team) currently use AI-powered tools? (multiple choice)

Fig. 3. Phases of deployment of AI-supported tools in the development process.

The Most Common Areas of Application for AI in Everyday Development Work. The majority of participants (n = 59; 51%) stated that they mainly use AI for code generation. Error diagnosis was also a common application, mentioned by 41 people (35%). Other tasks, such as data analysis, test automation and user analysis, were mentioned less frequently.

Changes to Everyday Working Life Through the Sse of AI. The majority of participants (n = 99; 32%) stated that using AI-supported tools leads to greater efficiency in routine tasks. Additionally, many participants reported that less manual coding is required and that more time is spent on review and control tasks (n = 68; 22%). Forty participants (13%) reported an increase in conceptual tasks, such as prompt design or tool selection. Other changes mentioned include greater demands on the technical understanding of AI systems and increased responsibility for AI-generated code. A complete overview is shown in Fig. 4.

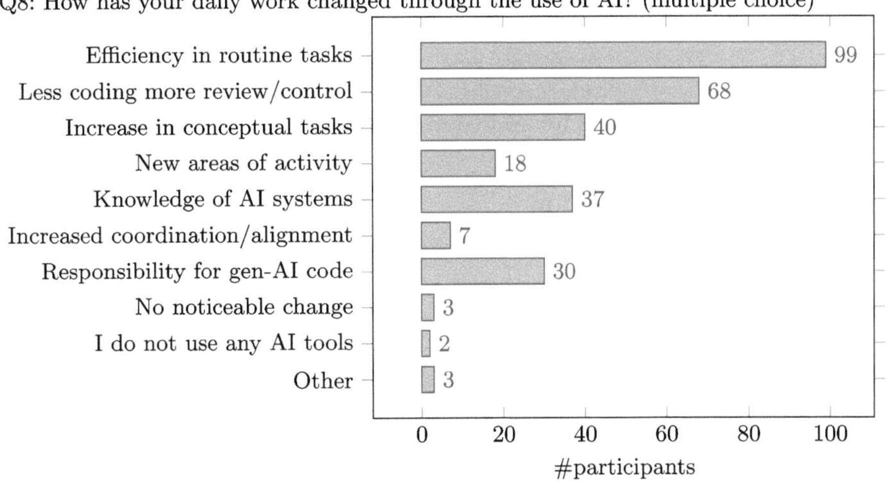

Fig. 4. Changes to everyday working life through the use of AI

Challenges of Using AI in the Development Process. The most common challenge cited by participants when using AI-supported tools was the difficulty of formulating effective prompts, or a lack of knowledge about prompting (n = 54; 25%). Other frequently mentioned challenges were a lack of transparency in AI decisions (n = 47; 22%) and poor integration with existing workflows (n = 36; 17%).

Further challenges were mentioned in the 'Other' response option. These included concerns about incorrect or unusable results, AI systems tendency to hallucinate and the use of outdated knowledge. Participants also criticised the sometimes high effort involved in creating prompts, which, in some cases, was greater than manual implementation. Other issues raised related to security, the danger of younger developers placing uncritical trust in generated content and difficulties with larger projects where the tools' performance reaches its limits.

Use of AI-Supported Tools in Everyday Development Work. The most frequently used AI application among participants was the free version of Chat-GPT (n = 70; 23%). GitHub Copilot and Copilot X were also used frequently (62 mentions, or 20%), followed by ChatGPT Plus (39 mentions, or 13%). Microsoft Copilot was used almost as frequently, with 38 mentions. Other tools, such as Gemini, Cursor and specialised tools like Amazon CodeWhisperer and Tabnine, were used significantly less frequently.

Types of AI Use in Code Generation. Participants use AI-supported tools most frequently for the autonomous generation of individual code blocks or snippets (n = 91; 27%). These suggestions are used just as frequently during the coding process, for example through inline completions in development environments (n = 77; 23%). Many people also mentioned the automatic generation of complete functions or modules (n = 64; 19%). Other uses include generating test code and providing support for code documentation.

4.1   Qualitative Evaluation

The following evaluations refer to questions 13, 14 and 15, which were open-ended. The qualitative analysis aimed to systematically record the evaluation criteria, experiences and perspectives of the developers mentioned in the free-text answers. To this end, the answers were evaluated using content analysis and grouped into recurring themes and categories. To provide an authentic insight into the assessments and reasons given by the respondents, the central themes are illustrated with direct quotes from respondents.

Perceived Quality of AI-Generated Code. Question 13 was: *Please briefly explain what you base your assessment of code quality on (e.g. comprehensibility, maintainability, efficiency).* The aim of this open-ended question was to identify the criteria developers use when assessing the quality of AI-generated code.

The evaluation shows that the quality of AI-generated code is predominantly assessed using established software quality criteria. Aspects such as comprehensibility, maintainability, functionality, efficiency, and integration into existing systems are given particular focus. A particularly positive aspect highlighted is that the generated code is often easy to read and includes comments. Many participants therefore find it a helpful starting point or source of inspiration for developing their own solutions further. Around a quarter of the responses also point to the time-saving advantages of quickly available suggestions, which allow problems to be tackled more quickly.

However, more than half of the responses emphasise that using AI code involves considerable post-processing effort. Problems frequently mentioned include outdated or faulty functions, insufficient efficiency and difficulties in implementing complex logic. Around a third of respondents emphasise that the generated code can rarely be used directly in productive applications, requiring adjustments almost always. Some responses even suggest that existing solutions have been worsened rather than improved by AI suggestions.

Overall, the picture is ambivalent: while there are clear advantages, such as time savings and comprehensibility, for simple code snippets or standardised tasks, problems tend to arise more frequently with more complex requirements, architectural issues, or when used in production. This makes it clear that the practical benefits of generative AI tools depend heavily on the specific use case and the developers' experience.

Opportunities Through the Use of AI in Software Development. Question 14 was: In your opinion, what are the greatest opportunities offered by the use of AI in software development? Analysis of the free-text responses shows that increased efficiency, the automation of routine tasks, and support with development tasks are perceived as the greatest opportunities.

The evaluation shows that the greatest opportunities for using AI in software development are seen primarily in increased efficiency, the automation of repetitive tasks and support in error analysis. In addition, developers expect relief from standard tasks, the opportunity to focus more on creative or complex activities, and potential for quality improvement and innovation.

Risks and Difficulties in the Use of AI in Software Development. Question 15 was: *What risks or difficulties do you see in this?* The evaluation shows that numerous challenges and uncertainties are perceived in connection with AI-supported software development.

The results bases on the answers of the participants willing to take part in the survey. The results shows that mainly experienced experts already using AI for SE has answered the questions. Otherwise experience would not be available, but this also means, people who are not willing to use AI for SE are not taken into account in the survey.

The qualitative evaluation makes clear that the risks and difficulties in dealing with AI for software development are seen in particular in the loss of knowledge, poor code quality, lack of control, security issues and long-term dependence on AI systems. The need for critical reflection and careful review of generated solutions is emphasised by numerous participants. Nevertheless is AI for most of the responding people a powerful tool for development support.

4.2   Answer to Research Questions and Discussion of Results

The survey in the given context provides detailed insight in the utilization of Gen-AI tools in Austria. In the following we will map the results to our research questions and discuss the impact.

RQ1: In Which Phases of the Software Development Process Is Generative AI Used? Generative AI tools are mainly used in the middle of the software development process, especially during implementation phase. This phase has by far the highest intensity of gen-AI use. This high rate indicates that gen-AI plays a particularly important role in the operational implementation of technical solutions. But gen-AI is also used frequently in the design phase for example, to support the structuring of solution approaches or the preparation of technical concepts.

In contrast, early phases such as requirements analysis or project definition are mentioned much less frequently. This indicates that generative AI has so far played a subordinate role in conceptual or planning-related stages of the development process. Its use in later phases such as operation and maintenance is equally low, although there is potential for automation and quality assurance in the long term.

In summary, it can be said that the use of generative AI is currently focused primarily on the central technical phases of software development – in particular design, implementation, and testing.

RQ2: How Does the Use of Gen-AI Tools Influence the Professional Practice and Role Understanding of Software Developers The survey results show that the role profile of software developers is changing significantly as a result of the use of generative AI tools. A key finding is the shift in activities. Routine tasks such as writing standard code or manual error analysis become less important, while monitoring, testing, and conceptual tasks are gaining in importance. Instead of creating content entirely on their own, many developers are increasingly taking on the role of control authorities who evaluate, adapt, and integrate content generated by gen-AI. This means that the activity is shifting in part from direct creation to quality and integration assurance.

This change is also reflected in the increasing importance of prompt engineering [8]. The ability to formulate clear and effective instructions is becoming a new key competence in everyday working life. At the same time, responsibility for the content and technical accuracy of AI-generated results is increasing, leading to greater vigilance, especially in safety-critical areas.

At the same time, an area of tension is becoming apparent: while many respondents see the reduction of routine tasks as an opportunity for more creativity and strategic thinking, there are also concerns about the possible loss of skills due to excessive dependence on generative AI. Securing technical expertise and problem-solving skills in the long term therefore remains a key issue when dealing with gen-AI tools.

Overall, the role of many developers is shifting toward a moderating, steering, and reflective position in the development process. The classic idea of a specialist who exclusively implement software is being supplemented by new requirements: analytical thinking, critical evaluation of AI results, and a deep understanding of the results are becoming increasingly important.

RQ3: What Are Software Developer Experiences with Using Gen-AI Tools in Practice? The third research question focuses on the reality of use and experiences with gen-AI tools. The results show that software developers' experience is ambivalent: on the one hand, clear advantages are seen in everyday use, but on the other hand, there are critical reservations regarding quality, reliability, and long-term effects. The quality of the generated content is predominantly rated as medium to high. Results are often considered helpful, but in need of post-processing. Expertise is still needed in order to classify and adapt the results.

5   Summary and Outlook

This paper examines the current utilization of gen-AI in software engineering in Austria. It focuses particularly on gen-AI's use in development phases, its impact on everyday work, and experiences of using these tools in practice.

For an insight in practical utilization, an approach combining quantitative and qualitative elements was adopted. This was implemented in an online survey with response of 116 people working in software development. The questionnaire included closed questions about frequency, phases of use, and perceived changes; as well as open questions about opportunities, risks, and quality assessments.

The results show that generative AI is primarily used in technical phases of software development, particularly implementation, design and testing. Routine activities such as writing or checking code are increasingly being automated, while supervisory, reflective and conceptual tasks are becoming more prevalent. This changes the role of software developers, who are acting less as implementers and more as controllers and supervisors.

Experiences with gen-AI tools are mixed: positive aspects include increased efficiency, support in learning new technologies, and relief from standard tasks. However, there are also considerable reservations regarding the loss of expertise, the lack of transparency in AI decision-making processes, and the quality issues with the generated code, which often requires reworking. Overall, this study shows that generative AI is already a relevant tool in the software development process, offering potential for increased efficiency and innovation, but also introducing new risks and requirements.

The insight into current utilization of gen-AI on the one hand raises further open research questions (long-term effects of gen-AI on job roles, team dynamics, and the quality of software-based products) but also is important for education and companies (Integrating prompt engineering in education, Education in critical evaluation of AI results, Companies have to adapt their role profiles and expertise, More empirical data on performance indicators applying gen-AI for SE).

Furthermore, legal issues require clarification, such as copyright when using AI-generated content, liability for incorrect or security-relevant decisions, and how to handle sensitive data contained in prompts or training data. Compliance with existing data protection regulations, particularly the General Data Protection Regulation (GDPR), is also a key issue.

References

1. Alevizos, V., et al.: Integrating artificial open generative artificial intelligence into software supply chain security. In: 2024 5th International Conference on Data Analytics for Business and Industry (ICDABI), pp. 200–206. IEEE (2024)
2. Banh, L., Holldack, F., Strobel, G.: Copiloting the future: how generative ai transforms software engineering. Inf. Softw. Technol. **183**, 107751 (2025)
3. Barenkamp, M.: Künstliche intelligenz in der softwareentwicklung. Wirtschaftsinformatik Manag. **12**(2), 120–129 (2020)
4. Barenkamp, M., Rebstadt, J., Thomas, O.: Applications of ai in classical software engineering. AI Perspect. **2**(1), 1 (2020)
5. Beywl, W., Balzer, L.: Fragebogen erstellen. In: evaluiert (E-Book). hep verlag, Switzerland (2018)
6. Coutinho, M., Marques, L., Santos, A., Dahia, M., França, C., de Souza Santos, R.: The role of generative AI in software development productivity: a pilot case study. In: Proceedings of the 1st ACM International Conference on AI-Powered Software, AIware 2024, pp. 131–138. Association for Computing Machinery, New York (2024)
7. Fan, A., et al.: Large language models for software engineering: survey and open problems. In: 2023 IEEE/ACM International Conference on Future of Software Engineering (ICSE-FoSE) (2023)
8. Keuthen, T.: Prompt Engineering im Geschäftsprozessmanagement: Innovation mit KI als Schlüssel zur Effizienz, pp. 11–76. Springer Fachmedien Wiesbaden, Wiesbaden (2025)
9. Mairinger, S.: Wie ki den arbeitsalltag von developern beeinflusst: Herausforderungen und künftige trends. Bachelor thesis, University for Applied Sciences Upper Austria, Campus Hagenberg (2025)
10. Maurya, H., Agrahari, A., Kumar, A.: Human-ai collaboration: cognitive challenges in interacting with generative ai agents (2024)
11. Muratovic, F., Kearns-Manolatos, D., Alibage, A.: Generative ai in software development: challenges, opportunities, and new paradigms for quality assurance. Computer **58**(7), 31–39 (2025)
12. Necula, S-C.: Artificial intelligence impact on the labour force – searching for the analytical skills of the future software engineers (2023)
13. Russo, D.: Navigating the complexity of generative ai adoption in software engineering. ACM Trans. Softw. Eng. Methodol. **33**(5) (2024)
14. Sauvola, J., Tarkoma, S., Klemettinen, M., Riekki, J., Doermann, D.: Future of software development with generative AI. Autom. Softw. Eng. **31**(1), 26 (2024)
15. Tufano, M., Agarwal, A., Jang, J., Moghaddam, R.Z., Sundaresan, N.: Autodev : automated ai-driven development (2024)

Automating Documentation of Complex Data Processing Flows with Large Language Models

Parisa Mahya[1]([✉]), Jorge Martinez-Gil[1], Mario Winterer[1],
Cornelia Neumüller[2], and Matthias Krump[2]

[1] Software Competence Center Hagenberg GmbH, Softwarepark 32a,
4232 Hagenberg, Austria
{parisa.mahya,jorge.martinez-gil,mario.winterer}@scch.at
[2] Raiffeisen Software GmbH, Goethestraße 80, 4020 Linz, Austria
{cornelia.neumueller,matthias.krump}@r-software.at

Abstract. Modern software systems increasingly consist of complex, multi-stage data processing flows that integrate artifacts such as code, database queries, and parameters. Maintaining accurate and up-to-date documentation of such systems is challenging due to the dynamic nature and system evolution. This article presents an LLM-based framework for automating documentation of complex data processing flows. The prototype system leverages modular agents and multi-level caching to generate both task-level and process-level documentation. Evaluation using the LLM-as-a-judge approach demonstrates accurate and coherent results on real-world data processing specifications.

Keywords: Workflow Documentation · Large Language Models · Agents · Software Process Automation · Prompting · LLM-as-a-Judge

1 Introduction

Modern data-intensive applications rely heavily on complex software systems, i.e., computational pipelines implemented in software systems that automate sequences of data-related tasks. These data processing flows often integrate heterogeneous artifacts such as database queries, parameterized configurations, and source code.

While such workflows are crucial for operational efficiency and decision-making throughout the software life-cycle, their documentation and maintenance remain major challenges. Manually created documentation requires significant human effort, often becomes incomplete or outdated, and struggles to evolve alongside rapidly changing systems [1,6,9,14]. These limitations lead to significant challenges in reproducibility, knowledge transfer, and system transparency.

Recent advances in large language models (LLMs) have demonstrated remarkable capabilities in analyzing code, queries, and unstructured data to generate human-readable documentation and summarization [2,5,7]. Prior research

© The Author(s), under exclusive license to Springer Nature Switzerland AG 2026
M. Dorner et al. (Eds.): SWQD 2026, LNBIP 581, pp. 113–124, 2026.
https://doi.org/10.1007/978-3-032-24216-7_7

has shown promising results in applying LLMs to the area of code summarization and documentation, where models generate natural language descriptions of functions, classes, and scripts [5,8]. However, existing methods largely focus on isolated code artifacts (e.g., individual functions or files), ignoring the inter-dependencies that exist across data processing stages. As a result, current systems fail to capture the holistic context—how data flows, transforms, and interacts across components.

To bridge this gap, we propose an LLM-powered framework for automated end-to-end documentation of complex software data processing flows. Rather than focusing solely on individual artifacts, our approach constructs a holistic view of a data processing flow, analyzing both the local behavior of individual steps and the flow of data across them. The system ingests structured data processing specifications that include source code, database queries, and configuration metadata, constructs a process graph, and produces: (1) a step-level description of each task's purpose, inputs, and outputs, and (2) a process-level summary that captures inter-task dependencies and overall purpose.

The development of the proposed system is conducted for software developers and system architects from a financial institution, who are responsible for maintaining complex banking services and software.

To enhance efficiency, the system incorporates a multi-level caching mechanism that reuses previously generated descriptions, reducing redundant analysis and improving performance. The quality of the results is then evaluated using an LLM-as-a-judge approach, enabling scalable, consistent, and multidimensional assessment of the generated documentation.

The main contributions of this work are threefold. First, we present a **modular LLM-powered prototype system** that unifies task-level descriptions, process-level summaries, and structured reporting across heterogeneous artifacts, including source code, database queries, and configuration files. Second, we introduce a **dataflow-aware documentation approach** that captures not only the behavior of individual tasks but also the inter-dependencies among data processing steps, resulting in coherent, end-to-end representations of overall system functionality. Finally, we propose an **LLM-based evaluation framework** that incorporates multi-level caching to improve efficiency and supports scalable, consistent, and cost-effective assessment of documentation quality.

The remainder of this article is organized as follows. Section 2 reviews relevant studies and papers on documentation automation and evaluation strategies. Section 3 provides background information on the users, requirements, and data processing structures addressed by the system. Section 4 describes the proposed system in detail, Sect. 5 presents and discusses the evaluation results, and Sect. 6 concludes the paper and outlines directions for future work.

2   Related Work

Automated documentation of software systems has been studied from multiple perspectives. In this section, we review the two most relevant areas to our work:

automated code summarization and documentation, and evaluation methodologies, including those leveraging LLM-as-a-judge techniques.

2.1 Automated Code Summarization and Documentation

Creating and maintaining accurate technical documentation in continuous software development (CSD) is often time-consuming and challenging due to the frequent system changes that occur. To address this issue, Birru et al. [1] present CodeDocSync, an LLM-based approach that automatically updates documentation in response to code modifications through code summarization and a chatbot. Similarly, Miranda et al. [4] propose a tool that leverages LLM to automatically summarize code contributions extracted from version control repositories.

Prompt optimization and context management have also been shown to enhance summarization quality. Fang et al. [6] introduce EP4CS, an Enhanced Prompting framework for code summarization that combines dynamic prompt optimization with syntax-aware code interpretation, achieving notable improvements over baseline models and human evaluations. Su et al. [13] propose a context-aware summarization model that incorporates caller methods to better capture a code snippet within the overall program, improving summary accuracy and relevance. Finally, Xia et al. [16] present DeepKnowCode, integrating deep learning techniques with LLMs and crowd-sourced KNOWledge to support developers describing both code behavior and practical usage guidelines.

Although the existing approaches substantially improve code-level summarization, they focus solely on the function or file level, neglecting dependencies between components. Our work extends beyond these boundaries by targeting process-level documentation and capturing the flow of data across multiple tasks.

2.2 Evaluation Methodologies

The evaluation of LLM-generated documentation and summarization has emerged as a critical step in such systems. Traditional metrics such as BLEU and ROUGE often fail to capture all aspects of documentation, such as practical usefulness or faithfulness. To address these limitations, studies have proposed LLM-based evaluations that reason about summaries in context.

Wu et al. [15] propose CoDERPE, a novel role-playing approach in which LLMs assess the quality of code summaries across various dimensions such as coherence, consistency, fluency, and relevance, showing strong correlation with human judgments. Song et al. [12] introduce FineSurE, a fine-grained LLM-based evaluation framework measuring completeness, conciseness, and faithfulness. Other works adopt complementary approaches: Mastropaolo et al. [10] propose a contrastive learning-based method that emphasizes semantic correctness; Robinson and Kummerfeld [11] directly prompt an LLM for a holistic scoring; and Crupi et al. [3] explore LLM-based evaluation as a scalable alternative to costly human assessment. Collectively, these studies demonstrate the effectiveness of the LLM-as-a-judge approach for the evaluation of code documentation.

Building on these insights, our work adopts the LLM-as-a-judge approach for evaluating data processing documentation.

3   Background

This section provides background information on the users, requirements, and the data processing flow addressed by the system.

3.1   Industrial Context

The proposed system is developed for a banking software company, targeting software engineers and system architects working in this environment. The bank's software system consists of several hundreds of microservices managed by dozens of teams responsible for their development and maintenance. The company maintains a large structured knowledge base about its system, containing information like service inter-dependencies, team responsibilities, or application scopes. To make use of this knowledge, experts can flexibly define complex data processes to query, transform, and visualize the required information. Currently, there are 68 real-world data processes, reflecting the diversity and complexity of its microservice ecosystem.

However, these processes lack appropriate documentation and are hard to understand. The main goal of the proposed system is to automatically generate the missing documentation to make the data processes accessible to and usable for all software engineers of the company.

3.2   Data Processing Flow Structure

In this article, the term data processing flow refers to machine-executable processes composed of interdependent tasks, such as data analysis and transformation, defined in any structured format. Each data processing specification comprises multiple interconnected tasks, including source code snippets, database queries, or configuration parameters.

A data processing flow is represented as a directed acyclic graph (DAG), where each node corresponds to an individual processing task, and the edges denote control and data dependencies between tasks, as illustrated in Fig. 1.

In the example shown in Fig. 1, each node represents a distinct artifact type, such as a query, transformation code, or configuration, while the directed edges denote the data flow between them.

A data process consists of different node types. **Upstream nodes** are tasks whose output feeds as input to other tasks/nodes (e.g., in Fig. 1, Node 1 provides data to Node 3). A **Downstream node** takes the outputs of the upstream nodes as inputs (e.g., Node 5 consumes results from Node 3 and 4). **Root nodes** are tasks without upstream dependencies, representing an entry point in the graph (e.g., Nodes 1 and 2 act as roots). Finally, **Converging nodes** have multiple upstream dependencies that combine data or results from several preceding nodes (e.g., Node 3 aggregates outputs from Nodes 1 and 2).

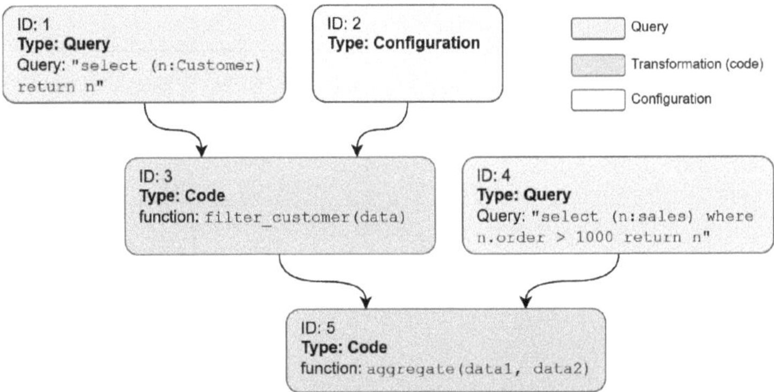

Fig. 1. Data processing graph example, consists of queries, transformations (code), and configuration artifacts.

4   System Architecture

The proposed prototype system is implemented as a modular pipeline that transforms heterogeneous data processing flows into structured, reusable documentation. This modular design enables flexibility across diverse artifact types such as code, queries, and configurations.

An overview of the architecture illustrated in Fig. 2 comprises four main components: the *data processing parser* extracts the graph from the data processing flow, the *description generator* produces task-level documentation, the *summary generator* creates an overall data processing graph summary, and the *reporting* module outputs the final structured documentation. These components are supported by an integrated *caching layer* and the actual documentation *agents*. The *caching* layer minimizes redundant analysis by reusing prior results, while the agents dynamically tailor documentation generation to each artifact type, ensuring context-aware and precise outputs.

4.1   Agents

A distinctive feature of the system is its prompting mechanism, which tailors the documentation generation to the type of artifact being analyzed. Instead of using a single, generic prompt for all tasks in the graph, the system employs customized task-specific agents, each associated with a tailored prompt template that reflects the characteristics of its target artifact type.

In this context, an agent represents a role-specific prompting strategy that guides the LLM to interpret and describe an artifact appropriately. This approach enables the LLM to produce documentation that is precise, semantically grounded, and context-aware, even in a heterogeneous data processing flow.

While state-of-the-art LLMs are capable of producing structured output like JSON, we decided not to use this feature, as structured output tends to

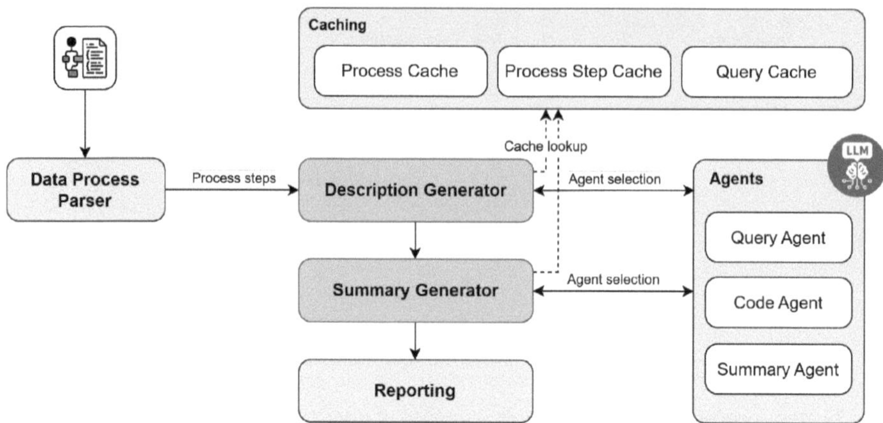

Fig. 2. An overview of the system architecture.

be shorter and less detailed than unstructured text. So instead, the model is prompted to just adhere to specific headlines.

The use of multiple agents eliminates the limitations of "one-size-fits-all" prompting, reducing redundancy and the likelihood of hallucinated content. Each agent captures the purpose, input parameters, expected outputs, and behavioral summary, considering contextual information from upstream steps. Unlike ordinary agents, these agents share their message history, so that the entire history of an upstream node agent is passed to the downstream node agent (instead of just passing the final documentation of the upstream node).

The system defines three primary agents to handle different artifact types.

Query Agent. This agent is specialized for analyzing data queries and generating a textual description that outlines the query's purpose, inputs, outputs, and summary as demonstrated in Prompt 1

Listing 1. Instructions for Query Agent (abridged)

```
You are an expert in graph databases and query languages.
You are given a query. Provide a description in the following format:
1. **Short Description**: A brief overview of what the query does.
2. **Input Types**: A list of expected inputs (e.g., parameters ...
3. **Output Types**: The output that the query produces. (e.g. ...
4. **Summary**: A concise explanation of the query's behavior ...
```

Code Agent. The code agent analyzes code snippets and describes the logic of a function overview, structured as a function overview, inputs, outputs, and a summary. Although the example in Prompt 2 illustrates a JavaScript-based snippet, the approach itself is language-agnostic. This agent can be easily adapted to other programming languages (e.g., Python, Java, R) by adjusting the prompt to that language.

Listing 2. Instructions for Code Agent (abridged)

```
You are given the JavaScript function of a data transformation
    process. It takes a data array as input and performs some
    transformation on it. Your task is to analyze ...
1. **Short Description**: A brief overview of the function's ...
2. **Input**: Description of the items of the input data array.
3. **Output**: Description of the result produced by the function.
    Focus directly on describing the structure and content ...
4. **Summary**: A concise summary of the function's behavior ...
```

Summary Agent. The summary agent synthesizes all previously generated descriptions into a process-level summary, as shown in Prompt 3. It uses the combined histories of all upstream node agents to generate a holistic summary of the data process graph, purpose, and results.

Listing 3. Instructions for Summary Agent

```
You are a data processing expert. Summarize the entire workflow ...
1. **Overall Purpose**: The overall objective of the workflow.
2. **Data Flow**: How data moves and transforms through the pipeline.
3. **Output**: The structure and nature of the final output.
4. **Final Summary**: A concise synthesis of the entire process.
```

This agent produces an accurate and cohesive summary by using localized documentation.

4.2   Caching

A multi-level caching mechanism improves scalability and efficiency by reusing previously generated documentation. As agents pass their conversation history to downstream node agents, every cache entry contains not just the final description of an artifact, but also the entire history of its agent. Cache eviction can be controlled by specifying a maximum cache age or manually deleting the folder that holds the cache items.

The caching operates at three levels. The *Query cache* stores descriptions for query nodes. The *Process step cache* maintains the histories for individual transformation and configuration nodes (which also include the descriptions of their upstream nodes). The *Process cache* stores the process descriptions and summaries, supporting reproducibility and regeneration of global reports when structures remain unchanged.

Together, these caches create a hierarchical reuse strategy that reduces latency, lowers the operational costs of the system, and promotes consistent documentation.

4.3   Description Generator

The description generator reproduces task-level documentation by traversing the parsed data processing graph in its logical execution order. For each task, it generates structured natural-language descriptions, capturing its functionality, inputs, outputs, and summary. This component leverages previously generated documentation as contextual history, propagating it to downstream nodes to preserve semantic continuity across the processes.

This component takes as input the data processing graph and processes the nodes in topological order, beginning with the root nodes. In this step, each root node is documented independently, as there are no upstream nodes. The appropriate agent is automatically selected based on the artifact type to ensure context-specific analysis. For downstream tasks, the description generator incorporates the conversation history of upstream nodes, enabling LLM to interpret and describe each task relative to the computational dependencies. For the converging nodes, their histories are aggregated into a shared context that captures the description of multiple data flows.

This context-aware design ensures that documentation remains coherent, avoids redundancy, and accurately reflects execution semantics. By grounding each task's documentation in the contextual history, the system minimizes hallucination and improves interpretability. Consequently, the generated documentation provides both detailed task-level and process-level documentation.

4.4   Summary Generator

While the description generator focuses on producing localized documentation of individual tasks, the summary generator is designed to synthesize these fragments into a coherent, system-level account of the data process. Leveraging LLMs, it moves beyond isolated descriptions and provides a higher-level and comprehensive summary that captures the purpose, functionality, output of the process, and flow of the entire process.

The summary generator operates by aggregating all task-level documentation and its dependencies as contextual information from the cache and incorporating it in a summary agent. This agent is responsible for emphasizing the high-level objective of the process by considering the contextual history and producing a holistic overview summary of the process. This holistic view is particularly important for users who need to understand the intent and outcome of a process without navigating the fine-grained documentation of individual tasks.

The strength of the summary generator lies in its contextualization. By considering connections between upstream and downstream tasks, it highlights how local operations collectively contribute to global system behavior. The generated results bridge the gap between technical documentation and conceptual understanding. It allows engineers to verify correctness and completeness, while providing non-technical users with a high-level overview of the system.

In general, the generated descriptions and summaries from the previous tasks are consolidated into a structured schema that preserves the order of tasks in the data processing graph and adds the generated documentation to each task as metadata.

5   Evaluation Results

This section outlines the evaluation setup and discusses the results.

5.1   Evaluation

As discussed earlier, traditional metrics such as BLEU or ROUGE are limited to similarity measurements using ground-truth texts. While these metrics are useful for benchmarking, they fail to capture the system behavior from multiple perspectives. To address these limitations and provide a more robust assessment, we adopt an *LLM-as-a-judge* approach that scores generated documentation from multiple dimensions.

We employ *GPT-4o-mini*, a general-purpose LLM with string code understanding capabilities and a competitive price-performance ratio, to generate both task-level and process-level documentation. For the evaluation, we select multiple LLMs rather than the one used for documentation to serve as independent judges: *GPT-4-o, LLaMA-4-Scout 17B, LLaMA 3.3 70B*, and *Qwen 2.5 Coder 32B*. These models differ in architecture, size and training focus which supports a mode robust assessment of the documentation quality. Presenting each LLM judge with the original data processing specifications, including tasks and their dependencies, and the corresponding generated documentation, it then evaluates the documentation based on five criteria: accuracy, comprehensibility, coherence, redundancy, and completeness. Ratings are assigned on a Likert scale (1–5). The evaluations focus on assessing whether the task-level descriptions faithfully reflect the behavior of each task.

In addition, we conducted the authors of data processes to perform an expert plausibility review of samples to get a rough overview of the appropriateness and correctness of the proposed results.

5.2   Preliminary Results

Our evaluation is conducted on 68 real-world data processing flows from the bank's software system, representing realistic and complex data processes and artifact scenarios. Each data processing flow contains between 1 and 24 tasks, with an average of 5.51 tasks per flow. Across all flows, the dataset includes an average of 4.88 transformation code artifacts and 1.79 cypher query artifacts per flow. The distribution reflects the heterogeneous nature of real-world data processing flows, ensuring the practicality of the system.

The quantitative results are reported as mean $\pm$ standard deviation, summarizing both the central tendency and variability of the evaluation scores. For each judge model m and evaluation criterion c, the mean score $\bar{s}_{m,c}$ is computed.

Table 1. LLM-as-a-judge evaluation of the generated documentation across five criteria. Scores are reported as mean ± standard deviation on a 1–5 Likert scale.

Criterion	GPT-4o	LLaMA-4 Scout 17B	LLaMA 3.3 70B	Qwen 2.5 Coder 32B	Mean $\bar{s}_{.,c}$
Accuracy	4.71 ± 0.20	4.24 ± 0.50	4.48 ± 0.45	4.55 ± 0.42	4.50
Comprehensibility	5.00 ± 0.00	4.22 ± 0.53	4.48 ± 0.49	4.60 ± 0.34	4.58
Coherence	4.86 ± 0.33	4.65 ± 0.47	4.98 ± 0.13	4.54 ± 0.37	4.76
Redundancy	4.40 ± 0.34	4.01 ± 0.49	4.20 ± 0.36	4.25 ± 0.46	4.22
Completeness	4.44 ± 0.25	4.55 ± 0.54	4.05 ± 0.43	4.56 ± 0.36	4.40
Overall $\bar{s}_m$	**4.68**	**4.33**	**4.44**	**4.50**	**4.49**

The standard deviation $\sigma_{m,c}$ quantifies the consistency of the evaluations.

An overall score $\bar{s}_m$ is also computed by averaging the arithmetic mean over all criteria C.

Table 1 summarizes the evaluation results. Each cell reports the mean ± std of the ratings assigned by a judge model. The mean represents the average quality of the generated documentation on a criterion across all data processing flows, while the standard deviation reflects the consistency of the model assessment. Lower standard deviation means a more stable and better relationship evaluation. Among individual models, *GPT-4-o* achieves the highest overall average ($\bar{s}_m = 4.68$), showing strong semantic and structure alignment of the generated documentation. LLaMA-4-Scout 17B produces low scores ($\bar{s}_m = 4.33$), which reflects a stricter evaluation tendency due to a smaller instruction tuning dataset.

Across evaluation criteria, the results are consistent. Coherence achieves the highest cross-model mean ($\bar{s}_{.,c} = 4.76$), depicting that the system preserves the logical flow and connectivity in the descriptions. Comprehensibility and accuracy also score high, indicating that the generated descriptions are understandable and faithful to the underlying tasks and artifacts.

The generated documentation obtains an overall mean score of 4.49 out of 5, demonstrating accuracy, coherence, and contextual consistency across all evaluated flows. The low variances in our evaluation indicate that the system is robust and maintains the documentation quality at all levels.

The expert plausibility review indicated that the generated documentation samples were generally correct and representative, with no severe errors identified.

6   Conclusion and Future Work

This paper presented a prototype LLM-powered system for automating the documentation of complex software data processing flows. Instead of focusing on an isolated artifact for summarization and documentation, the system integrates agents, multi-level caching, and contextual generation to produce consistent task- and process-level documentation.

The significance of this work lies in simplifying the use of process analysis techniques for software developers and architects. Our approach contributes toward making advanced data-driven process analysis more accessible to organizations that may not have dedicated process mining teams.

The results from the LLM-as-a-judge confirm the feasibility of LLM-based automation for large, heterogeneous data processing flows. Although promising, there are still areas for further exploration. First, as the current system considers that data processing specifications and dependencies are structured, future work may investigate approaches to parse unstructured flows and their relationships. Second, although the evaluation uses multiple LLMs as judges, future work should incorporate structured human assessments to validate subjective dimensions such as readability and practical usefulness.

Moreover, future research will explore how an LLM-based evaluation framework can be utilized not only for assessment but also for self-improvement of the documentation generation process. By integrating feedback from the LLM-as-a-judge evaluations, the system could iteratively refine its prompts and caching strategies. This feedback loop would enable continuous optimization of the generated documentation's accuracy and coherence, ultimately leading to a more adaptive and self-improving documentation system.

Acknowledgments. We thank the anonymous reviewers for their help in improving the manuscript. The research reported in this paper has been funded by the Federal Ministry for Innovation, Mobility and Infrastructure (BMIMI), the Federal Ministry for Economy, Energy and Tourism (BMWET), and the State of Upper Austria in the frame of the SCCH competence center INTEGRATE (FFG grant no. 892418) in the COMET - Competence Centers for Excellent Technologies Programme managed by Austrian Research Promotion Agency FFG.

References

1. Birru, H., Cicchetti, A., Latifaj, M.: Supporting automated documentation updates in continuous software development with large language models. In: Proceedings of the 20th International Conference on Evaluation of Novel Approaches to Software Engineering - vol. 1: ENASE, pp. 92–106. INSTICC, SciTePress (2025)
2. Chakrabarty, S., Pal, S.: Readmeready: free and customizable code documentation with LLMs - a fine-tuning approach. J. Open Source Softw. 10(108), 7489 (2025)
3. Crupi, G., Tufano, R., Velasco, A., Mastropaolo, A., Poshyvanyk, D., Bavota, G.: On the effectiveness of LLM-as-a-judge for code generation and summarization. IEEE Trans. Softw. Eng. **51**(08), 2329–2345 (2025)
4. de Miranda, F., Ferrao, R.C., Soler, D.P., Graglia, M.A.V.: Llm-based individual contribution summarization in software projects. In: Proceedings of the 2024 on ACM Virtual Global Computing Education Conference V. 2, SIGCSE Virtual 2024, pp. 307–308. Association for Computing Machinery, New York (2024)
5. Dvivedi, S.S., Vijay, V., Pujari, S.L.R., Lodh, S., Kumar, D.: A comparative analysis of large language models for code documentation generation. In: Proceedings of the 1st ACM International Conference on AI-Powered Software, pp. 65–73 (2024)
6. Fang, M., Yuan, X., Li, Y., Li, H., Fang, C., Du, J.: Enhanced prompting framework for code summarization with large language models. Proc. ACM Softw. Eng. **2**(ISSTA), 1630–1653 (2025)

7. Jelodar, H., Meymani, M., Razavi-Far, R.: Large language models (llms) for source code analysis: applications, models and datasets. arXiv preprint arXiv:2503.17502 (2025)
8. Macke, W., Doyle, M.: Testing the effect of code documentation on large language model code understanding. In: Duh, K., Gomez, H., Bethard, S. (eds.) Findings of the Association for Computational Linguistics: NAACL 2024, Mexico City, Mexico, June 2024, pp. 1044–1050. Association for Computational Linguistics (2024)
9. Makharev, V., Ivanov, V.: Code summarization beyond function level. In: 2025 IEEE/ACM International Workshop on Large Language Models for Code (LLM4Code), pp. 153–160. IEEE (2025)
10. Mastropaolo, A., Ciniselli, M., Di Penta, M., Bavota, G.: Evaluating code summarization techniques: a new metric and an empirical characterization. In: Proceedings of the IEEE/ACM 46th International Conference on Software Engineering, ICSE '24, New York, NY, USA. Association for Computing Machinery (2024)
11. Robinson, J., Kummerfeld, J.K.: Simple and effective baselines for code summarisation evaluation. arXiv preprint arXiv:2505.19392 (2025)
12. Song, H., Su, H., Shalyminov, I., Cai, J., Mansour, S.: FineSurE: fine-grained summarization evaluation using LLMs. In: Ku, L.W., Martins, A., Srikumar, V. (eds.) Proceedings of the 62nd Annual Meeting of the Association for Computational Linguistics, Bangkok, Thailand, August 2024, vol. 1: Long Papers, pp. 906–922. Association for Computational Linguistics (2024)
13. Su, C.Y., Bansal, A., Huang, Y., Li, T.J.J., McMillan, C.: Context-aware code summary generation. J. Syst. Softw. **231**, 112580 (2026)
14. Virk, Y., Devanbu, P., Ahmed, T.: Calibration of large language models on code summarization. Proc. ACM Softw. Eng. **2**(FSE) (2025)
15. Wu, Y., et al.: Can large language models serve as evaluators for code summarization? IEEE Trans. Softw. Eng. (2025)
16. Xia, M., Maharjan, S., Song, M.: Automated code summarization by training large language models with crowdsourced knowledge. In: 2025 IEEE/ACIS 23rd International Conference on Software Engineering Research, Management and Applications (SERA), Los Alamitos, CA, USA, May 2025, pp. 126–133. IEEE Computer Society (2025)

Software Testing and AI

Improving the Quality of GitHub Copilot Generated Unit Tests

Max Schallermayer[1(✉)] and Markus Schnappinger[2]

[1] Technical University of Munich (TUM), Munich, Germany
`schaller@in.tum.de`
[2] msg systems ag, Ismaning, Germany
`markus.schnappinger@msg.group`

Abstract. Unit tests are essential for software quality control, but remain costly and tedious to write. AI coding assistants like GitHub Copilot can generate unit tests automatically, yet the practical effectiveness of such tests is poorly understood. Prior work has mostly focused on AI models in isolation, leaving open how actual tools like Copilot perform in realistic developer workflows.

This paper presents a systematic study of Copilot-generated unit tests for Java across five real-world projects. We evaluate three factors for improving test quality: (i) prompts to prevent compile errors, (ii) prompts emphasizing testing best practices and fault detection, and (iii) the choice of the underlying AI model. Our evaluation combines compilation rate, line coverage, and mutation coverage, providing both syntactic and fault-detection perspectives. A custom tool allows for test generation, prompt variation, and evaluation without human intervention.

We find that prompts aimed at preventing compile errors are not beneficial in practice. Goal-setting prompts that instruct Copilot to maximize fault detection lead to a sharp decline in compilation success, limiting the number of usable test classes. However, for those classes that do compile, these prompts consistently yield higher mutation coverage than both the standard prompt and even developer-written baselines, highlighting their potential for strong fault-detection effectiveness if compilation challenges are addressed. The choice of LLM is most influential: GPT-4.1 achieves the highest compilation rate, while Anthropic Sonnet variants (e.g., Sonnet 3.7, Sonnet 4) deliver higher mutation coverage and greater fault-detection capability, albeit at the cost of more frequent compile errors. This creates a practical trade-off: developers seeking stronger fault sensitivity may prefer Sonnet models, provided they can accommodate higher error rates, while those prioritizing fewer compile errors may favor GPT-4.1. Finally, we show how simple and pragmatic post-processing can substantially increase the practical usability of generated tests. This study provides actionable guidance for practitioners using GitHub Copilot, providing empirical results and translating them into concrete decisions about prompts, models, and repair strategies.

Keywords: AI-Assisted Software Engineering · GitHub Copilot · Test Generation

© The Author(s), under exclusive license to Springer Nature Switzerland AG 2026
M. Dorner et al. (Eds.): SWQD 2026, LNBIP 581, pp. 127–146, 2026.
https://doi.org/10.1007/978-3-032-24216-7_8

1   Introduction

Unit testing is a cornerstone of modern software engineering, enabling early fault detection and long-term maintainability. Yet, writing comprehensive unit tests remains tedious and time-consuming. Automated test generation aims to reduce this burden while preserving software quality.

GitHub Copilot is among the most widely used AI coding assistants. It integrates into developers' IDEs and can, among other features, generate unit tests for a given class under test. Most prior work prompts LLMs directly rather than evaluating Copilot within the development environment, leaving open questions about real-world applicability to developers' workflows. Moreover, while broader LLM research demonstrates that prompt design and model choice substantially affect output quality [11,14], Copilot-focused evaluations typically use only a single prompt and a single underlying model, leaving unexplored whether these factors could similarly improve Copilot's performance. This paper addresses these gaps. Our study combines a pre-study to establish a baseline with controlled experiments varying prompts and models. To evaluate the practical benefit of the generated tests, we refer to their compilation rate, coverage metrics, and mutation coverage.

Our study finds that Copilot's test generation for Java is strongly influenced by prompt design and model choice: Warning Copilot about common compilation pitfalls does not consistently improve outcomes; its benefits are project-dependent. Advising to apply testing best practices results in fewer compiling tests. But if they do compile, these tests exhibit higher fault sensitivity. The choice of underlying LLM is most impactful, with GPT-4.1 achieving the highest compilation rate and Anthropic Sonnet variants delivering superior mutation coverage, revealing a trade-off between syntactic correctness and fault detection. Simple post-processing further increases the usability of generated tests.

Our systematic study quantifies these effects across real-world projects, providing actionable guidance for practitioners and establishing a mutation-centric evaluation baseline for Copilot in realistic workflows. In the spirit of open science, our tool to control GitHub Copilot and all results are shared in [12].

2   Related Work

Automated unit test generation has gained significant attention in recent years. While traditional search-based and heuristic-driven approaches, have been widely studied, recent research has just begun to explore the effectiveness of large language models (LLMs) to generate software tests. For example, EvoSuite [4] is a search-based tool that generates unit tests for Java code. It uses a genetic algorithm to search for tests that maximize code coverage. Tang et al. [17] compared the unit test generation capabilities of ChatGPT using GPT-3.5 Turbo with Evo-Suite. They found that ChatGPT generated compilable tests in 69.9% of cases. In contrast, EvoSuite has been found to produced non-compilable test suites in only about 3.4% of the cases [13]. Schäfer et al. [11] evaluated the effectiveness of

LLMs for automated unit test generation in JavaScript. They introduced TEST-PILOT, a tool that adaptively changes the prompt given to the LLM by providing different forms of context, including function signatures, implementations, documentation, and usage examples of the method under test. They found that this improved prompting strategy increased statement coverage substantially, reaching a median of 70.2%. By contrast, our study focuses on GitHub Copilot. It assembles the necessary code context automatically [10], which allows aiming at higher-level instructions in the prompt, such as warning against common mistakes or asking for tests that maximize fault detection.

In [14], Siddiq et al. generated Java unit tests for JUnit by prompting the LLMs GPT-3.5 Turbo and StarCoder [8]. They found that, without fixing the generated code through heuristics, 43% of the generated test classes compiled successfully for GPT-3.5 Turbo and 70% for StarCoder. This work highlights that the choice of model can substantially influence the quality of generated tests, which motivates our own experiments with different LLMs. However, the models they studied (GPT-3.5 Turbo and StarCoder) are now out of date compared to currently available models such as GPT-4.1, Claude Sonnet, or Gemini 2.0.

El Haji et al. [3] generated Python unit tests with Copilot. They deleted the body of existing developer-written test methods and used Copilot manually inside a code editor to fill the gaps. The authors generated tests both with and without surrounding test code and with different commenting strategies. Using surrounding tests as context and a minimal commenting strategy, they found that in 30.4% of cases the tests had syntactic errors, in 34.8% of cases they failed due to incorrect assertions, and in 21.7% they passed as expected. The authors speculated that in their experimental setup, Copilot did not consider the code under test and instead only the surrounding test code. In our work, we explicitly attach the class under test as context before generating the test class to provide Copilot with the necessary information.

Sundqvist [16] investigated the use of GitHub Copilot for generating tests aimed at detecting real bugs in the Defects4J dataset. They employed a single prompt and restricted their evaluation to GPT-4 as the underlying model. In their experiments, only 37% of the generated tests were directly usable without developer intervention. Of these tests, merely 6% were able to reveal real bugs. However, when developers assisted by fixing errors in the generated code, the proportion of usable tests increased to 80% and the bug detection rate rose to 18%. Their study differs from ours in two important aspects: they do not vary prompts or models, and they focus on real bug detection rather than mutation testing as a proxy for fault detection.

Wang et al. [20] provide a benchmark for project-level unit test generation called *ProjectTest*. They evaluate nine LLMs, including GPT-4, GPT-o1, Claude 3.5 Sonnet, and Gemini 2.0 Flash. However, their evaluation focuses on compile rates and coverage as quality metrics, whereas we additionally consider mutation coverage. Furthermore, *ProjectTest* does not vary the prompts used.

Gap: In summary, although research on automated unit test generation with LLMs is expanding, only a limited number of studies have examined GitHub Copilot in depth. Existing works typically rely on a single LLM and a constant prompt, without systematically analyzing how variations in prompt design or model choice influence results. Moreover, prior evaluations have concentrated on metrics such as syntactic correctness, line coverage, or real bug detection, while neglecting mutation coverage as a proxy for fault detection. This leaves a gap in understanding the practical effectiveness of Copilot, which is particularly relevant given its role as a widely used, developer-facing tool. Our study addresses this gap by systematically varying prompts and models within Copilot and by incorporating mutation coverage alongside established quality metrics.

3   Study Design

To structure our investigation, we first conducted a preliminary assessment of Copilot in its default configuration. The following subsection details this pre-study and its findings.

3.1   Pre-Study

We conducted a pre-study to evaluate Copilot's ability to generate Java unit tests using its default model (GPT-4o) and the preset command (`/tests`).

Our results showed that Copilot-generated test classes frequently failed to compile successfully, limiting their immediate usability. On average, only 62% of the generated test classes compiled, and of those, 65% contained exclusively passing test methods. This means that only about 40% of the generated classes were directly usable for fault detection without manual fixes. Provided the nature of our dataset (Sect. 3.4), we assume the system under test to be correct. Hence, all generated tests should initially passed.

For the subset of classes that did compile and pass, we measured mutation coverage to assess their fault-detection capability (Sect. 3.3). We found that developer-written tests achieved an average mutation coverage of 59%, compared to 54% for Copilot-generated classes. While Copilot-generated test classes achieved comparable or even higher mutation coverage in about half of the cases, developer-written tests clearly outperformed them in the other half.

Overall, Copilot shows potential as a test generation tool, but the quality of generated tests in the baseline configuration can be improved.

3.2   Research Questions

Building on the findings of the pre-study, this study aims to enhance Copilot-generated unit tests to make them more useful for developers. In particular, we investigate three possible actions developers can take to improve the output of GitHub Copilot: (1) modifying the prompt to prevent previously observed compile errors, (2) modifying the prompt to explicitly maximize fault detection capabilities, and (3) choosing an appropriate LLM used by Copilot.

RQ1: What is the impact of adding error-prevention prompts that warn against common pitfalls? In our pre-study, recurring compile errors included type mismatches, inheritance mistakes, and hallucinated methods/variables. We test whether prompt engineering can improve generated test quality by warning Copilot against these pitfalls.

RQ2: What is the impact of using goal-setting prompts that instruct Copilot to maximize fault detection? We examine whether instructing Copilot to follow testing best practices, such as boundary cases, equivalence partitioning, and precise assertions, improves test effectiveness.

RQ3: What is the impact of using different underlying LLMs on the quality of Copilot-generated test classes? Copilot supports multiple LLMs. We investigate whether alternative models (e.g., GPT o3-mini, Claude 3.5 Sonnet, Gemini Flash) generate higher-quality test classes than the default model.

3.3   Evaluation Metrics

To answer our research questions, we rely on a set of quantitative metrics capturing both syntactic correctness and fault-detection capability. Compilation rate and mutation coverage were used in our pre-study, too; for the main investigation, we also analyze the number of test methods and lines of code.

Compilation Rate. Compilation Rate is the ratio of successfully compiled test classes to total generated classes. It considers test classes instead of single test methods, since compilation errors can affect the entire class.

$$\text{Compilation Rate} = \frac{|Successfully\ Compiled\ Test\ Classes|}{|Total\ Number\ of\ Generated\ Test\ Classes|} \tag{1}$$

Mutation Coverage. Mutation coverage [5] measures how well a test suite detects faults by introducing small changes (mutations) and checking if tests fail. Detected mutations are "killed"; undetected ones "survive." This metric is widely recognized as a proxy for fault detection effectiveness [13]. To introduce faults and compute mutation coverage, we use PIT [1], a mutation testing framework for Java.

$$\text{Mutation Coverage} = \frac{|Killed\ Mutants|}{|Total\ Number\ of\ Mutants|} \tag{2}$$

Line Coverage Line coverage [22] measures the proportion of executable source lines exercised by at least one test method: While mutation coverage is a stronger indicator of fault detection, line coverage is a useful complementary metric.

$$\text{Line Coverage} = \frac{|Covered\ Lines|}{|Total\ Executable\ Lines|} \tag{3}$$

Number of Test Methods. The number of test methods counts methods annotated with `@Test` or `@ParameterizedTest` in a generated test class.

Lines of Code (LOC). LOC measures the size of a generated test class. Tracking test methods and LOC is important as it helps interpreting mutation coverage scores [9].

3.4   Dataset

The dataset is based on Defects4J [6], a repository of real-world Java projects with known faults and patches. Defects4J is widely used dard prompt across [7,15,17–19], making our results comparable to prior work. We focus on fault-free versions of the systems, interpreting failing Copilot tests as test errors, not system faults [3,11,14]. Thus, we assume the system under test is correct and all generated tests should initially pass. We then introduce artificial mutations and check if tests detect them.

Projects must be implemented in Java, use Maven, and rely on JUnit 5. Of 17 Defects4J projects, 13 met these criteria. To avoid bias towards the Jackson system family, we selected at most one of them, leaving 11 possible projects, from which we randomly selected five.

For prompting strategy experiments, we included all eligible classes, yielding 604 test classes. We only considered classes with a direct mapping from a class under test (CUT) to an existing developer-written test class.

For LLM variation experiments, we restricted to at most 30 test classes per project due to Copilot's monthly quota for premium requests (Table 1).

Table 1. Selected projects and meta info

Project	Version Hash	Version Date	Keyword	n Classes
JFreeChart	21922c1c	23 June 2024	Chart/Visual	332
Commons-CLI	1a074e40	31 December 2024	CLI parsing	24
Commons-Collections	c61f84a0	01 January 2025	Datastructures	188
Jackson-Core	58feb270	12 December 2024	JSON processing	28
Jsoup	33d0d46d	01 December 2024	HTML parsing	30

3.5   Tooling and Experiment Execution

GitHub Copilot is an AI-powered code completion tool integrated into IDEs such as Visual Studio Code. Unlike direct prompting of an LLM, Copilot automatically leverages surrounding project code and editor state to produce tailored suggestions. Our tooling and prompts are available in our replication package [12].

Previous work [3,21] manually interacted with Copilot in the editor to generate outputs. This manual approach is tedious and error-prone. To generate tests at scale, we implemented a Visual Studio Code extension that interacts with Copilot to generate test classes. Our tool writes the prompt into the chat window, attaches the class under test as context, and starts generation.

After the tests are created, we apply two trivial pre-processing steps before compiling them. First, we locate the package declaration and move it to the top of the file. Second, we use the tool `javaimports` [2] to add missing import statements. During initial experiments, Copilot struggled both with correct package declaration at the top of the file and with import statements. These steps alter the generation of Copilot and increase the compilation rate. However, these errors are trivial to fix for most developers or can even be mitigated automatically by an IDE. In our study, we focus on severe syntactic errors that are not easily fixable. After generating and pre-processing the test class, we then compile, build and execute the test class with Maven and save the output.

With a reproducible pipeline for generating, preprocessing, and executing Copilot-generate test classes, we next investigate the research questions outlined in Sect. 3.2.

3.6   Handling Failing Tests

Copilot may generate test classes that compile successfully but contain failing tests. In this study, we assume the system under test to be correct, and therefore treat such classes as faulty output by Copilot and exclude them from mutation testing. To validate this assumption and ensure that failing tests do not indicate actual bugs in the system under test, we manually sampled 10 random test failures and analyzed their root causes. In all 10 cases, the failures arose from incorrect assumptions in Copilot's assertions, confirming that test failures should be attributed to faulty generation rather than system defects.

3.7   LLM Choice

Prior studies show model choice substantially impacts compilation rate and correctness of generated tests [14]. We systematically evaluate multiple models, which are state-of-the-art as of the time of this study.

All models used the same dataset (Sect. 3.4) and test generation pipeline. To keep setup comparable, we used identical prompts for all models (see [12]). Table 2 lists the LLMs and their metadata. Notably, the models vary in context window size and reasoning abilities.

3.8   Compile Error Optimized Prompt

A key observation in our pre-study was frequent compilation failures in Copilot-generated test classes. We analyzed compilation errors from using Copilot without improvements, identified common mistakes and designed an improved prompt warning against these errors. Our hypothesis is that targeted prompting will reduce compilation errors and increase compilation rate. Table 3 summarizes the most common errors and their frequency.

Table 2. Evaluated LLMs and metadata

Model	Provider	Context Window	Reasoning Capability
GPT-4o (pre-study)	OpenAI	63,833	No
GPT-4.1	OpenAI	111,452	No
GPT-o3-mini	OpenAI	63,833	Yes
Sonnet 3.5	Anthropic	81,644	No
Sonnet 3.7	Anthropic	89,833	No
Sonnet 3.7 Thinking	Anthropic	89,833	Yes
Sonnet 4	Anthropic	111,836	Yes
Gemini-2.0-flash	Google	127,833	No

Table 3. Most frequent compilation error messages in Copilot-generated test classes (GPT-4.1, standard prompt)

Error message	Frequency
"cannot find symbol"	69
"is not abstract and does not override abstract method"	47
"incompatible types"	24
"method does not override or implement a method from a supertype"	18
"cannot be applied to given types"	17
"package .* does not exist"	12

The error `cannot find symbol` is the most frequent error. It often results from Copilot referencing private or non-existent members, reflecting hallucinations. The error `is not abstract and does not override abstract method` occurs when a generated class extends an abstract class or implements an interface but fails to implement all required methods. The error `incompatible types` indicates type mismatches, such as wrong argument types or incompatible assignments. The message `method does not override or implement a method from a supertype` is triggered when Copilot adds an `@Override` annotation without a corresponding method in the superclass or interface. The error type `cannot be applied to given types` arises when Copilot invokes a method with incorrect parameters. Eventually, `package .* does not exist` reflects missing or incorrect import statements, often due to hallucinated libraries or package names.

Improved Prompt. Based on this analysis, we designed an improved prompt (available in the replication package [12]) to guide Copilot away from frequent pitfalls. The prompt warns against referencing non-existent members, misusing inheritance, and incorrect method calls. It encourages adherence to JUnit 5 conventions and avoidance of unnecessary external libraries. The prompt includes the `#codebase` tag to help Copilot search for related code.

3.9   Goal-Based Prompt

In addition to baseline and compile-error optimized prompts, we designed a third strategy to steer Copilot toward more thorough test suites (available in the replication package [12]). We explicitly instruct the model to generate tests sensitive to faults: if a bug is introduced, at least one test should fail. The prompt emphasizes exhaustiveness and variety.

The prompt reflects two established test design strategies. First, it highlights boundary and numeric edge cases, encouraging Copilot to generate inputs at extreme values, special constants, and edge conditions. Second, it introduces equivalence partitioning, asking for representative cases from distinct input categories. Instructions include using precise assertions and checking return values, exceptions, and side effects.

The goal is for Copilot to produce test classes that systematically explore the input space and validate behavior under diverse conditions. We do not mention mutation analysis directly, to avoid biasing the model, but expect a more comprehensive suite will improve fault detection.

4   Results

We now present the outcomes of applying our three strategies compile error optimized prompts, prompts with testing objectives, and LLM choice–to the dataset. For each, we analyze compilation success, coverage, and mutation testing, comparing to developer-written baselines where applicable. This assesses the effectiveness of different approaches for improving Copilot-generated unit tests.

4.1   Impact of Compile Error Optimized Prompts

Figure 1 shows compilation rates for the standard prompt versus the prompt designed to reduce compilation errors.

In three projects, the improved prompt slightly increases compilation rate; in two, the rate decreases marginally. Overall, there is no clear improvement in compilation rate using the specialized prompt.

Figure 2 presents mutation coverage, line coverage, and test suite size per project, comparing developer-written tests with Copilot-generated tests using the standard prompt, compile error prompt, and goal-based prompt. Each vertical band represents a metric; each horizontal line corresponds to a prompt. The y-axis is scaled to 01. For mutation and line coverage, the mapping is direct; for number of test methods and lines of code, values are normalized, with minimum and maximum annotated for interpretability.

Across all projects, the compile error optimized prompt yields more usable test classes than the standard prompt. For commons-cli and jsoup, the compile error prompt achieves notably higher mutation and line coverage. These are also the projects with increased compile rate (Fig. 1). For the other three projects, both prompts perform similarly, with no consistent advantage. No improvement

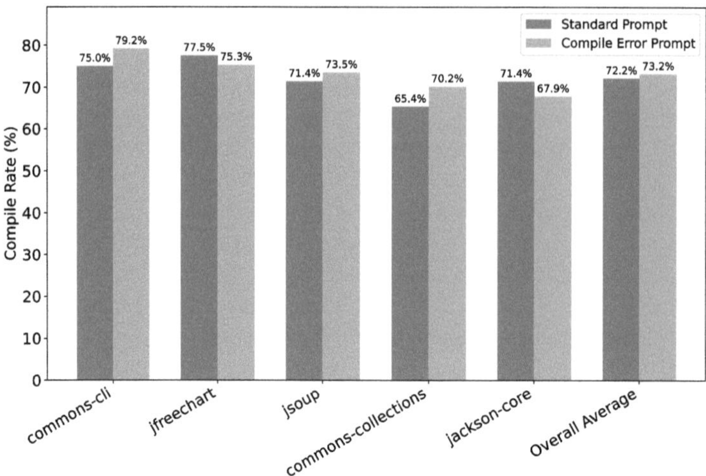

Fig. 1. Comparison of compilation rates between the standard prompt and the compile error prompt.

in mutation coverage is seen for commons-collections, despite increased compile rate. Developer-written tests consistently achieve higher mutation coverage than Copilot-generated tests. The compile error prompt does not degrade coverage compared to the standard prompt.

Overall, the effect of the compile error prompt on compilation rate is inconclusive, with some projects improving and others decreasing. Mutation and line coverage are not reduced by the compile error prompt.

4.2   Impact of Prompt with Testing Objectives

Figure 3 shows the goal-based prompt strongly decreases compilation rate across all projects except commons-cli, where it remains unchanged. As visualized in Fig. 2, for commons-cli, the goal-based prompt produces higher coverage metrics and larger test suites than the standard prompt. For other projects, it results in lower coverage and smaller test suites.

Due to the drop in compilation rate, aggregated mutation coverage may not reliably indicate effectiveness. Many generated test classes do not compile or contain failing tests, so they cannot be included in the full suite for project-level mutation testing. When mutating the entire project, some classes lack runnable Copilot test classes to catch mutants. To provide a fairer comparison, we also measure mutation coverage per test class, i.e. mutating only the corresponding class under test and executing only its associated test class.

In Fig. 4, each boxplot shows the distribution of mutation coverage values from per-class evaluation. Each class under test is mutated independently, and only its corresponding test class is executed. When considering single test classes, the goal-based prompt achieves higher median mutation coverage than both

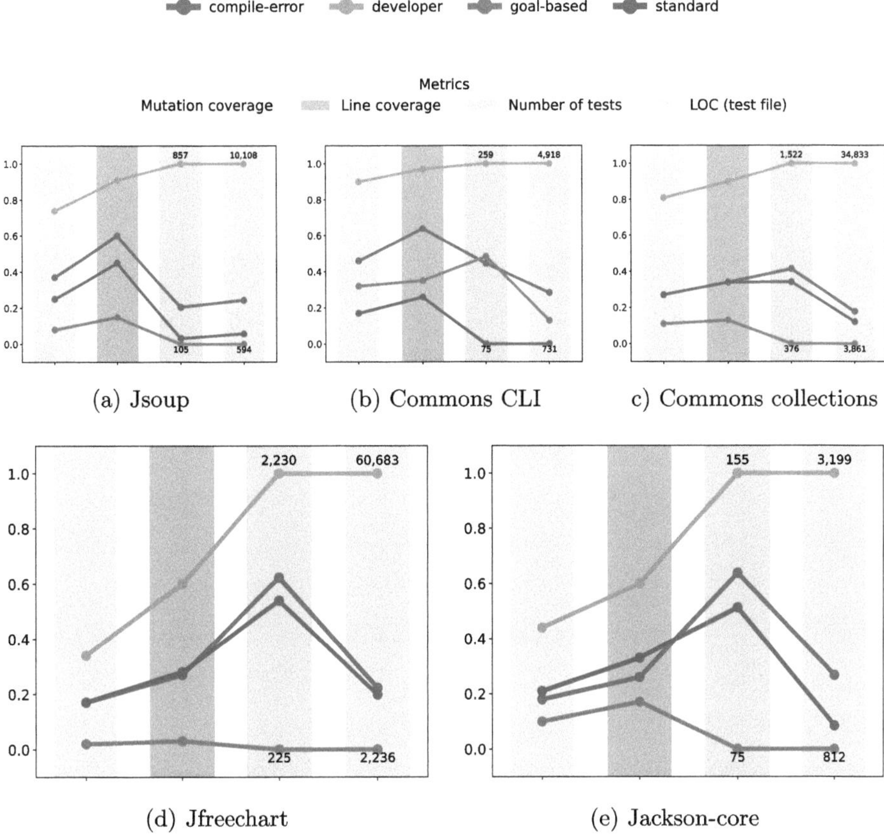

Fig. 2. Mutation coverage, line coverage, and test suite size per project for the developer tests and for the Copilot-generated tests with the standard prompt, compile-error prompt, and goal-based prompt.

developer-written tests and the standard prompt across all projects. This suggests that, although fewer test classes compile, those that do show particularly high fault-detection capabilities (Table 1).

4.3   Impact of LLM Choice

Having analyzed the effects of compile error prompts and goal-based prompts, we now turn to our third strategy: varying the underlying large language model. The lowest compilation rate observed was 50% for Sonnet 3.7 on jackson-core; the highest was 83.3%, achieved by GPT-4.1 and o3-mini on commons-cli. While GPT-4.1 achieves the highest average compilation rate across all projects (74.4%), its performance varies substantially at the project level. In some cases, such as jackson-core and jfreechart, other LLMs outperform it. Notably, the rea-

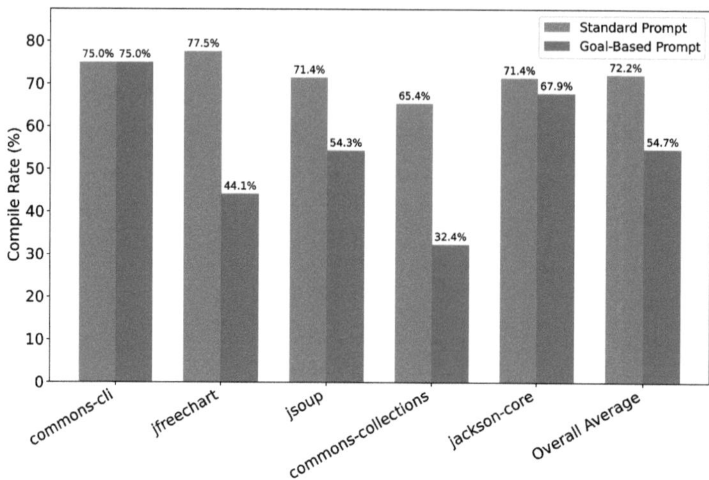

Fig. 3. Comparison of compilation rates between the standard prompt and the goal-based prompt.

Table 4. Compilation rates (rounded) across projects and LLMs

	GPT 4o	GPT 4.	Sonnet 3.7	Sonnet 3.5	Sonnet-3.7 -thinking	Sonnet 4	o3-mini	Gemini-2.0 -flash
jsoup	59	71	54	66	63	66	69	66
jackson-core	63	71	50	75	79	68	57	75
commons-cli	38	83	67	67	71	79	83	79
commons-collections	81	74	71	69	69	71	77	66
jfreechart	73	71	66	80	69	60	74	74
Average across projects	63	74	62	71	70	69	72	72

soning models o3-mini and Sonnet-3.7-thinking have average compilation rates of 72.1% and 69.9%, not exceeding the best non-reasoning models (Fig. 5).

Across all projects, developer-written tests achieve the highest mutation coverage (average 64.6%), ahead of the best Copilot-backed LLMs (e.g., Sonnet-3.7-thinking and Sonnet 4 at $\approx$ 44.4%). Also, developer-written tests have the largest test suite size in 4 of 5 projects. Thus, the developer baseline remains strongest in fault detection and typically among the largest suites.

Ranking LLMs by mutation coverage and averaging the ranks across projects, GPT-4.1 and o3-mini perform worst overall, with average ranks of 7.4 and 7.2, respectively (lower rank is better). The strongest AI models are Sonnet-3.7-thinking (average rank $\approx$ 2.6), Sonnet-3.7/Sonnet 4 (both $\approx$ 3.2), followed by Gemini-2.0-flash and Sonnet-3.5. Models generating more tests tend to achieve higher mutation coverage, but large suites do not guarantee higher coverage. This is illustrated by two cases: (i) For jfreechart: GPT 4.1 produces a large suite (1,307 tests) but achieves low mutation coverage (17%), far below developers (2,230 tests, 34%) and several smaller LLM suites. (ii) For jackson-core: Sonnet 4

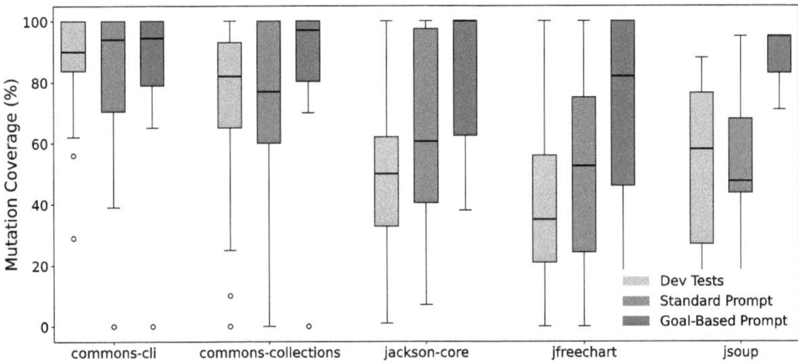

Fig. 4. Per-class mutation coverage comparison between developer-written tests, standard prompt, and goal-based prompt.

yields more tests (284) than developers (155), yet its mutation coverage (41%) does not surpass the developer baseline (44%).

5   Discussion

5.1   Implications for Developers

Our results have several practical implications for developers using Copilot for unit test generation. We evaluated three strategies: prompts optimized to reduce compile errors, goal-oriented prompts to maximize fault detection, and LLM variation, each with different strengths and limitations. Our results can be summarized as follows: (i) Prompts to prevent compile errors are not considered beneficial in practice; (ii) Prompts setting the goal to find faults and adhere to testing best practices **can** improve per-class quality but require strategies to address compilation failures; (iii) Choosing an appropriate LLM has the largest impact, with GPT 4.1 best for compilation and Sonnet models best for fault detection.

Compile Error Oriented Prompting. With respect to RQ1 (What is the impact of adding error-prevention prompts that warn against common pitfalls?), our study shows that such prompts do not yield systematic improvements. The corresponding prompt explicitly warned Copilot against common sources of compilation failure. However, this strategy did not improve compilation rates by large margins; in some projects it even reduced them. Moreover, the types of compilation errors observed remained largely unchanged compared to the standard prompt. This indicates Copilot continued making the same mistakes despite the additional guidance. Mutation coverage outcomes were inconclusive, with minor gains in some projects and losses in others. Taken together, these findings suggest that the compile error prompt cannot be recommended as a practical strategy for developers: It adds prompt complexity without providing consistent benefits.

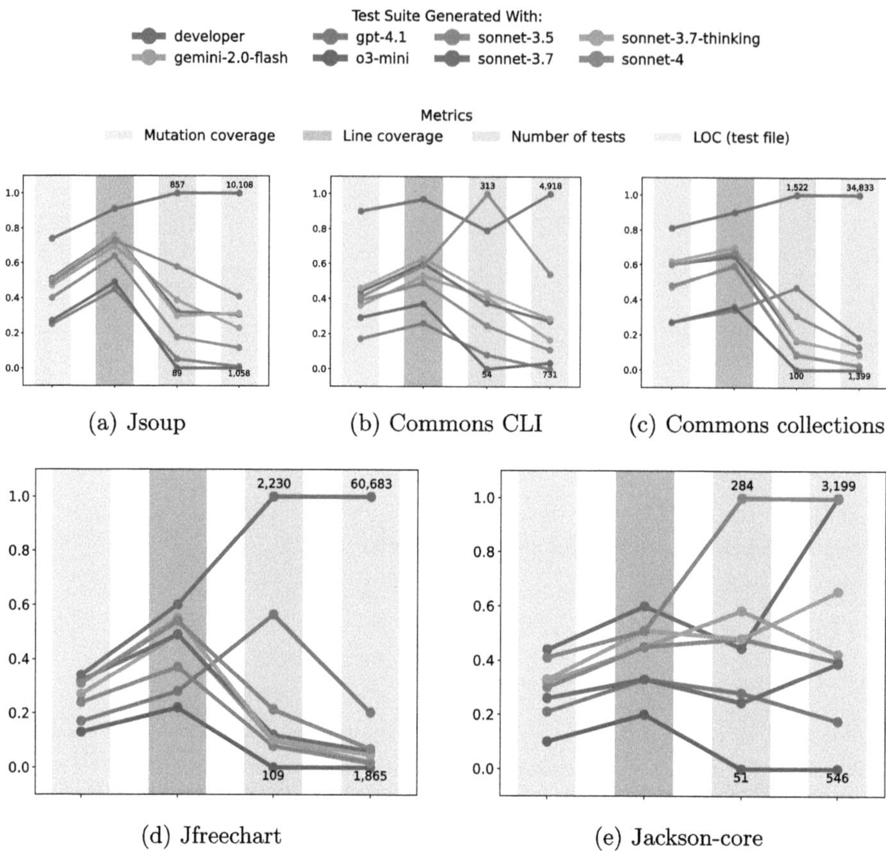

Fig. 5. Mutation coverage, line coverage, and test suite size per project for the developer tests and for Copilot-generated tests. The Copilot tests were all generated using the same standard prompt but with different LLMs.

Setting Fault Detection as a Goal. With respect to RQ2 (What is the impact of using goal-setting prompts that instruct Copilot to maximize fault detection?), we provide a nuanced answer. We found such prompts produced lower aggregated mutation coverage than the standard prompt. This outcome is largely attributed to its sharply reduced compilation rate, which meant that far fewer test classes could be run to detect mutations. To obtain a clearer picture, we also analyzed mutation coverage at the level of individual test classes. Here, the goal-setting prompt showed promising results: across all projects, the distribution of per-class mutation coverage was higher than for both the standard prompt and the developer baseline. This suggests that when test classes compile successfully, the goal-setting strategy can lead to tests with high fault-detection capability. The central challenge is therefore to mitigate the increased number of compilation failures.

Choice of LLM. With respect to RQ3 (What is the impact of using different underlying LLMs on the quality of Copilot-generated test classes?), our results demonstrate that model choice has a clear and measurable effect. While GPT 4.1 emerged as the strongest option for reliable compilation, other models like Sonnet 3.7 and Sonnet 4, offer superior mutation coverage and greater fault-detection capability.

Compilation rates were highest for GPT 4.1, confirming its suitability as a baseline for developers primarily concerned with syntactic correctness and ease of use. Interestingly, reasoning-enabled models such as o3-mini and Sonnet-3.7-thinking, which are often perceived as superior, did not outperform GPT 4.1 in terms of compilation success.

Considering mutation coverage, GPT 4.1 consistently performed worse than alternative model, with the best-performing models being Sonnet-3.7-thinking, Sonnet 3.7, and Sonnet 4. These models not only achieved higher coverage but also produced more usable tests per class, despite lower average compilation rates. This indicates that although fewer classes compile, the classes that do succeed are more thorough and contain larger test suites.

It is also important to consider cost and availability. Requests to GPT 4.1 are (as the time of this study) included in GitHub Copilot's standard usage, whereas premium models such as the Sonnet family count against a limited monthly quota of premium requests. Thus, while Sonnet models may offer better fault-detection capability, their use may be constrained in practice by pricing models and request limits.

For developers, our findings result in a fundamental trade-off: If the priority is to maximize fault-detection probability and they are willing to tolerate a higher number of compile errors, Sonnet models are the more promising choice. If developers prioritize syntactic correctness and thus ease of use, they are best served by GPT 4.1.

5.2   Outlook: Handling Compilation Errors and Failing Tests

A recurring limitation in our study was the relatively low compilation rate of Copilot-generated test classes, which directly restricts the number of tests available for mutation testing and, ultimately, fault detection. In addition, we observed failing test methods even when classes did compile. Since we assume the system under test to be correct, such failing tests represent errors in the generated suite rather than genuine faults. From a developer's perspective, encountering such issues would likely lead to attempts at fixing the generated test code rather than discarding it entirely. To approximate this behavior, we experimented with a simple strategy. Instead of repairing the faulty logic, we removed all test methods that either triggered compilation errors or failed at runtime. In practice, this translates to developers pragmatically commenting out non-compiling generated tests in order to at least use the remaining generated tests.

We applied this technique exemplarily to the results of the jsoup project generated with the goal-based prompt. The improvements were substantial. Mutation coverage increased from 8% to 55%, while line coverage rose from 15% to

77%. The usable test suite also grew considerably, from 105 test methods (594 LOC) to 560 test methods (4,733 LOC). As reported in Sect. 4, the goal-setting prompt without that post-processing reduced the compile rate for jsoup from 71.4% (standard prompt) to 54.3%. Applying the repair strategy, the compilation rate reached 80%. Notably, the rate did not reach 100% due to structural errors that affect the test class itself instead of individual test methods. A typical example are test classes that fail to implement all required abstract methods. In that case, the entire class is rendered unusable.

These results suggest that even simple, pragmatic repair strategies can drastically improve the usability of Copilot-generated test classes. This highlights the potential for lightweight automated or semi-automated post-processing steps to bridge the gap between raw Copilot output and tests. We therefore recommend further investigation into more advanced repair strategies, which could amplify these benefits without discarding as much generated content.

5.3   Threats to Validity

A key threat to validity is the use of mutation coverage as a proxy for fault-detection effectiveness. Prior work notes that mutation scores can be misleading, especially when test suite size is controlled, and that strong gains in real-fault detection appear only at very high mutation scores [9]. However, our claims are comparative within the same projects and classes, not absolute on real faults. We use mutation coverage to compare prompts and LLMs on a fixed codebase, thus framing mutation coverage as a relative attribute. Also, we report the amount of generated tests and their LOC alongside mutation coverage. This allows readers to interpret coverage in context, not isolation. Eventually, we argue that while larger suites often correlate with higher mutation coverage, size alone does not explain outcomes. For example, some larger suites underperform (e.g., jfreechart with GPT 4.1), and more tests do not always surpass the developer baseline (e.g., jackson-core with Sonnet 4).

High mutation coverage scores may result from generating a large quantity of test cases rather than from high individual test quality. While we acknowledge this limitation for developer-written test suites, automated generation can produce many tests quickly and cheaply. Even if coverage gains are size-driven, they still improve fault detection. Thus, quantity of tests is not a drawback for automated techniques.

Our study uses open-source projects from Defects4J. Copilot and the LLMs may have been trained on similar code, potentially inflating performance by reproducing known patterns. Thus, our findings may not transfer to proprietary software. However, this affects all models equally, so comparative results remain fair.

By the nature of LLMs, Copilot generations are non-deterministic; repeated runs can yield different results. This threatens the stability of observed results. All strategies and LLMs were executed under the same automation and tooling. In our pre-study, we repeated experiments ten times for one projects and found compilation and pass rates to be consistent between runs. Thus, we decided to run each configuration once per project in the main study.

5.4   Future Work

As of now, low compilation rates remain a bottleneck. We showed that removing non-compiling test methods can substantially improve usability, compilation rates, and mutation coverage. Future work should explore advanced approaches, such as adding compiler errors to the context of the prompt, automatically applying Copilot's `/fix` command, or agentic methods that iteratively repair tests. Beyond error prevention and goal setting, techniques like chain-of-thought prompting or few-shot exemplars may further improve correctness and effectiveness.

In this study, we investigated prompting strategies and model choice separately. Next, their combined effect should be examined, e.g., whether reasoning-enabled models respond better to error-prevention or goal-setting prompts.

We considered mutation coverage a proxy for fault detection, not a substitute for real defect detection. As prior work has showed that Copilot-generated tests can detect real bugs in Defects4J [16], future work could apply our methodology to assess impact on real fault detection. Possible overlaps with training data should be explicitly considered in that case.

6   Conclusion

This paper presented a systematic study of GitHub Copilot's ability to generate unit tests and practical strategies for improving their effectiveness. Starting from a baseline evaluation on real-world Java projects, we investigated three factors: Avoiding compile errors through prompts, setting the goal to maximize fault detection capabilities, and the choice of the underlying LLM.

To enable large-scale, reproducible studies, we developed a custom Visual Studio Code extension that automates interaction with GitHub Copilot via the IDE plugin. This allows for systematic test generation, prompt variation, and evaluation across hundreds of classes, overcoming the limitations of manual Copilot usage in prior work. Our evaluation combined compilation success, structural coverage, and mutation coverage to capture both syntactic correctness and fault-detection capability.

Our findings provide several actionable insights for practitioners. First, prompts designed to prevent compile errors do not reliably improve outcomes and add unnecessary complexity. Second, prompts that set fault detection as an explicit goal can lead to higher mutation coverage for those test classes that compile, but overall reduce the number of usable tests due to increased compilation failures. Third, the choice of LLM is decisive: GPT-4.1 offers the most robust compilation rates, while Anthropic Sonnet models (such as Sonnet 3.7 and Sonnet 4) deliver superior mutation coverage and fault-detection capability, though at the expense of more frequent compile errors. This creates a practical trade-off for developers: Those seeking maximum fault sensitivity may benefit from Sonnet models if they can tolerate higher error rates and premium usage constraints, whereas those prioritizing reliability and ease of integration may prefer GPT-4.1. Finally, we demonstrate that pragmatic post-processing, such as removing non-compiling or failing test methods, can substantially enhance the usability and effectiveness of Copilot-generated test suites.

Looking forward, our results suggest that Copilot can already provide useful unit tests, but that non-compiling tests still pose a problem. Future work should explore iterative repair strategies, combinations of prompting techniques with reasoning-enabled models, and more advanced prompting strategies.

7 Open Science

To support transparency and reproducibility, we provide all artifacts and data associated with this study in a replication package [12]. In detail, we share the custom VS Code extension used to automate test generation with GitHub Copilot and the raw data from these generations. This includes Git repositories with the generated code, Maven build outputs, and mutation coverage reports, as well as a Jupyter notebook to process that data and produce the figures presented in this paper. Eventually, the used prompts are shared, too.

Disclosure of Interests. The authors have no competing interests to declare that are relevant to the content of this article.

References

1. Coles, H., Laurent, T., Henard, C., Papadakis, M., Ventresque, A.: PIT: a practical mutation testing tool for Java (demo). In: Proceedings of the 25th International Symposium on Software Testing and Analysis, ISSTA 2016, pp. 449–452. Association for Computing Machinery, New York (2016). https://doi.org/10.1145/2931037.2948707
2. Couvrat, N.: Javaimports (2025). https://github.com/nicolascouvrat/javaimports
3. El Haji, K., Brandt, C., Zaidman, A.: Using GitHub copilot for test generation in python: an empirical study. In: Proceedings of the 5th ACM/IEEE International Conference on Automation of Software Test (AST 2024), pp. 45–55. ACM, Lisbon (2024). https://doi.org/10.1145/3644032.3644443
4. Fraser, G., Arcuri, A.: EvoSuite: automatic test suite generation for object-oriented software. In: Proceedings of the 19th ACM SIGSOFT Symposium and the 13th European Conference on Foundations of Software Engineering, ESEC/FSE '11, pp. 416–419. Association for Computing Machinery, New York (2011). https://doi.org/10.1145/2025113.2025179
5. Jia, Y., Harman, M.: An Analysis and Survey of the Development of Mutation Testing. IEEE Trans. Softw. Eng. **37**(5), 649–678 (2011). https://doi.org/10.1109/TSE.2010.62

6. Just, R., Jalali, D., Ernst, M.D.: Defects4J: a database of existing faults to enable controlled testing studies for Java programs. In: Proceedings of the 2014 International Symposium on Software Testing and Analysis, pp. 437–440. ACM, San Jose (2014). https://doi.org/10.1145/2610384.2628055

7. Kang, S., Yoon, J., Yoo, S.: Large Language Models are Few-shot Testers: Exploring LLM-based General Bug Reproduction (2023)

8. Li, R., et al.: Starcoder: may the source be with you! arXiv preprint arXiv:2305.06161 (2023)

9. Papadakis, M., Shin, D., Yoo, S., Bae, D.H.: Are mutation scores correlated with real fault detection? a large scale empirical study on the relationship between mutants and real faults. In: Proceedings of the 40th International Conference on Software Engineering, ICSE '18, pp. 537–548. Association for Computing Machinery, New York (2018). https://doi.org/10.1145/3180155.3180183

10. Rosenkilde, J.: How GitHub Copilot is getting better at understanding your code (2023)

11. Schäfer, M., Nadi, S., Eghbali, A., Tip, F.: An empirical evaluation of using large language models for automated unit test generation. IEEE Trans. Softw. Eng. **50**(1), 85–105 (2023)

12. Schallermayer, M., Schnappinger, M.: Replication package for "improving the quality of copilot-generated unit tests" (Oct2025). https://doi.org/10.5281/zenodo.17436491

13. Shamshiri, S., Just, R., Rojas, J.M., Fraser, G., McMinn, P., Arcuri, A.: Do automatically generated unit tests find real faults? An empirical study of effectiveness and challenges. In: 2015 30th IEEE/ACM International Conference on Automated Software Engineering (ASE), pp. 201–211. IEEE (2015)

14. Siddiq, M.L., Santos, J.C.S., Tanvir, R.H., Ulfat, N., Rifat, F.A., Lopes, V.C.: Using large language models to generate JUnit tests: an empirical study. In: Proceedings of the 28th International Conference on Evaluation and Assessment in Software Engineering, pp. 313–322 (2024). https://doi.org/10.1145/3661167.3661216

15. Sobreira, V., Durieux, T., Madeiral, F., Monperrus, M., de Almeida Maia, M.: Dissection of a bug dataset: anatomy of 395 patches from Defects4J. In: 2018 IEEE 25th International Conference on Software Analysis, Evolution and Reengineering (SANER), pp. 130–140 (2018). https://doi.org/10.1109/SANER.2018.8330203

16. Sundqvist, E.: AI-assisted unit testing: empirical insights into github copilot chat effectiveness and collaborative benefits. Master's thesis, Linnaeus University (2024)

17. Tang, Y., Liu, Z., Zhou, Z., Luo, X.: ChatGPT vs SBST: a comparative assessment of unit test suite generation. IEEE Trans. Softw. Eng. **50**(6), 1340–1359 (2024). https://doi.org/10.1109/TSE.2024.3382365

18. Tufano, M., Drain, D., Svyatkovskiy, A., Deng, S.K., Sundaresan, N.: Unit test case generation with transformers and focal context. arXiv preprint arXiv:2009.05617 (2021)

19. Wang, J., Huang, Y., Chen, C., Liu, Z., Wang, S., Wang, Q.: Software testing with large language models: survey, landscape, and vision. IEEE Trans. Softw. Eng. **50**(4), 911–936 (2024). https://doi.org/10.1109/TSE.2024.3368208

20. Wang, Y., et al.: ProjectTest: a project-level LLM unit test generation benchmark and impact of error fixing mechanisms. arXiv preprint arXiv:2502.06556 (2025). https://doi.org/10.48550/arXiv.2502.06556

21. Yetistiren, B., Ozsoy, I., Tuzun, E.: Assessing the quality of GitHub copilot's code generation. In: Proceedings of the 18th International Conference on Predictive Models and Data Analytics in Software Engineering, pp. 62–71. ACM, Singapore (2022). https://doi.org/10.1145/3558489.3559072
22. Zhu, H., Hall, P.A.V., May, J.H.R.: Software unit test coverage and adequacy. ACM Comput. Surv. **29**(4), 366–427 (1997). https://doi.org/10.1145/267580.267590

LLM Agents for Autonomous System Testing: A Semi-structured Literature Review

Stefan Fischer[1]([envelope]) [iD] and Werner Kloihofer[2] [iD]

[1] Software Competence Center Hagenberg GmbH (SCCH), Hagenberg, Austria
stefan.fischer@scch.at
[2] PKE Holding AG, Computerstraße 6, 1100 Vienna, Austria

Abstract. System-level software testing is essential to ensure that complex systems function correctly when all components interact, yet it remains labor-intensive and error-prone. Recent advancements in Large Language Models (LLMs) offer the potential to automate and enhance system-level testing by generating test cases, reasoning about system behavior, and supporting adaptive exploration. This paper presents a semi-structured review of literature on LLM-based autonomous testing agents, focusing on their architectures, interactions with the tested systems, and testing objectives. We identify common limitations in current approaches, like hallucinations, limited contextual understanding, incomplete test oracles, and challenges in navigating complex system states. Based on these findings, we discuss future research opportunities.

Keywords: Literature-review · Software Testing · System-Testing · Large-Language-Models · AI-Agents

1 Introduction

System-level software testing is a critical yet challenging aspect of software engineering. It ensures that complex systems function as intended when all components interact [12]. Traditionally, system-level testing has been performed manually, requiring significant human effort to design, execute, and maintain test cases [PS10]. This manual approach is not only time-consuming but also prone to human error, leading to inconsistent test results and limited coverage [PS10] [2].

Recent advancements in *Large Language Models* (LLMs) offer promising avenues to address these persistent challenges. LLMs, capable of understanding and generating human-like text, can automate test generation, reason about system responses, and support adaptive exploration of system behavior [7,10]. Unlike conventional automation tools, LLMs can interpret natural language documentation, infer intent from examples, and generalize across diverse testing contexts [14]. Wang et al. [12] show that LLMs have already been effectively applied in various testing activities, including unit test generation, test oracle creation, system test input generation, bug analysis, and automated repair.

© The Author(s), under exclusive license to Springer Nature Switzerland AG 2026
M. Dorner et al. (Eds.): SWQD 2026, LNBIP 581, pp. 147–167, 2026.
https://doi.org/10.1007/978-3-032-24216-7_9

Beyond individual LLM applications, there is increasing interest in multi-agent architectures where several AI-based agents collaborate, guide each other, and iteratively refine test strategies. Amalfitano et al. note that such collaborative agent systems, often inspired by cognitive models, can enhance the robustness and adaptability of testing processes [2]. These developments mark a shift from LLMs as passive code generators toward autonomous, goal-directed testing agents capable of complex reasoning and coordination.

Motivated by these trends, this paper reviews the emerging landscape of LLM-based autonomous system-level testing agents. We synthesize existing approaches, highlight their architectural and operational characteristics, and identify open challenges that limit their wider adoption. Based on these insights, we outline research opportunities to guide future work in this rapidly evolving area. Our contributions are as follows:

- **Semi-structured Review:** Categorization of existing studies on LLM-based testing agents, focusing on architectures, autonomy levels, and interactions with the *System under Test* (SUT).
- **Identification of Challenges:** Discussion of limitations faced by LLM-based testing agents.
- **Research Opportunities:** Outline of potential avenues for future research based on observed limitations.

By addressing these aspects, this work aims to support the evolution of autonomous testing methodologies and to pave the way for more robust and efficient software testing practices.

2   Background and Related Work

2.1   Large Language Models (LLMs)

LLMs are pre-trained Transformer-based models with hundreds of millions to trillions of parameters, capable of generating high-quality text and performing reasoning over natural language inputs [6]. Prominent examples include GPT-3, GPT-4, Codex, LLaMA, and Claude. LLMs demonstrate emergent capabilities such as in-context learning and multi-step reasoning when scaled beyond a certain parameter threshold, which enables them to perform generative and planning tasks that are relevant for software engineering applications, including test generation and autonomous agent behavior [13].

Recent advancements in multi-modal LLMs allow models to interpret visual and graphical information, such as screenshots or *Graphical User Interface* (GUI) representations. Models like GPT-4 Vision, Claude, and LLaVA can perceive visual states and generate action sequences to interact with software environments, enhancing performance in system-level testing and autonomous GUI navigation [11].

Several surveys have examined the use of LLMs in software testing [3,4,10]. Notably, Wang et al. [12] reviewed 102 studies and categorized LLM applications according to software testing tasks, such as test case preparation, program repair, and bug detection. They also analyzed which LLMs were used, how they were prompted or fine-tuned, and how traditional testing techniques were combined with LLMs. Their survey highlights trends in prompt engineering, integration with conventional testing methods, and open challenges such as limited test coverage, the oracle problem, and difficulties in rigorous evaluation. While Wang et al. focus on *what* testing tasks LLMs support, our work examines *how* autonomous agents are structured and utilized for system-level testing.

Beyond testing-oriented surveys, He et al. [7] conducted a systematic review of 71 studies on LLM-based multi-agent systems across the software development lifecycle. Their analysis shows how collaborative agents with specialized expertise can autonomously decompose software tasks, cross-validate outputs, and scale to complex projects. Through two case studies, they demonstrate that such systems enhance robustness and fault tolerance via debate and validation mechanisms, mitigating hallucination and improving the reliability of autonomous software engineering workflows.

2.2 System-Level Software Testing

System-level testing evaluates the behavior of a complete software system to identify defects that may affect its functionality, reliability, or user experience [12]. It typically involves activities such as test planning, test case design, execution, and result analysis. System-level testing can cover functional, usability, performance, accessibility, or security aspects, and generally operates over fully integrated components or the complete application under realistic usage scenarios. Compared to unit or integration testing, it emphasizes end-to-end behavior, interactions among components, and responses to real inputs and outputs [1].

To facilitate system-level testing, various automation frameworks and tools are commonly used. These include browser- and GUI-based frameworks such as Selenium[1], Playwright[2], Appium[3], UIAutomator2, Android Debugging Bridge (ADB)[4], PyAutoGUI[5] and PyWinAuto[6]. In the context of LLM-based testing agents, these tools provide interfaces through which agents can perform actions, observe system states, and evaluate test outcomes, enabling end-to-end autonomous or semi-autonomous testing.

2.3 Autonomous LLM Agents for Testing

Recent research has explored the use of LLMs as autonomous agents that can independently plan and perform testing activities on complex software systems [5]. Such agents perceive the system state–through structured, symbolic, or

---

[1] https://www.selenium.dev/.

[2] https://playwright.dev/.

[3] https://appium.io/.

[4] https://android.googlesource.com/platform/packages/modules/adb/.

[5] https://pyautogui.readthedocs.io/.

[6] https://github.com/pywinauto/pywinauto.

visual representations–reason about testing strategies, and execute actions ranging from low-level interactions (e.g., API calls, GUI clicks) to high-level tasks such as feature exploration or end-to-end scenario testing.

LLM agents are logical entities that use an LLM to perform role-specific tasks. Each agent has a clearly defined responsibility (e.g., generating inputs, selecting GUI elements, or evaluating outputs), can interact with other agents, humans, or external tools, and executes actions or tool calls according to its assigned role. Multiple agents may share the same underlying LLM–what distinguishes them are their goals, context, and instructions rather than the model itself. Zhang et al. [14] provide a comprehensive survey of LLM-powered GUI agents, highlighting the synergy between LLMs as the "brain" and automation tools as the "hands" of autonomous GUI agents. Their work demonstrates how multi-modal LLMs can interpret complex GUI elements, execute actions based on natural language instructions, and generalize across dynamic workflows. They categorize existing approaches by key components such as data collection for model training, action model development, and framework support.

Autonomous testing refers to testing approaches in which such agents actively make decisions to guide the testing process. Instead of merely producing static test data, autonomous agents plan and adapt their actions based on system feedback, observed states, or testing goals. They operate toward high-level objectives such as achieving coverage, discovering faults, or exploring novel system behaviors. Feldt et al. [5] introduced a conceptual taxonomy for LLM-based testing agents, positioning them along a spectrum of autonomy from simple completion and infilling to fully conversational agents capable of planning and executing actions through middleware tools. Their work demonstrates how LLMs can assist developers by reasoning about specifications, filling in test details, and engaging in interactive dialogues to uncover faults. They identify key benefits such as reduced developer effort and enhanced reasoning about test outcomes but also highlight challenges including hallucinations and the need for human oversight in highly autonomous settings.

3   Method

This work follows a lightweight, semi-structured literature review approach inspired by evidence-based software engineering practices [8]. While systematic mapping and review methodologies aim to ensure rigor and reproducibility through detailed protocols, our goal was to balance structure with flexibility, enabling us to capture a rapidly evolving and interdisciplinary research landscape. Our process was informed by the general framework of Petersen et al. [9], including the formulation of research questions, literature search and screening, data extraction, and categorization.

3.1   Research Questions

RQ1: How are LLM-based testing agents architected and orchestrated? *Rationale:* This question examines the architectural organization of

LLM-based testing agents–the number of agents involved, how they collaborate or operate independently, and how orchestration frameworks or auxiliary utilities facilitate coordination.

RQ2: How do LLM-based agents interact with and test the SUT? *Rationale:* This question investigates how LLM agents perceive, reason about, and act upon the SUT. It focuses on the mechanisms linking the LLM to the SUT–how the agent observes system state, plans and executes actions, and evaluates system behavior.

RQ3: What are the current limitations and open challenges for reliable and generalizable LLM-based testing agents? *Rationale:* This question addresses the key barriers that limit the reliability and generalization of LLM-based testing. By identifying such limitations, we aim to motivate future work toward improving robustness, verifiability, and the development of evaluation metrics for autonomous testing performance and reliability.

3.2   Literature Search and Screening

To identify relevant research on LLM-agent-driven system testing, we conducted a semi-structured literature review. The process was designed to balance breadth and efficiency, focusing on collecting representative studies and organizing them into a coherent taxonomy.

Scope. We targeted studies that explicitly use LLMs for system-level testing tasks. Papers were excluded if they did not employ LLMs, or if their use of LLMs was unrelated to system-level testing. To capture recent developments, the search covered publications from *June 2020* (the release of GPT-3) to *18th September 2025* (when the search was performed).

Inclusion and Exclusion Criteria. Studies were included if they: (i) explicitly employed one or more LLMs, (ii) used LLMs as part of an autonomous or semi-autonomous testing agent, and (iii) targeted system-level testing tasks, such as end-to-end, integration, or GUI-based testing. Studies were excluded if they: (a) focused solely on unit testing or static analysis, (b) used LLMs only for documentation, code completion, or other non-testing objectives.

Search Strategy. We queried major digital libraries, including the ACM Digital Library, IEEE Xplore, SpringerLink, Wiley Online Library, and Google Scholar (which also indexes arXiv preprints). The primary query combined terms related to LLMs and autonomous testing:

```
("large language model" OR "GPT-3" OR "GPT-4" OR ChatGPT OR
"LLM agent") AND ("system testing" OR "system-level testing"
OR "software testing" OR "test case generation" OR "automated
testing")
```

Specific model names (e.g., GPT-3, GPT-4) were included because early studies often referred to concrete models rather than using the more general term *LLM*. Additional filters were applied in IEEE and Springer to restrict results to software testing topics, and in Wiley to limit to computer science articles. Given the large number of unrelated results in ACM Digital Library, we refined the query to focus on agentic testing frameworks:

```
("agentic AI" OR "LLM orchestration" OR "LLM agent") AND
("system testing" OR "autonomous testing" OR "interactive
testing" OR "agent-based testing" OR "automated testing")
```

For broader coverage, we also applied this refined query to Google Scholar and employed a practical stopping criterion: the review of results was terminated once three consecutive pages yielded no new relevant studies.

Screening and Selection. All identified studies were initially screened based on title, abstract, and in a second *detailed screening* phase we looked at the full text to ensure relevance. After the detailed selection, we performed *backward snowballing* by examining the references of included papers. The number of papers identified and retained at each stage is summarized in Sect. 4.

3.3 Data Extraction and Classification

To capture relevant information from the selected studies, we defined a structured data extraction process. We created a guideline document to clarify the meaning of each classification term and a spreadsheet to record the extracted data.

The spreadsheet included fields covering bibliographic information (year, venue, publication type), application context (domain, testing target, testing focus), and details about the LLM-based testing setup, including agent framework, number and type of LLM agents, orchestration or automation frameworks used, agent architecture and collaboration, level of autonomy, oracle mechanism(s), granularity of actions, and state representation for the LLM.

4 Results

In this section, we present the results of our literature search. The process and number of papers remaining after each phase are summarized in Fig. 1. In total,

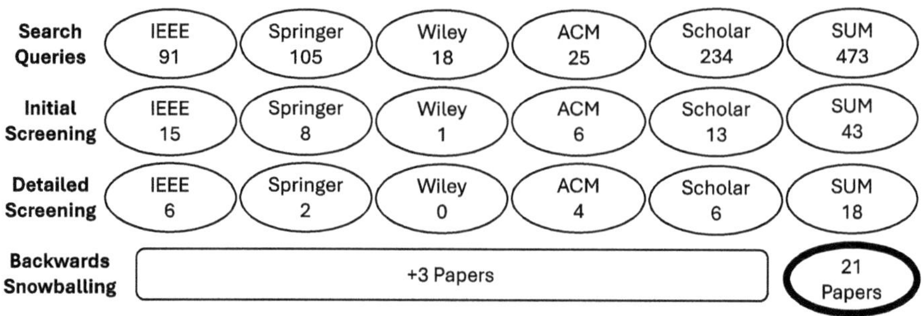

Fig. 1. Overview of the paper collection process.

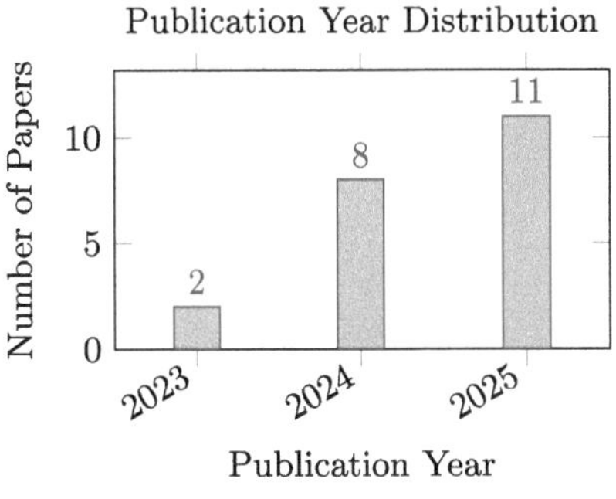

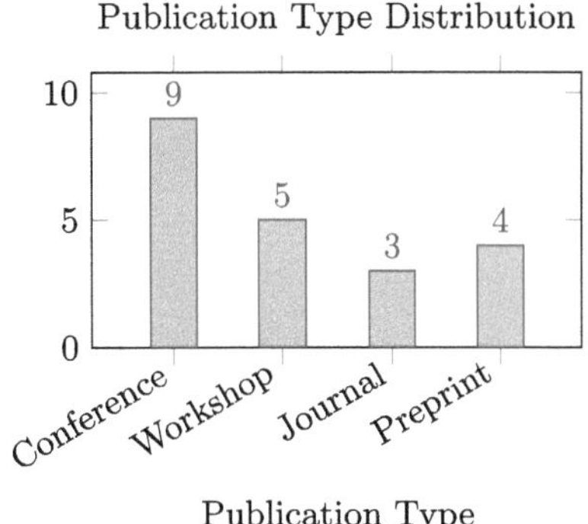

Fig. 2. Distribution of selected publications by year and publication type.

the search returned 473 studies. After the *initial screening* of titles and abstracts, 43 studies remained for detailed review. Subsequent *full-text screening* reduced this number to 18, and *backward snowballing* added three additional papers, resulting in a final corpus of 21 studies. For the Google Scholar search, the halting criterion of three consecutive result pages without a relevant hit was reached after page 11 (110 results), at which point no further publications were considered. All intermediate results and the final classification can be found in our online appendix[7]. Figure 2 summarizes the publication years and venue types. The earliest studies appeared in 2023, even though our search window began in June 2020–likely reflecting the time required to develop and evaluate LLM-based approaches after the release of GPT-3 and to publish them through peer review. Most studies were published at conferences (nine), followed by workshops (five) and journals (three), with an additional four relevant preprints meeting our inclusion criteria.

In Table 1 we list the applications types that were tested in the studies along with the automation frameworks used in the studies listed. Study [PS14] did not mention the automation framework, however the authors describe using *browser-use* which according to its documentation uses *Playwright* internally. Therefore, we classified [PS14] as using *Playwright*. The two outliers from this classification are [PS7] which tests a smart TV platform, and [PS4] testing the LLVM compiler via the CLI. All approaches, besides [PS4], are testing through the GUI.

Table 2 classifies the studies by the testing focus. The majority of studies (15) set out to find issues in the *functional* behavior of the *SUT*. The second largest group of five studies is assessing *usability*. [PS8] is the only study in our results that tests both *functionality* and *usability*. [PS4] is the only one testing *robustness* and solely detects crashes. [PS12] is focused on assessing *accessibility* of *iOS* mobile applications.

---

[7] https://github.com/software-competence-center-hagenberg/2026-SWQD-Autonomous-Testing.

Table 1. Application types and corresponding automation frameworks used in the analyzed studies. "NA" indicates papers where no automation framework was mentioned.

Application Type	Automation Framework	Studies
Web applications	Selenium	[PS1], [PS6], [PS13], [PS15]
	Playwright	[PS9], [PS10], [PS14]
	Not specified	[PS11], [PS16]
Mobile applications	UIAutomator2 &	[PS3], [PS5], [PS17],
	Android Debug Bridge	[PS19], [PS20], [PS21]
	XCTest	[PS12]
Desktop applications	PyAutoGUI	[PS7], [PS8]
	PyWinAuto	[PS18]
	NA	[PS2]
Specialized platforms	Tira[a]	[PS7]
	NA	[PS4]

[a] https://home-electro.com/products/tira-21.

Table 2. Testing focus of the analyzed papers.

Testing Focus	Studies
Functional	[PS1], [PS2], [PS3], [PS5], [PS6], [PS7], [PS8], [PS9], [PS10], [PS15], [PS16], [PS17], [PS19], [PS20], [PS21]
Robustness	[PS4]
Usability	[PS8], [PS11], [PS13], [PS14], [PS18]
Accessibility	[PS12]

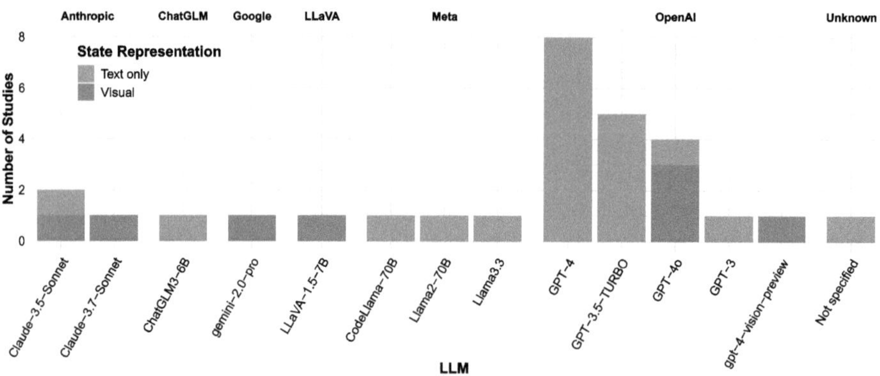

Fig. 3. Number of studies using different LLMs, grouped by provider. Bars are stacked to indicate the type of state representation the LLM received: text-only versus visual (multimodal) input.

Table 3. Agent architectures and their subtypes in the analyzed studies. The type multi-agent collaborative is further split by collaboration method.

Agent Architecture	Studies
Single-agent iterative	[PS1], [PS2], [PS4], [PS8], [PS19]
Single autonomous agent + auxiliary LLM	[PS5], [PS6], [PS7], [PS11], [PS14]
Multi-agent collaborative	—
- Message passing	[PS15], [PS17], [PS18], [PS21]
- Shared memory	[PS3], [PS11], [PS20]
- Orchestrator	[PS9], [PS11], [PS12], [PS16]
Multi-agent independent	[PS13]

Figure 3 shows the number of studies using each LLM, grouped by provider. Each bar represents a specific LLM, with colors indicating whether the study used the LLM for text-only analysis or also for visual/multimodal analysis. The most commonly used LLMs are from *OpenAI*, followed by the *Claude* models from *Anthropic* and different models from *Meta* and then other providers with models only used in single studies. Multimodal LLMs are used in six of the studies ([PS6], [PS10], [PS14], [PS16], [PS18], [PS20]), which include analyzing screenshots in their approaches. Only one study, [PS2], mentioned using *fine-tuning* the *GPT-3* model to improve its performance for their experiments testing a Python GUI application.

In our study, we identified four main types of agent architectures used for autonomous testing with LLMs. We list the studies for each architecture in Table 3. The four architectures we distinguished are:

- **Single-agent iterative:** A single logical agent executes test actions in a closed loop, iteratively observing the system state and determining the next action based on its reasoning. This architecture was used in five studies.
- **Single autonomous agent with auxiliary LLM utilities:** A primary executor agent drives the testing process, while additional LLM instances serve as auxiliary utilities, e.g., for generating test inputs, validating outputs, or providing an agent persona. Five studies used this architecture.
- **Multi-agent collaborative:** Multiple logical agents with distinct roles actively coordinate during testing. This was the most common architecture, found in eleven studies. Collaboration can be realized through:
  - *Message passing:* Agents communicate by explicitly sending messages with state updates or requests.
  - *Shared memory:* Agents access a common memory space to share observations, intermediate results, or planned actions.
  - *Orchestrator:* A central coordinating agent manages task allocation and synchronizes the actions of individual agents.
- **Multi-agent independent:** Multiple agents operate independently in separate sessions, without active coordination or sharing of information. This

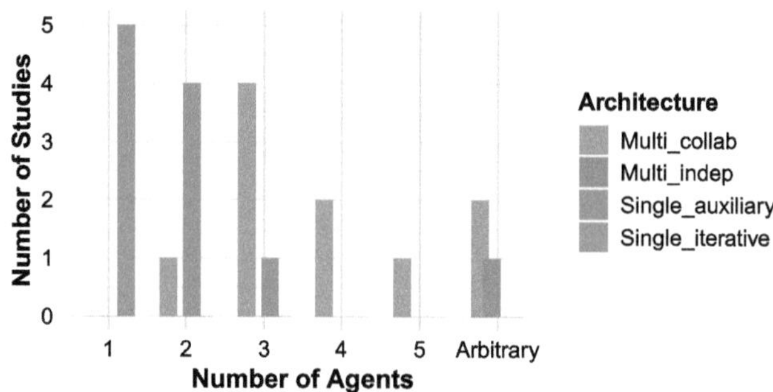

Fig. 4. Distribution of the number of agents in studies, grouped by architecture.

architecture was observed in only one study, where it was used for A/B testing of variations of an e-commerce web application, with an arbitrary number of agents assigned different personas.

These architectures reflect varying degrees of complexity and interaction between the agents. Figure 4 shows the distribution of the number of agents used in the analyzed studies, grouped by agent architecture. For the *Single autonomous agent + auxiliary LLM* architecture, the count includes the primary autonomous agent as well as any auxiliary LLMs used for other tasks. It is worth noting that only two studies ([PS9] and [PS15]) mentioned implementing their agents using a dedicated *agent framework*–both based on *AutoGen*[8]–while the remaining works constructed their own ad hoc architectures.

In our analysis, we classified the testing agents by their *level of autonomy*, which reflects the degree of human involvement in defining testing goals and guiding the agent's behavior. The studies assigned to each category are listed in Table 4. We distinguished the following three levels:

- **Fully human-specified goals:** The LLM executes tests based on explicit, predefined test cases or detailed natural-language instructions provided by humans. The model acts primarily as an executor rather than an autonomous decision-maker. Two studies adopted this mode.

Table 4. Levels of autonomy of the testing agents in the analyzed studies.

Level of Autonomy	Studies
Fully human-specified goals	[PS2], [PS9]
Semi-autonomous	[PS4], [PS5], [PS7], [PS8], [PS10], [PS11], [PS12], [PS13], [PS14], [PS15], [PS17], [PS18], [PS21]
Fully autonomous	[PS1], [PS3], [PS6], [PS16], [PS19], [PS20]

---

[8] https://microsoft.github.io/autogen.

- **Semi-autonomous:** The LLM is provided with high-level testing objectives or partial guidance (e.g., a target functionality and optionally its expected behavior), but independently decides how to achieve these goals. This setup allows adaptive exploration while keeping the overall test intent human-directed. The majority of studies (13) fall into this category.
- **Fully autonomous:** The LLM agent independently determines what aspects of the system to test, plans its actions, and decides when to terminate exploration, without human-provided goals. This setting represents the highest degree of autonomy and was observed in six studies.

In addition to the agent architecture and level of autonomy, we further classified the analyzed approaches according to their *oracle mechanism*, *granularity of actions*, and *state representation*, defined as follows:

Oracle Mechanism. The oracle defines how the outcome of a test execution is evaluated and what constitutes a fault. We identified the following types, which are not mutually exclusive:

- **Explicit:** Predefined expectations, typically via natural-language test descriptions or assertions.
- **LLM intrinsic:** The LLM decides whether a behavior indicates a fault based on its reasoning or general knowledge.
- **Simple crash detection:** Failures detected through system signals such as crashes or unhandled exceptions.
- **Human-in-the-loop:** A human confirms or rejects whether the observed outcome corresponds to a fault.
- **Metric-based:** Test outcomes judged using quantitative metrics such as completion time, error rates, usability scores, or performance counters.

Granularity of Actions.

- **Low-level:** Fine-grained interactions such as clicks, taps, scrolls, text input, or individual API calls.
- **High-level:** Abstract actions such as complete test scenarios, user tasks, or complex feature invocations.

State Representation.

- **Complete structural:** Full structured views of the interface or system, e.g., DOM trees or view hierarchies.
- **Filtered context:** Relevant subsets selected to reduce input complexity.
- **Visual:** Screenshots or rendered views, optionally annotated.
- **Symbolic or abstracted:** Abstracted representations emphasizing semantic or actionable aspects such as widgets, controls, or summarized pages.

While we do not list the individual studies for each category due to space constraints, Fig. 5 presents an overview of how these dimensions co-occur with different autonomy levels. We show three separate heatmaps, each illustrating

Level of autonomy		Number of papers	State Representation				Oracle					Granularity	
			Complete structural	Filtered Context	Visual	Symbolic/Abstracted	Explicit	LLM intrinsic	Crash detection	Human	Metric-based	Low-level	High-level
Level of autonomy	Fully human-specified	2	2				2					1	1
	Semi-autonomous	13	2	7	3	8	6	5	1	4	5	11	2
	Fully autonomous	6		4	3	3		6			1	4	2
	SUM	21	4	11	6	11	8	11	1	4	6	16	5

Fig. 5. Heatmaps showing the relationship between the *Level of Autonomy* and other classification dimensions across the analyzed studies. Each cell indicates the number of papers exhibiting a specific combination of characteristics. The rows correspond to different autonomy levels, while the columns represent (from left to right) the total number of papers, the type of *State Representation* used for the LLM, the employed *Oracle* mechanisms, and the *Granularity of Actions*. The final row summarizes the overall distribution of papers across categories.

the co-occurrence between *autonomy level* and one of the other dimensions. Each heatmap uses a color gradient where red indicates a higher number of studies, green a lower number, and yellow intermediate values, allowing for a quick visual comparison across categories.

From the heatmaps, several trends emerge. *Fully human-specified* agents use *explicit* oracles specified in their input and simpler state representations. *Semi-autonomous* agents show the greatest diversity in *state representations* and *oracle mechanisms*, reflecting a balance between human guidance and autonomous reasoning. *Fully autonomous* agents more frequently employ structural or *symbolic representations* and *LLM-intrinsic* oracles, aligning with their need to independently evaluate system behavior. *Low-level* actions are more common overall than *high-level* actions, both appearing in all *autonomy levels*. Overall, these patterns highlight how *autonomy* influences the choice of *state representation, oracle type*, and how LLM-based agents adapt their strategies based on the degree of human involvement.

5   Discussion

In this section, we summarize our findings in relation to the research questions and discuss their implications, highlighting current limitations and potential directions for future research.

5.1   RQ1: Agent Architecture and Orchestration

The studies reveal that LLM-based testing agents employ a range of architectures, from single-agent iterative designs to multi-agent collaborative systems. Multi-agent collaboration is the most common, reflecting the need for coordination and division of tasks in complex system-level testing. Single-agent approaches are used primarily in simpler scenarios or when auxiliary LLMs support specific sub-tasks. We found one instance of a independent multi-agent architecture used for parallel exploration in A/B testing.

5.2   RQ2: Agent System Interaction

LLM-based testing agents interact with the SUT using automation frameworks, state representations, and action strategies. Most studies focus on functional GUI testing, with fewer addressing usability, accessibility, or robustness. Oracle mechanisms vary, including explicit human-defined expectations, LLM intrinsic reasoning, simple crash detection, or metric-based evaluation, sometimes with human-in-the-loop support. No approaches mentioned using complex system specifications. Actions range from low-level interactions (clicks, taps, scrolls) to high-level workflows, while state representations include structural, filtered, visual, and symbolic abstractions. Overall, these mechanisms are combined to enable perception, reasoning, and action, with trade-offs between autonomy, reliability, and task complexity shaping each approach.

5.3   RQ3: Open Challenges and Current Limitations

To answer this research question, we analyzed the primary studies to identify recurring limitations and open challenges in current approaches.

Hallucination and Reliability of LLMs: A common limitation identified across multiple studies is the unreliability of LLM outputs, often stemming from hallucination and non-deterministic behavior [14]. Due to their generative nature, LLMs can produce invalid or misleading testing outcomes [PS4]. Empirical studies have shown that agents may modify or reinterpret test cases, making invalid tests appear executable or incorrectly reporting failing tests as successful [PS9]. Additionally, LLM-based agents have been observed to misinterpret verification tasks or incorrectly validate assertions, leading to false confirmations of system correctness [PS10].

Limited Contextual Understanding: A recurring limitation of current LLM-based testing agents is their restricted understanding of the system context. Agents often fail to correctly interpret the verification task or to obtain all necessary information from the environment. For example, [PS10] report instances where agents incorrectly validated assertions or missed critical details due to misunderstandings of the intended verification. Similarly, [PS12] highlights that agents can lack sufficient knowledge about application structure or fail to determine when to terminate a task, leading to incomplete or erroneous exploration of the SUT. Another limitation in this category is the narrow set of actions supported by some approaches agents. Many approaches are restricted to basic interactions such as "click" and "type" ([PS11], [PS12], [PS18]). This constraint prevents the agents from fully interacting with the SUT, limiting their ability to perceive state changes or explore alternative workflows. Tasks that require more complex interactions, such as scrolling, or hovering, remain largely unaddressed, which can reduce the fidelity and completeness of autonomous testing.

False Positives and Interpretation Errors: LLM-based testing agents have been observed to generate false positives and misinterpret system behaviors across multiple studies. [PS9] reported that GPT models occasionally marked tests as failed when human analysis found them to be successful. Similarly, [PS10] found that agents frequently misjudged whether system states satisfied expected conditions, incorrectly validating assertions. False positives were also linked to insufficient contextual understanding. [PS14] noted that agents sometimes incorrectly attributed failures to defects in the SUT rather than to limitations of the automation framework. A portion of false positives stemmed from reasonable but incorrect assumptions, particularly when temporal or domain context was lacking. [PS20] corroborated these observations, reporting false positive faults caused by misinterpretation of dynamic content or complex interactions.

Planning and Navigation Challenges: LLM-based testing agents currently face limitations in planning and navigating complex software systems. Agents often struggle to maintain coherent execution sequences, explore multi-application scenarios, and handle deeply nested or dynamically rendered interfaces. For example, [PS3] reports difficulties when leaving the tested application to access related functionalities. [PS10] highlights errors with agents performing unnecessary actions, or executing steps out of order, which disrupts workflows and reduces reliability. Similarly, [PS12] notes that agents may lack sufficient knowledge about the application or understanding of when to stop, limiting effective exploration. [PS14] further observes that agents often terminate exploration before encountering deeply embedded faults, particularly in dynamic or multi-page interfaces. These findings indicate that current LLM-based agents may have limited capability to plan and execute complex, long-horizon testing tasks reliably.

Usability and Human Behavior Simulation: Simulating human interactions for testing remains a significant challenge. Several studies report that automated agents struggle to fully capture nuanced human behaviors and usability considerations. [PS8] highlight limitations in detecting gesture behavior, noting that while automated approaches can theoretically identify usability errors, the completeness and scope of detected issues remain uncertain. Their study comparing a simulated user to multiple human participants revealed notable discrepancies, emphasizing that simulated users cannot fully replace human testing. Accessibility issues could also be missed if the simulation is not integrated early in the testing process. [PS11] report additional concerns regarding model and data biases in usability-focused LLM agents, which can further compromise the accuracy and fairness of simulated user interactions. Similarly, [PS13] stress that simulated behavior cannot fully replicate human cognition and can misinterpret complex or unconventional system structures, such as dynamic or irregular DOM elements in web applications. Overall, these findings indicate that while autonomous agents can support usability and human-centric testing, significant gaps remain in accurately modeling human behavior, ensuring completeness of error detection, and mitigating bias [3].

Limited Application Domains: Most reported work focuses on *web* or *mobile* applications (see Table 1), primarily testing the GUI. LLM-based testing agents have rarely been applied to other domains, such as API testing, embedded systems, or real-time software [6]. This may be partly due to the availability of mature automation frameworks for GUI testing and the latency constraints of LLMs, which can hinder their applicability in time-sensitive or resource-constrained environments [14].

General-purpose LLMs often lack the domain-specific knowledge necessary to reason effectively about specialized systems, which can reduce the quality and reliability of generated tests [6]. Even within supported domains, agents struggle to generalize across diverse system interfaces [14]. Variations in GUI layouts, dynamic content, or application-specific interaction patterns can easily break previously functional agents. Frequent updates, A/B tests, or redesigns of user interfaces further exacerbate this problem, often requiring retraining for each new application or major interface change [14]. These limitations indicate that current approaches remain sensitive to environmental variations and may have limited robustness in handling unseen systems or configurations.

5.4   Research Opportunities

More Reliable Test Oracles: Determining correct expected outcomes remains a major challenge in LLM-based testing, particularly for crash-free or non-trivial behaviors [12]. Most existing approaches rely either on the LLM to infer the correct behavior or on a human-provided oracle for each task. This reliance contributes to false positives, as LLMs may make incorrect assumptions when specifications are incomplete or missing [PS9], [PS10], [PS14], [PS20].

We did not find approaches that explicitly leverage formal system specifications as test oracles. One potential solution is *Retrieval-Augmented Generation* (RAG), where LLM agents consult documentation, previous test cases, or human demonstrations to validate expected outcomes [14]. Integrating formal or semi-formal specifications could further improve the correctness and reliability of autonomous test oracles.

Improved Test Planning: Current LLM-based testing agents often explore systems incrementally, step by step, which limits their ability to execute coherent, long-horizon test sequences [PS3], [PS10], [PS12], [PS14]. This restriction leads to navigation errors, missed deep system states, and inefficient coverage. Planning could be improved using similar strategies as for test oracles: consulting system specifications or documentation, or employing RAG approaches to access prior knowledge, user manuals, or example workflows [14]. Constructing internal application models–capturing pages, actions, and transitions, as in [PS7]–could provide a high-level overview, enabling more effective planning.

Another promising direction is transferable test planning, where knowledge of typical test scenarios is transferred across applications within the same domain, or even across domains, to inform exploration strategies. Techniques like *transfer learning* and *meta-learning* can help generalize planning across applications [14], supporting adaptation of LLM-based testing to domain-specific inputs and behaviors [12].

Fine-Tuning and Multi-modal Adaptation: Current LLM-based testing agents predominantly rely on general-purpose models, with only one study in our set performing fine-tuning on GPT-3 [PS2]. This limits their effectiveness, particularly in multi-modal testing scenarios involving screenshots or GUI representations, where standard LLMs may misinterpret visual layouts or dynamic interface elements. While one study suggested integrating visual inputs such as screenshots and spatial layouts [PS13], six studies in our set ([PS6], [PS10], [PS15], [PS16], [PS18], [PS20]) already use screenshots for multi-modal LLMs. However, none report any fine-tuning. Task- and domain-specific fine-tuning could enhance LLM understanding of system states and actions. Curated multi-modal datasets combining screenshots, GUI structures, and corresponding actions or expected outcomes could enable more accurate reasoning about visual and interactive system aspects. Fine-tuned models could better detect UI changes, interpret complex layouts, and reduce hallucinations or misinterpretations, improving both the reliability and coverage of autonomous GUI tests.

Dynamic Integration with Traditional Testing Techniques: While LLM-based autonomous agents can explore and test systems independently, several limitations persist, such as restricted action sets ([PS11], [PS12], [PS18]), difficulties in navigating deeply nested system states ([PS12], [PS14]), and handling complex workflows ([PS3], [PS10]). To overcome these challenges, agents could dynamically integrate or invoke traditional testing techniques when needed [12]. For example, they could switch to classical testing methods or pre-defined scripts to handle parts of the system that require complex interactions, such as multistep forms, deep navigation paths, or GUI elements not easily accessible through standard actions. Similarly, human-developed test scripts or auxiliary functions could be called to manage tricky scenarios, like login procedures with multi-factor authentication or domain-specific setup sequences, enabling testing beyond the LLM's intrinsic capabilities. Agents could selectively employ specialized testing tools, such as automated input generators, formal verifiers, or stress-testing frameworks, on system components where purely LLM-driven exploration is insufficient. Such a hybrid approach would allow autonomous agents to retain their generative flexibility while leveraging the precision, reliability, and domain-specific knowledge of existing testing techniques. The agent itself could determine when to invoke these complementary methods–for example, when encountering unreachable states, complex interactions, or situations prone to hallucinations– thereby improving overall test coverage, reliability, and efficiency.

Focus on Non-functional Testing: In their literature review on the general use of LLMs in software testing, Wang et al. [12] observed that existing studies primarily target functional testing, with little to no focus on performance, usability, or other non-functional aspects. Although we identified several studies addressing usability ([PS8], [PS11][PS11], [PS13], [PS14], [PS18]) and accessibility ([PS12]), most of them were still primarily classified as functional testing. Future research could extend LLM-based agents toward non-functional testing by integrating specialized analysis tools or domain models for tasks such as performance monitoring, load generation, or user experience evaluation. Such integration could enable LLM agents not only to execute functional workflows but also to reason about system responsiveness, stability under stress, and interface quality–thereby broadening the applicability of autonomous testing beyond purely functional correctness.

5.5   Threats to Validity

Several threats may affect the validity and generalizability of our semi-structured literature review. **Selection of Sources:** We limited our search to a set of specific paper repositories and relied on carefully constructed search queries. Relevant studies may have been missed if they were not indexed in the selected repositories or if they did not match the query terms. **Classification Scheme:** Our classification of agent architectures, autonomy levels, interaction mechanisms, and other dimensions is based on our interpretation of the reported studies. Alternative schemes or finer-grained distinctions might lead to different categorizations. **Inclusion and Exclusion Criteria:** The criteria used to select studies for review may have introduced bias. Certain types of work focusing on adjacent but related topics may have been excluded, potentially limiting the completeness of the review. **Data Extraction and Single-Researcher Bias:** All screening, coding, and data extraction steps were performed by a single researcher. No inter-rater agreement or secondary validation was conducted, which introduces the risk of subjective interpretation or inadvertent errors affecting consistency and reliability. To mitigate this threat, we applied well-defined inclusion and exclusion criteria consistently, carefully documented all decisions, and provide a publicly available appendix containing the intermediate results, allowing others to review and verify our process. While these measures do not eliminate subjectivity, they improve transparency and reproducibility of the review.

6   Conclusion

This paper presented a semi-structured review of LLM-based autonomous agents for system-level software testing. Our analysis revealed a growing diversity in agent architectures, autonomy levels, and interaction strategies, reflecting a field that is rapidly evolving yet still in an exploratory phase. While the reviewed approaches demonstrate that LLMs can reason about complex systems and autonomously execute meaningful tests, several limitations persist – including restricted action capabilities, incomplete oracles, and difficulties in maintaining context across long interaction sequences.

These findings suggest that LLM-based testing agents are not yet a substitute for traditional automation but rather a complementary paradigm that can enhance adaptability and reasoning in testing workflows. Future research should therefore focus on hybrid architectures that integrate LLM-driven exploration with established testing techniques, improved grounding mechanisms to reduce hallucinations, and better handling of complex, stateful interactions.

List of Primary Studies

[PS1] Zimmermann, D., Koziolek, A.: Gui-based software testing: An automated approach using GPT-4 and selenium webdriver. In: 38th IEEE/ACM International Conference on Automated Software Engineering, ASE - Workshops. pp. 171174. IEEE (2023). https://doi.org/10.1109/ASEW60602.2023.00028

[PS2] Zimmermann, D., Koziolek, A.: Automating gui-based software testing with GPT- 3. In: IEEE International Conference on Software Testing, Verification and Validation, ICST - Workshops. pp. 6265. IEEE (2023). https://doi.org/10.1109/ICSTW58534.2023.00022

[PS3] Yoon, J., Feldt, R., Yoo, S.: Intent-driven mobile GUI testing with autonomous large language model agents. In: IEEE Conference on Software Testing, Verification and Validation, ICST. pp. 129139. IEEE (2024). https://doi.org/10.1109/ICST60714.2024.00020

[PS4] Wang, T., Wang, R., Chen, Y., Yu, L., Pan, Z., Zhang, M., Ma, H., Zheng, J.: Enhancing black-box compiler option fuzzing with LLM through command feedback. In: 35th IEEE International Symposium on Software Reliability Engineering, ISSRE. pp. 319330. IEEE (2024). https://doi.org/10.1109/ISSRE62328.2024.00039

[PS5] Feng, S., Lu, H., Jiang, J., Xiong, T., Huang, L., Liang, Y., Li, X., Deng, Y., Aleti, A.: Enabling cost-effective UI automation testing with retrieval-based llms: A case study in wechat. In: Proceedings of the 39th IEEE/ACM International Conference on Automated Software Engineering, ASE. pp. 19731978. ACM (2024). https://doi.org/10.1145/3691620.3695260

[PS6] Wang, S., Wang, S., Fan, Y., Li, X., Liu, Y.: Leveraging large vision-language model for better automatic web GUI testing. In: IEEE International Conference on Software Maintenance and Evolution, ICSME. pp. 125137. IEEE (2024).https://doi.org/10.1109/ICSME58944.2024.00022

[PS7] Azimi, M.Y., Yilmaz, C.: Model-based test execution from high-level natural language instructions using GPT-4. Softw. Qual. J. 33(1), 15 (2025).https://doi.org/10.1007/S11219-025-09712-9

[PS8] Goetz, M.: Enhancing the validation of human factors in user interface software testing with AI. In: Kurosu, M., Hashizume, A. (eds.) Human-Computer Interaction - Thematic Area, HCI. Lecture Notes in Computer Science, vol. 15769, pp. 5976. Springer (2025). https://doi.org/10.1007/978-3-031-93861-0_4

[PS9] Bergsmann, S., Schmidt, A., Fischer, S., Ramler, R.: First experiments on au- tomated execution of gherkin test specifications with collaborating LLM agents. In: Proceedings of the 15th ACM International Workshop on Automating Test Case Design, Selection and Evaluation, A-TEST. pp. 1215. ACM (2024). https://doi.org/10.1145/3678719.3685692

[PS10] Chevrot, A., Vernotte, A., Falleri, J., Blanc, X., Legeard, B., Cretin, A.: Are autonomous web agents good testers? Proc. ACM Softw. Eng. 2(ISSTA), 206228 (2025). https://doi.org/10.1145/3728879

[PS11] Lu, Y., Yao, B., Gu, H., Huang, J., Wang, Z.J., Li, Y., Gesi, J., He, Q., Li, T.J., Wang, D.: Uxagent: An LLM agent-based usability testing framework for web design. In: Proceedings of the Extended Abstracts of the CHI Conference on Human Factors in Computing Systems, CHI EA. pp. 545:1545:12. ACM (2025).https://doi.org/10.1145/3706599.3719729

[PS12] Taeb, M., Swearngin, A., Schoop, E., Cheng, R., Jiang, Y., Nichols, J.: Axnav: Replaying accessibility tests from natural language. In: Proceedings of the CHI Conference on Human Factors in Computing Systems, CHI. pp. 962:1962:16. ACM (2024). https://doi.org/10.1145/3613904.3642777

[PS13] Wang, D., Hsu, T., Lu, Y., Gu, H., Cui, L., Xie, Y., Headean, W., Yao, B., Veeragouni, A., Liu, J., Nag, S., Wang, J.: AgentA/B: Automated and Scalable Web A/BTesting with Interactive LLM Agents. CoRR abs/2504.09723 (2025). https://doi.org/10.48550/ARXIV.2504.09723

[PS14] Ye, N., Yu, X., Xu, R., Peng, T., Yu, Z.: Ai agents for web testing: A case study in the wild. CoRR abs/2509.05197 (2025).https://doi.org/10.48550/ARXIV.2509.05197

[PS15] Almutawa, M., Ghabrah, Q., Canini, M.: Towards llm-assisted system testing for microservices. In: 44th IEEE International Conference on Distributed Computing Systems, ICDCS - Workshops. pp. 2934. IEEE (2024).https://doi.org/10.1109/ICDCSW63686.2024.00011

[PS16] Liu, C., Gu, Z., Wu, G., Zhang, Y., Wei, J., Xie, T.: Temac: Multi-agent collaboration for automated web GUI testing. CoRR abs/2506.00520 (2025).https://doi.org/10.48550/ARXIV.2506.00520

[PS17] Feng, S., Du, C., Liu, H., Wang, Q., Lv, Z., Wang, M., Chen, C.: Breaking Single-Tester Limits: Multi-Agent LLMs for Multi-User Feature Testing. CoRR abs/2506.17539 (2025).https://doi.org/10.48550/ARXIV.2506.17539

[PS18] Rosenbach, T., Heidrich, D., Weinert, A.: Automated testing of the GUI of a real-life engineering software using large language models. In: IEEE International Conference on Software Testing, Verification and Validation, ICST - Workshops. pp. 103110. IEEE (2025).https://doi.org/10.1109/ICSTW64639.2025.10962502

[PS19] Liu, Z., Chen, C., Wang, J., Chen, M., Wu, B., Che, X., Wang, D., Wang, Q.: Make LLM a testing expert: Bringing human-like interaction to mobile GUI testing via functionality-aware decisions. In: Proceedings of the 46th IEEE/ACM International Conference on Software Engineering, ICSE. pp. 100:1100:13. ACM (2024).https://doi.org/10.1145/3597503.3639180

[PS20] Liu, Z., Li, C., Chen, C., Wang, J., Chen, M., Wu, B., Wang, Y., Hu, J., Wang, Q.: Seeing is believing: Vision-driven non-crash functional bug detection for mobile apps. IEEE Trans. Software Eng. pp. 114 (2025).https://doi.org/10.1109/TSE.2025.3614469

[PS21] Feng, S., Du, C., Liu, H., Wang, Q., Lv, Z., Huo, G., Yang, X., Chen, C.: Agent for user: Testing multi - user interactive features in tiktok. In: 47th IEEE/ACM International Conference on Software Engineering: Software

Engineering in Practice, SEIP@ICSE. pp. 5768. IEEE (2025).https://doi.org/10.1109/ICSE-SEIP66354.2025.00011

Acknowledgement. The research reported in this paper has been funded by BMK, BMAW, and the State of Upper Austria in the frame of the SCCH competence center INTEGRATE (FFG grant no. 892418) part of the FFG COMET Competence Centers for Excellent Technologies Programme.

References

1. Alshahwan, N., Harman, M., Marginean, A.: Software testing research challenges: an industrial perspective. In: IEEE Conference on Software Testing, Verification and Validation, ICST, Dublin, Ireland, pp. 1–10. IEEE (2023). https://doi.org/10.1109/ICST57152.2023.00008
2. Amalfitano, D., Coppola, R., Distante, D., Ricca, F.: AI in GUI-based software testing: insights from a survey with industrial practitioners. In: 17th International Conference on the Quality of Information and Communications Technology, QUATIC Pisa, Italy. CCIS, vol. 2178, pp. 328–343. Springer, Cham (2024).https://doi.org/10.1007/978-3-031-70245-7_23
3. Bayrı, V., Demirel, E.: AI-powered software testing: the impact of large language models on testing methodologies. In: 4th International Informatics and Software Engineering Conference (IISEC), pp. 1–4 (2023).https://doi.org/10.1109/IISEC59749.2023.10391027
4. Boukhlif, M., Kharmoum, N., Hanine, M.: LLMs for intelligent software testing: a comparative study. In: 7th International Conference on Networking, Intelligent Systems and Security, NISS 2024. Association for Computing Machinery, New York, NY, USA (2024). https://doi.org/10.1145/3659677.3659749
5. Feldt, R., Kang, S., Yoon, J., Yoo, S.: Towards autonomous testing agents via conversational large language models. In: 38th IEEE/ACM International Conference on Automated Software Engineering, ASE Luxembourg, pp. 1688–1693. IEEE (2023). https://doi.org/10.1109/ASE56229.2023.00148
6. Haque, M.A.: LLMs: a game-changer for software engineers? BenchCouncil Trans. Benchmarks Standards Eval. **5**(1), 100204 (2025). https://doi.org/10.1016/j.tbench.2025.100204
7. He, J., Treude, C., Lo, D.: LLM-based multi-agent systems for software engineering: literature review, vision, and the road ahead. ACM Trans. Softw. Eng. Methodol. **34**(5), 124:1–124:30 (2025). https://doi.org/10.1145/3712003
8. Kitchenham, B.A., Dybå, T., Jørgensen, M.: Evidence-based software engineering. In: 26th International Conference on Software Engineering (ICSE), pp. 273–281. IEEE Computer Society (2004). https://doi.org/10.1109/ICSE.2004.1317449
9. Petersen, K., Feldt, R., Mujtaba, S., Mattsson, M.: Systematic mapping studies in software engineering. In: 12th International Conference on Evaluation and Assessment in Software Engineering, EASE, University of Bari, Italy. Workshops in Computing, BCS (2008). http://ewic.bcs.org/content/ConWebDoc/19543
10. Santos, R., Santos, Í., de Magalhães, C.V.C., de Souza Santos, R.: Are we testing or being tested? Exploring the practical applications of large language models in software testing. In: IEEE Conference on Software Testing, Verification and Validation, ICST, Toronto, ON, Canada, pp. 353–360. IEEE (2024). https://doi.org/10.1109/ICST60714.2024.00039

11. Thomas, A., Ramesh, K., Mohan, S.: Multimodal LLM agents: exploring LLM interactions in software, web and operating systems. In: Submitted to CS598 LLM Agent Workshop (2025). https://openreview.net/forum?id=YGLOpASCY5
12. Wang, J., Huang, Y., Chen, C., Liu, Z., Wang, S., Wang, Q.: Software testing with large language models: survey, landscape, and vision. IEEE Trans. Softw. Eng. **50**(4), 911–936 (2024). https://doi.org/10.1109/TSE.2024.3368208
13. Wei, J., et al.: Emergent abilities of large language models. Trans. Mach. Learn. Res. **2022** (2022). https://openreview.net/forum?id=yzkSU5zdwD
14. Zhang, C., et al.: Large language model-brained GUI agents: a survey. Trans. Mach. Learn. Res. **2025** (2025). https://openreview.net/forum?id=xChvYjvXTp

Author Index

B
Biffl, Stefan   42
Bludau, Peter   25

D
Daxerer, Christoph   82

E
Elberzhager, Frank   65

F
Fischer, Stefan   147

G
Gerbershagen, Matthias   65
Ginkel, Joshua   65

K
Kloihofer, Werner   147
Krump, Matthias   82, 113

M
Mahya, Parisa   113
Mairinger, Simon   101

M
Martinelli, Matteo   42
Martinez-Gil, Jorge   82, 113
Muccini, Henry   3

N
Neumüller, Cornelia   82, 113

P
Picone, Marco   42
Pretschner, Alexander   25

R
Rahmani, Hossein   42

S
Schallermayer, Max   127
Schnappinger, Markus   127

W
Winterer, Mario   82, 113

Z
Ziebermayr, Thomas   101

© The Editor(s) (if applicable) and The Author(s), under exclusive license
to Springer Nature Switzerland AG 2026
M. Dorner et al. (Eds.): SWQD 2026, LNBIP 581, p. 169, 2026.
https://doi.org/10.1007/978-3-032-24216-7

MIX
Papier aus verantwortungsvollen Quellen
Paper from responsible sources
FSC® C105338

FSC
www.fsc.org

If you have any concerns about our products,
you can contact us on
ProductSafety@springernature.com

In case Publisher is established outside the EU,
the EU authorized representative is:
Springer Nature Customer Service Center GmbH
Europaplatz 3, 69115 Heidelberg, Germany

Printed by Libri Plureos GmbH
in Hamburg, Germany